D0065133

EDUCATED
AND IGNORANT

EDUCATED AND IGNORANT

෧

Ultraorthodox Jewish Women and Their World

. . . .

Tamar El-Or

translated by Haim Watzman

Lynne Rienner Publishers   ෧   Boulder & London

Photographs by Yair El-Or

Published in the United States of America in 1994 by
Lynne Rienner Publishers, Inc.
1800 30th Street, Boulder, Colorado 80301

and in the United Kingdom by
Lynne Rienner Publishers, Inc.
3 Henrietta Street, Covent Garden, London WC2E 8LU

Library of Congress Cataloging-in-Publication Data
El-Or, Tamar.
    Educated and ignorant : ultraorthodox Jewish women and their world
    / by Tamar El-Or.
    p.   cm.
    Includes bibliographical references and index.
    ISBN 1-55587-393-6 (alk. paper)
    ISBN 1-55587-396-0 (pbk. : alk. paper)
    1. Orthodox Judaism—Israel. 2. Women, Jewish—Israel—Religious
life. 3. Hasidim—Israel. 4. Jewish religious education of girls—
Israel. 5. Talmud Torah (Judaism) I. Title.
BM390.E4   1993
296.8'32'082—dc20   93-13332
                                       CIP

British Cataloguing in Publication Data
A Cataloguing in Publication record for this book
is available from the British Library.

Printed and bound in the United States of America

 The paper used in this publication meets the requirements
of the American National Standard for Permanence of
Paper for Printed Library Materials Z39.48-1984.

In memory of Julie Freedman

Contents

· · · 🌿 · · ·

Preface

· · · 🙰 · · ·

As I was reading the final proofs of this work, my eldest son came up to me and inquired whether this would be a book that people could read. Perhaps he was trying to picture the audience toward which the book was directed—would the material be accessible only to researchers and students, or also to those who came to it simply out of curiosity? (He may just have wanted to know whether he would be expected to read it!) In fact, my concerns were similar. I wished both to tell a story and search for its meaning, both to present primary material—the record of my fieldwork—and to offer reflective and critical analysis.

While the story is of a particular place and a particular society, its implications extend to the entire set of contexts in which it lies and out of which it developed. The book progresses from the local to the general, from the society under study to ultraorthodox society as a whole, and thence to all of Israeli society.

🙰

This book is based on a doctoral thesis prepared for the Department of Sociology and Anthropology at Bar-Ilan University. I owe thanks to my advisers, Dafna Yizraeli and Haim Hazan, as well as to Phyllis Palgi, Daliah Moore, and Gideon Kunda. I must also thank the editors at Am Oved—Haim Be'er, Nira Harel, Eli Shaltiel, Ilana Shamir, and Zehava Kana'an—for their perceptive and attentive reading and editing of the Hebrew-language manuscript. Am Oved published the Hebrew version in September 1992.

This edition is a translation of the Hebrew version, with comments and clarifications added for the English-language reader. I owe special thanks to the translator, Haim Watzman, for his superb work, which is faithful to the spirit of the book and to both languages.

My thanks to the Rosita and Isteban Herczeg Fund for Gender Studies of the Hebrew University of Jerusalem for the grant that enabled translation of the book.

The endnotes to each chapter include commentary of a purely academic nature. Since the subject matter may be of interest to a nonacademic audience, I have tried to incorporate some basic social science terms and expressions into the descriptive and interpretive narrative. Readers are invited to skip passages that are for them superfluous.

The English version of this book is dedicated to the memory of Julie Freedman and to her family. At the age of sixteen I won a scholarship from the Reform Jewish community of the United States and spent six months at the Freedman's home in Birmingham, Michigan. There I studied at a public high school, looked for after-school work to supplement my allowance, and experienced something of the life of an American teenager. In many ways this was a formative period that broadened my personality, and that continues to influence me today. Alone at such a complicated age, far from home, in a different and strange world, I was lucky to find with the Freedmans a family in every sense of the word. The sorrow, pain, and recovery they have undergone in the twenty years since then have only brought us closer.

This research project, which was intertwined with my private life, was made possible by the support of my family. My thanks and love to my mother, Yona Freiman; to my husband, Yair; and to my sons, Uri and Shaul.

I have not expressed my thanks to the women I studied. I am aware that this book does not convey my gratitude in a way they would appreciate.

ஃ

As the Hebrew version of the book was being prepared for print, the elections to the Thirteenth Knesset took place. The sense that a new political age has begun still needs to stand the test of reality. Nevertheless, a significant change in the status of the ultraorthodox communities is already apparent, both among themselves and in Israeli society. Among the Gur Hasidim, the subjects of this study, things have also changed.

I learned of the death of Rebbe Simha Bonim Alter, the fifth in the Gur Hasidim line of spiritual leaders, from a telephone call I received in early July in a miserable hotel room in Lublin, Poland. The next day I traveled to the city of Gora-Kalwaria, the Gur Hasidic sect's birthplace. I visited the study hall that had been turned into a carpentry shop and the rebbe's house, now a gynecological clinic. Polish children on vacation from school were happy to show us the way to the Jewish cemetery. Among the tall summer weeds, the broken and upended headstones, and the reconstructed burial monument of the family of rebbes, we found the town's only Jew and told him the news.

Tamar El-Or

Translator's Note

· · · ❧ · · ·

The term "ultraorthodox," commonly used to refer to the Hasidim and Misnagdim, those observant Jews who are distinguished from the "modern Orthodox" by their distinctive dress and, generally, their absolute rejection of modern secularism and of Zionism, is an unfortunate word. It implies that those it refers to are somehow more observant than other observant Jews, when what is at issue is not the extent of observance, but rather two rival conceptions regarding the essence of Judaism. I have therefore preferred the Hebrew term *haredi* (plural, *haredim*), literally "the [God]fearing." It is a more value-neutral term and the one that they themselves prefer.

Other terms have been retained in Hebrew, with explanations in context or in the endnotes when any possible translation seemed inadequate or misleading. I have tried to keep these to a minimum.

Haim Watzman

Introduction

· · · 🐦 · · ·

The Road to
the Development

Dr. Ovadia locked the door of the waiting room, letting no one else in. Those sitting inside had already been waiting for nearly two hours. Old Dr. Ovadia, adored by his patients, was the only GP in the area, and that winter had brought on a lot of flu. The *haredi* woman sitting opposite, a two-year-old girl on her knees, smiled at me and at Shaul, my one-year-old son—a smile of shared afflictions soon to be ministered to. Sitting beside us in the small room were an elderly couple, a teenager, and one middle-aged woman.

The usual waiting room conversation had already been exhausted. We sat mutely. I looked at the haredi woman, with her tailored woolen suit and the short blonde wig. I noticed the small hands holding the baby, the cut nails, the pale skin of her face, and her watery green eyes.

"You're from the Development?" I heard myself asking.

"Yes, but I don't like the neighborhood doctor so we like to come here, a lot from the Development come here."

"They don't go to Bene Brak?" I wondered, referring to the Tel Aviv suburb where haredim predominate.

"Maybe some are used to the doctor there, but why go so far? We live here."

There, I encouraged myself, you see, she answers. Go on, tell her, tell her that you pass by frequently, and that you would really like to go in, confess to her that you are waiting for the day you can visit.

You know, maybe this will sound strange, but I've gone by your neighborhood so many times, on the way to the swimming pool or to the drug store. I would so much like to go into the Development. But you know how it is, the secular think that the religious people don't want them to go among them, everyone is closed off in their own neighborhood.[1]

It seemed to me that she blushed a little—her pale skin gave away change.

1

Woman: Why closed off? Nobody was ever thrown out.

I: I work at the university, and I'm interested in the subject of
education. I think about you a lot. About the way you educate your
children. Especially about the mothers, about the small children.
I just finished a study of children in a well-off suburban community,
and I say to myself all the time that the next thing I would like to
do is learn something about your education. But I always convince
myself that they won't let me in, that they won't agree to talk to me.

Woman: About our education? I suppose that really is something you
have to study, I never thought about it, for me it's obvious.

In the meantime a man in Hasidic dress had entered the room. He was
wearing a long black coat, under which were black pants tucked into black
socks, in black loafers. On his head was a medium-sized flat hat, and he
had a reddish beard and sidelocks concealed behind his ears. The man sat
down near the woman, a key chain and a membership booklet for the Mac-
cabee Health Plan in his hands.

Woman: Did you hear? She lives here and works at the university.
Says she wants to learn about our education, that she studies children
and their education. What do you say, would they let her in to us?

The man took a swift glance, then directed a second glance at me and
said:
"Why not? Have to try, I don't think they kick people out, have to
talk and try it."
"This is my brother," the woman informed me. "He has a carpentry
shop here in the area, he lives in the Development, too."
If they're open enough to talk with me, they must be modern enough
to have a telephone at home. I will chance the question.

I: Maybe you have a telephone number I could write down and call
you some time?

Woman: Sure, write it down, my name is Rivka Zilberstein.

I jotted Rivka Zilberstein's phone number down on a scrap of news-
print I tore out of *Der Spiegel*, the newspaper that the doctor's wife apparently read. At home I stuffed it into the sleeve of my appointment book
and did not use it for two years. At the end of each year I would push it
into the corner of my new diary, gazing at it as if it were a promise, a great
opportunity. I knew that I had an entry ticket.
I thought about the subject, which had been on my mind for a long
time. I thought of the professional conferences in Jerusalem during which

I had spent my time in the haredi neighborhoods instead of in the lecture rooms. Of the long summer nights in the yard with my father as he told stories and I conjured up pictures, pictures that melded with stories from Isaac Bashevis Singer and S. Y. Agnon. The focus was always people. Girls jumping rope in Mea She'arim, Jerusalem's old haredi neighborhood, wide satin ribbons in their braids, speaking Yiddish. Little girls speaking Yiddish! It fascinated me. Thick-bodied women standing behind wooden counters in corner grocery stores selling merchandise from which one could prepare delicacies like the ones Agnon describes in his stories. I knew that I had been seeking them out for a long time, and I knew very well that I wanted, through them, to touch the past. I was not searching for spirituality, I was not searching for faith—I wanted them, the human beings.

When I finally got around to calling Rivka Zilberstein, to my great relief she did not answer. I called again, with mixed feelings, a few more times, and the results were the same.

In order to prove, once and for all, that the opportunity was lost, I decided to go there.

So on a sun-drenched winter morning at the beginning of 1985 I put on a long skirt, a blouse closed around the neck, got into my antique Saab, and set out. The four-minute trip was a hard one. Something in the bottom of my stomach was bothering me. Deep inside I wanted the visit to end unsuccessfully. I steered the car into the parking lot between the apartment buildings. It was ten in the morning and all was still. There were no girls with braids, the laundry waving between the houses had disappeared, and there were no men rushing through the streets. Nothing, no one. A few minutes later a man came out of one of the houses and strode towards an old station wagon. I asked him if he knew someone named Rivka Zilberstein. My field notebook records:

"Zilberstein Rivka? They moved a year ago to Bene Brak."

Great, I thought, but really too bad. My face must have shown my disappointment, because he asked whether he could help me.

I told him that I had spoken to her once, and that I was interested in women's activities in the Development. I said that she had promised to help me. He looked at me, made a quick judgment, and decided.

"Look, I don't know what can be done, but you can go up to my wife, she's at home now, Waxman, Sarah Waxman."

On my way I thought about the profession called anthropology, about the chutzpah you have to get up in order to knock on a woman's door in the morning and ask permission to enter her life. The stone at the bottom of my stomach got heavier and slowed my steps up the dark stairway.

A woman of about thirty opened the door. She was busy mopping. Next to her was a boy of about four, and from behind her legs peeked a girl of about two. The woman was wearing a thin, checkered housecoat, and there was a carelessly tied kerchief on her head that she pushed forward every so often while we were talking.

I don't understand so well what you actually want, excuse me for
the house being this way, it's just that tonight we're having a *sheva
brachot* [one of the festive meals held each evening during the week
after a marriage to honor the new couple] and I haven't finished
getting ready yet, but come on, come on in to the living room.

I sat on the couch, facing six chairs piled onto a large dining table and
waiting for the mop to pass by so that they could return to their natural
state. Along the wall was a large cabinet full of books; some of the shelves
were protected by glass and contained silver implements and other orna-
mental objects.

Look, now the women are not very active here, you understand, at
the beginning when we came here we were newlyweds, so we had
clubs and meetings on Shabbat [the Sabbath], but now, thank God,
everyone has children, I have six for instance, may they be healthy,
so everyone is busy. Now a lot of new couples have moved into
the buildings across the way, and the girls there are starting to get
organized. What can I say, I don't know, but wait a second, look,
there's a very haredi woman here in the neighborhood, she's Rivka
Zilberstein's sister-in-law, you know what, go to her, maybe she can
help you, she lives two buildings up. Hannah Zilberstein.

"Very haredi?" And what was *she*, if not haredi? What did she mean by
the description "haredi"? By the time I got to Hannah Zilberstein's house
I had lost my will again—one had been enough for me this morning. I was
relieved when no sound came from Hannah's apartment.

Ten days went by before I returned to the apartment, and two and a
half years before I left it for good.

When I got up the courage to return, the light switch in the stairwell
was broken. I recorded what happened thereafter as follows:

I go up to the second-floor apartment, and a girl of about eight
descends past me, with a small boy on her back. The apartment
across from the Zilbersteins is being renovated, the door is gaping,
and two laborers are inside. I knock on the front door, and feel the
knocking in my chest. The door is opened by a woman dressed in
a plaid wool skirt, a gray blouse, and a kerchief of blue and white
squares. Her legs are in opaque, flesh-colored nylon stockings, and
her feet are in shabby, dirty clogs with thick platform soles.

Hannah: Yes, Sarah Waxman told me about you on Shabbat, but
time went by, I thought you forgot about the whole business. Listen,

I need to hear from you what you want, and to talk to my husband. He's not at home during the week, he comes back only on Thursday.

Behind her back I saw a bare apartment. A ladder stood in the foyer, a can of paint alongside. Maybe they're renovating, too, I thought. In the middle of the wall I saw a patch of exposed concrete—completely exposed, without any plaster, a naked rectangle.[2] A baby girl, about a year and a half old, was entwined around Hannah's legs; she was dressed in short wool pants and a sweater. Hannah left me on the landing, and our first conversation was conducted there, standing.

> *I*: Look, it's a little hard for me to tell you exactly what I want. It's not that clear to me, either. I know that I want to be here a little and see how you live, but actually the main thing that interests me is education. You know, with the secular there's a feeling that they haven't been very successful with education, that what they want to pass on to the next generation doesn't always get there. And when they look at you, at least from the outside, it seems as if you don't have any problem of that sort.

I stood there in the hallway, my legs tightly crossed, and I realized that I was already working. How does work begin? For an anthropologist, when does conversation stop and inquiry begin?

I felt that my body was tight, that I was not using it. My body, which I use to express myself beyond words, was turned in on itself and under the control of my speech. My sentences became vague, and they had large gaps that could be filled in by the woman facing me. I knew that I was play-acting a bit, that I was circumventing the essential. What I really wanted was the women, and I was talking about education. I would almost certainly look for the problematic and take a critical stance, and here I was playing up to and extolling their education. Still, at the same time, I spoke utterly naturally. The place I was standing and the woman I was speaking with gave the conversation its own authenticity.

Over time, the changes that began in me during my time at the Development became deeper. In Hannah's house, and in other houses, in public places, on the street, and at celebrations, I learned to move my body in a special way, to change my resolute tone of voice, and to remain silent a great deal. Slowly, from the minute I decided to go to the Development, during the short drive there, as I locked the car and began a slow walk to one of the houses, I would change. I became another woman.

> *Hannah:* If I don't call you by Shabbat, it means that my husband agreed, and you can come. I request that if you come, you dress the way you are now, in modest clothing.

I: For me this is a great opportunity. I hope your husband will understand that. Yes, of course I'll dress the way I should.

I left with weak knees. I knew that I had placed great hope in her, and I was sure that this woman did not take other people's hopes lightly, just as she does not take her own hopes lightly. The phone did not ring, and at the end of March, three weeks before Passover, my journey began. A personal journey towards other human beings, incarnated finally as scientific labor.

⟨⟩

"Anthropology?" people say. "You're an anthropologist? It must be so interesting." The picture it conjures up is of British researchers sitting crosslegged in a circle with a council of Africans deliberating over the sale of goats to the neighboring tribe, wild-bearded investigators in khaki like those shown in the television series "Disappearing World." Maybe they think of Margaret Mead and the adolescents of the New Guinea islands, of her popular books that took anthropology out of the ivory tower and confronted Americans with the mirror-image of Westernism and capitalism. "Yes," I answer. "It is the same anthropology, but it is entirely different."

Anthropology has undergone both marginal and fundamental changes since it began to occupy researchers at the end of the nineteenth century; now only one common characteristic remains: the anthropologists' personal contact with the people they are studying. This contact with people—observation of them, conversation with them, attention to them, reading what they have written—is unmediated. It is a network of relations with a group of human beings built up over time. It does not always involve a long journey, tropical weather, a jeep, and a tent. The sidewalks of New York, labor-intensive factories, immigrant neighborhoods in a European capital, and all kinds of bureaucracies can be fields of research—as can a Hasidic community.

Another characteristic common to most anthropological work is the necessary flexibility of the research questions. During one's time with the group under study, the original questions are likely to become unimportant, while others—which could not have been conceived of before meeting the subjects—emerge to take their places. What remains for the anthropologist is to try to decipher what has been experienced, remembered, collected, and documented.

My interest in haredi women had several catalysts. Some of these were academic, and these always remained in the background as I conducted my day-to-day contacts with the women, observed events, and recorded my emotions and spontaneous insights. My academic interests were in a constant process of give-and-take with the reality I studied. Areas that seemed significant to me at the beginning of the project—such as the women's daily routines, their lives as believing religious women, their intimate-family worlds, their sociopolitical status—had their importance tested in the reality I observed. During the course of the study I developed a strong antipathy to deliberately exposing private matters, such as the relations between wife and husband and between women and their bodies. Contrary to the prevalent image of anthropological work, and contrary to the expectations of my friends, colleagues, and family members, voyeurism was not my purpose. I was well aware that the material collected on my computer diskettes revealed a society and individuals for whom privacy was of utmost importance. As a result, I preferred to focus on social processes that are not centered on the individual.

A short time after beginning my regular visits with Hannah, I asked to widen my circle of acquaintances among the community women. I asked Hannah about the neighborhood activities held for women, and she promised that the "classes" would soon begin again. They did indeed begin again, to my good fortune, and they became my central arena for the observation of women as a "public." I saw young women who had, not long before, finished fourteen years of intensive study leave their homes and their small children, their housework, and the husband who had just returned from the *kolel* (a place for religious study by married men), from work, or from prayers, and go to attend a class. Women studying Jewish law, the Bible, or Jewish philosophy populated most of the material I had—and it was this social phenomenon that I wished to understand.

A sweeping phenomenon in the haredi sector is that of women spending what little free time they have attending classes. This is not a marginal manifestation that I just happened to run into at the Development; it is the state of affairs in haredi communities in Bene Brak, Tel Aviv, Jerusalem, the suburbs, and more distant communities as well. Just as a community is known for the *ulpanot* (religious schools for girls) and *yeshivot* (religious schools for boys) it supplies for its children, it is also known by the system of adult education it provides for its women and the variety of lessons it provides for its adult men.

It became clear to me that it was the haredi women's intellectual world and their studies that I wished to decipher. The haredi women's intellectual world is of recent make. Women, unlike men, are not commanded to study, so women in the haredi sector did not study in any institutionalized way until the second decade of this century. For men, knowledge, erudition, and scholarship are a means of enhancing their status, are the basis for the creation of leadership, and grant official sanction to male control of society.[3]

Such study, by far the greatest part of which is the study of the Talmud, is not the provenance of women today, either. I therefore wished to find out what purpose the community had in offering the women studies in other subjects, and what purpose the women themselves saw in study that a priori denied them the Talmudic sources of knowledge that allow men to achieve power, respect, and money.

This question requires an answer on both the descriptive and theoretical levels, focusing on three major areas:

1. *Literacy*. This term applies to the cultural and social significance of knowledge, from the deciphering of content and curricula, teaching methods, the dissemination or restriction of knowledge, through the constitution of consciousness and knowledge of individuals according to their social position. The examination of literacy also provides a historical survey of the place of knowledge in society, dwelling in particular on those junctures at which there have been significant changes in the ability of individuals and groups to approach its sources.

Here it is necessary to ascertain what the women's intellectual world includes. Are its boundaries negotiable? Are there women who wish to master new fields of knowledge that have hitherto been forbidden them? Are there situations in which women "steal" knowledge from their husbands and sons? What is the practical and ideological force of this literacy? Is the growing literacy of women changing the intracommunity or intrafamily division of power?

This female literacy is also of interest as a form of consciousness. Are women taught to think differently than men, to read the world in a way unique to them, and if so, do they consequently experience themselves as being literate or as being ignorant?

2. *Women*. The protagonists of this work are women—women in a society that determines many of its decisions and customs according to gender. Theory and research in the field of gender studies have aided my work.[4]

3. *The haredi community in Israel*. What is the specific (Gur Hasidic) and broader context of the women in the Development, the context in which they live and through which they experience and interpret their world? This work does not seek to study the haredi communities in Israel, but rather to understand some of their central characteristics in order to anchor the phenomenon under investigation (women's study) in the human domain significant to it.

These three elements create a triangle, with each of its points in a different contextual world. Literacy and the women form the two upper sides, and are connected by the bottom side, the foundation, which signifies the haredi Jewish community.

The tension between literacy and women is derived from the significance that haredi society gives to women's study, given the fact that they study a great deal. This tension, which will be shown to be a paradoxical factor in the life of the community and of the women themselves, is a discrete event in a chain of paradoxes that are the lot of the haredi community in Israel today.

The book moves along an avenue of paradoxes, from the private to the general, and contains four chapters. The first chapter will provide an acquaintance with the research population and the research methods. The second chapter will focus in detail on the paradox of education and ignorance. The third chapter will show the expressions of the paradox in the women's society, and the fourth chapter will be devoted to a general description of other paradoxes in which the haredi community in Israel finds itself caught, and will make an attempt to show how this mechanism of creating and finding a way out of paradoxes helps the haredi communities in Israel to distinguish themselves from their surroundings and to construct social boundaries, in particular between themselves and other Jews.

The daily lives of the women and their families, or the classic divisions of most anthropological studies—such as economics, power relations, the world of faith, and ritual—do not make separate appearances. They are integrated into the attempt to answer the research question at the center of the book and are addressed along the way. Descriptions of the daily reality of Gur Hasidic women allow the reader to acquire some sense of their relations with their children and spouses, their homes, their expectations, their anxieties, their celebrations, and their difficulties, as in any other human society.

These women belong to the community of Gur Hasidim. Before we go deeper into their world, we should become acquainted with that community, and with the place in which they live.

Notes

1. The orthodox/secular dichotomy used to describe Jewish/Israeli differences is not completely accurate. Jews in Israel who are not orthodox do participate in many traditional customs and procedures due to the Jewish nature of the state. Judaism should be understood as more than a religion: it encompasses history, nationality, language, and destiny. Therefore, the reader must be aware that describing someone as a secular, or nonorthodox, Jew is a complicated and sometimes vague matter.

2. I later learned that this bare patch is meant to be a memorial to the destruction of the Temple, and that in many haredi homes a section of the eastern wall is intentionally left exposed, without plaster or paint.

3. For a broader discussion of the social importance of study in modern Judaism, see Heschel 1966; Adler 1959; Finkelstein 1955.

4. I will not discuss the subject of gender studies here, but three important sources that deal with the connection between gender and culture should be noted: Zimbalist-Rosaldo 1975; Reiter 1975; MacCormack and Strathern 1980.

The Gur Hasidic Development in Tel Aviv

1

· · · 🙠 · · ·

The Gur Hasidim
and the Development

The women described in these pages are members of the Gur Hasidic sect. "Gur" refers to the Polish town Gora-Kalwaria, not far from Warsaw on the banks of the Vistula River, in which the sect's first spiritual leader (the *admor* or rebbe) established his court.

Hasidism evolved in Central Europe in the mideighteenth century. Despite the movement's declared allegiance to Jewish tradition, it constituted a social revolution in Jewish society, coming as a response to the great changes then occurring in the countries where most European Jews lived, and in the Jewish communities themselves.

Hasidism was an attempt to provide answers to modernism, to the development of the nation-state, to the secularizing Jewish enlightenment that was just then beginning, and to the first opportunities for Jews to mix with and play a role as citizens in non-Jewish society. It also wished to provide remedies for the ailments then afflicting the Jewish communities themselves—the corruption that plagued the rabbinic leadership and the destitution of the Jewish communities of Eastern Europe. On the ideological level, Hasidism was the first Jewish movement to wrestle with the constitution of selfhood in its modern sense—with issues such as the status of the individual in a hierarchical society, power relationships, and equality before the law. Hasidism offered a new social utopia based on the relationship between the individual Hasid and his saintly spiritual leader, on the divine and sublime aspect of each person without regard to his social standing, and on liberation from the traditional social structure. With the exception of the *Tania* by Rebbe Schneur Zalman of Liadi, the early Hasidim composed no clear, organized exposition of their ideas. Rather, these find expression in a rich tradition of homilies, books of moral instruction, works about the deeds of saintly Hasidim, and a rich oral literature.

The new movement divided Ashkenazi (European) Jewry into two major groups—the Hasidim and the Misnagdim (literally, "opponents," they are often referred to as "Lithuanians," after the area where they were strongest). Hasidism itself divided into different sects, or "courts," each

11

centered around a dynasty of rebbes and referred to by the name of the city or town in which the rebbe resided.

Hasidim were immediately distinguishable from other Jews by their appearance and behavior. Each sect had its unique dress, style of prayer, and rituals. While it is these external phenomena that attract attention, it is important to remember that they are expressions of a cosmology and theology that go far beyond dances, songs, and stories.

The Ashkenazi haredi community in Israel today still breaks down along the old fault lines between Hasidim and Misnagdim.[1] The two groups sometimes ally for political purposes; at other times they clash. In recent years the conflict between them has increased, most notably between the major Israeli Misnaged leader, Rabbi Eliezer Menachem Shach, and the Lubavitcher (Habad) rebbe, Rabbi Menachem Mendel Schneerson, whose court is in Brooklyn, New York. The Hasidim's reverence for their spiritual leaders has been magnified in Habad; the rebbe has encouraged a messianic fervor that has led many of his followers to proclaim that he is the Messiah. Rabbi Shach considers this the worst of heresies, and while he attacks Habad specifically, he clearly believes that this is the end result of what he considers the pagan cult of the rebbe in all Hasidic sects.

The Hasidic sects in Israel may be divided into two major groups. The smaller is the Ha'eda Haharedit, an irreconcilable opponent of Zionism, concentrated largely in and around the Jerusalem neighborhood of Mea She'arim. Encompassing groups like the Toldot Aharon Hasidim and the Satmer Hasidim, Ha'eda Haharedit refuses to cooperate with the Israeli state in any way. Its members refuse to vote or to be elected to national institutions; they also refuse government funds and consider the establishment of Israel as one of the major catastrophes of modern Jewish history.[2]

The second group includes Gur as well as the Vizhnitz Hasidim, the Belzer Hasidim, the Bratislaver Hasidim, and other smaller courts. These do not believe in Zionism, but play an ever-expanding role in the life and leadership of the country.[3]

The first Gur rebbe was Rebbe Yitzhak Meir Rutenberg, better known as the Rim, an acronym of his Hebrew initials. Considered a child prodigy, he studied when young under the *maggid* (preacher) of Kozhnitz. During his adolescence he decided it would be best for him to cut off his ties to the Kozhnitz court, where he felt "spoiled," and to accept the solicitations of the Pashisha court. The Rim established a Pashisha-style *beit-midrash*, or house of study, in Warsaw.

His wife, the daughter of a wealthy man, supported him by managing a store for woven goods in Warsaw, but the Polish rebellion led to financial hardship for his father-in-law and thus for the Rim himself. They became destitute and were forced to hide from their creditors. They changed their name from Rutenberg to Alter and were supported by the rebbe's rich brother. Upon the death of Warsaw's chief rabbi in 1840, the post was offered to the Rim, but he turned it down. At the death of Rebbe Mendele of Kotzk, the leader of Pashisha Hasidism, the remnants of the Pashisha community gathered under the Rim's leadership and became his disciples. His court centered around the large house of study built at the edge of the city, and when the movement had grown and his followers had multiplied, the rebbe searched for a small city to which they could move. From among the proposals that reached him, the Rim chose Gur, where his father had once been the community rabbi. This small town was close to Warsaw, with direct transportation to and from the capital, and it soon became the center of Polish Hasidism. Gur, which people claimed had been the site of rampant sexual profligacy, was transformed into a name that sprang to the lips of Hasidim like a prayer.

The Rim, the spiritual and social shepherd of the new generation, the "generation of deep learning," put special emphasis on religious study. If, originally, Pashisha Hasidism had been known for its love and, then, in its Kotzk incarnation, for its fear of God, Gur assumed a scholarly and scrupulously observant image. Gur Hasidism tried to distance itself from mysticism. The rebbe, unlike other Hasidic leaders, did not deal in miracles and did not collect tithes from his followers. Old customs were revived. Observance of the designated hours of prayer, for instance, which had slackened in Hasidism's first generation, was reinstated. Blowing the *shofar* during the month of Elul was resumed as part of the prayers of repentance leading up to Yom Kippur, and much time was devoting to study. The Hasidim of Gur emphasized the qualities of truth and humility, and worked hard to create a rational, solid, and meticulous self-image.

The Rim saw the exile of the Jews from the Holy Land as a divine retribution and a catastrophe. Yet he did not, like some other Hasidic leaders, consider Poland an incubator of Judaism. Even though Poland was kind to the Jews at the time, this did not turn his city into Gur Hasidism's Jerusalem.

The first admor encouraged Jews to travel to the land of Israel, and told his community to continue contributing to the support of the small Jewish community there. He even expressed his own desire to visit the Holy Land.

The real possibility of a return to Zion began to interest the generations that came after the first rebbe. His grandson, Rebbe Yehuda Arieh Leib Alter, known (as many Jewish religious scholars have come to be known) by the name of his major work, the *Sefat Emet*, lived in the era of the Hovevei Tsion, the earliest, pre-Herzl movement to call for the return of the Jewish people to the land of their fathers. The letters he wrote to his followers in response to these early Zionists reveal that he had mixed feelings about Jewish settlement in Palestine. On the one hand, he was happy to witness the Jewish reawakening that was prompting Jews to return to the Holy Land. On the other hand, he heard rumors that those who were going there were not living as observant Jews. He thus told his disciples, and advised all those who heard him, to conduct a thorough investigation of the possibilities of life in the Holy Land, both from the Jewish and economic aspects. The Sefat Emet was neither enthusiastic about nor opposed to the idea of the return to Zion. He chose a cautious attitude, neither rejecting settlement in the land of Israel nor encouraging his followers to move there.[4]

After the Balfour Declaration of 1917, the leaders of religious Judaism had to take a clear stand on the real possibility of Jewish settlement in Palestine. The Sefat Emet's son chose to take a position that differed from his father's. Rebbe Avraham Mordecai Alter, the third Gur rebbe, was known for his organizational talent. He was among the founders of Agudat Yisrael, an organization that attempted to unite all parts of the religious Jewish community, and of Agudat Shlomei Emunei Yisrael.[5] He visited Israel six times and considered himself (and was perceived as) a *Hovev Tsion*—a lover of Zion.

In the year 5671 (1921), the third admor promulgated an epistle that greatly influenced the movement of Gur Hasidim to Israel. Written under the influence of his first journey there, the rebbe praised the Holy Land, enumerated the religious and social justifications for settling in Israel, and calmed his readers' fears of the Arabs. "Almost everywhere we went they deferred to us; may we see just a bit of this among the residents of all countries. My opinion is that we can have good relations with them and live there in peace and security."[6]

Avraham Mordecai encouraged his disciples to invest their money in Palestine, to buy land, and to support construction projects such as the establishment of the town of Bene Brak. Starting in the mid-1920s, some of his followers began emigrating to the Holy Land. These Hasidim established social infrastructures in Tel Aviv, Jerusalem, and Bene Brak, communities that became a solid nucleus for their Hasidic movement after World War II. The admor and a part of his family succeeded in fleeing Poland when the Nazis invaded and settled in Israel.

The task of gathering together and revitalizing the sect's fragments after the Holocaust fell to the fourth admor, Avraham Mordecai's son. Rebbe Yisrael Alter, the "Beit Yisrael," was a stern, rigorous, and exacting leader; he made the Gurs into the strongest Polish Hasidic sect in Israel and the dominant force in Agudat Yisrael (which, after the foundation of the State of Israel, functioned as a political party representing the haredi community in the country's parliament, the Knesset). When Rebbe Yisrael Alter died in 1977, his brother, who had until then been a businessman, became admor. The major accomplishment of Rebbe Simha Bonim Alter was the organization and institutionalization of the movement after its postwar revitalization. As an experienced businessman, he foresaw that the "learning society" would force frugality on the haredi community. He continued to encourage men to study and women to refrain from taking anything other than teaching work, but also imposed new economic restrictions, largely on the younger generation.

The admor ordered that weddings, bar mitzvahs, and other celebrations be conducted on a more modest scale; that young couples buy smaller apartments; and that these apartments be located far from existing haredi towns and neighborhoods. At his bidding, Agudat Yisrael supported the Gur movement in obtaining government support for the construction of four housing developments—in Ashdod, Arad, Hatzor Hagelilit, and Tel Aviv—all but the last in peripheral cities. Each young couple was required to live far from parents and in-laws (that is, far from Bene Brak, central Tel Aviv, and Jerusalem), for at least five years. The rebbe himself, as well as men in key positions (heads of yeshivot, *kashrut* inspectors, and other functionaries), sent young couples to the new developments and helped them buy apartments there by offering loans on easy terms. Just a few years after the four developments first opened in 1974, some 800 Gur families were living in them. By leaving the established haredi communities for the Galilee and the Negev, they created centers of orthodoxy in the heart of the secular population.

The fifth admor, Rebbe Simha Bonim Alter, died in July 1992, after seven years of illness during which he was unable to carry out most of his responsibilities. (The field work for this study took place in 1985–1988, during his illness.) There were two candidates to replace him. The first was his half-brother, Rabbi Pinhas Alter, more than eighty years old, who stood at the head of the most important Gur yeshiva, the Sefat Emet Yeshiva in Jerusalem. Pinhas Alter served as the sect's political leader during the previous rebbe's illness. The second candidate was the fifth admor's son, Rabbi Ya'akov Alter, who lives in Bene Brak. He is thirty years younger than his uncle and had avoided public activity other than heading the major Gur yeshiva in Tel Aviv. The two of them agreed that Pinhas Alter would succeed his brother, and that Ya'akov would eventually have his turn. Even now, however, rumor has it that the Hasidim are not happy with their new leader and that they are urging Ya'akov to take his uncle's place.

The Gur Hasidim remain the largest and central component of Agudat Yisrael. When the Misnaged haredim split off from Agudat Yisrael before the 1988 Knesset elections, Gur became the only real power in the movement. While it cooperated in that election with the Habad Hasidim, the alliance was seen as a tactical one only. Habad has no real control over the resources of Agudat Yisrael and in the 1992 elections Habad remained neutral. The Agudat Yisrael newspaper, *Hamodia*, is for all intents and purposes the Gur newspaper, and Agudat Yisrael's offices are run for the most part by Gur Hasidim.

It is estimated that there are between 5,000 and 8,000 Gur Hasidic families in Israel. Accounting and statistics are a serious matter for haredi communities, since government subsidies are often appropriated on a per student, per person, or per family basis. For this reason, there is no way of knowing whether or not they keep precise records regarding matters like school enrollment. It would seem that they benefit from numerical obscurity, because it allows them to depict themselves as few or large in number, according to the demands of a given situation. It may be, however, that it is technically impossible for them to obtain such figures. The uncertainty may not necessarily be an attempt by the leadership to hide such information from the "evil eye"; it may just represent the difficulties of collating pieces of data from the multitude of people responsible for them—school principals, yeshiva directors, politicians. In any case, financial, political, and social matters are managed in accordance with estimates that approximate reality.

Only in the last decade did Gur establish itself as the largest and most important Hasidic group in Israel and take control of Agudat Yisrael. There are those who call them the "Cossacks"[7] because of their practice of wearing their pants tucked deep into their black socks. Others (especially the Lithuanians) call them the "Polish merchants" because of their reputation as practical people well-placed in the local economy, in contrast with, for instance, the eccentric Bratislaver Hasidim or extreme Hasidic sects that have cut themselves off from the secular world. The men did not spend long years studying in yeshivot; instead, they joined the family business when they reached their late twenties. The appointment of Simha Bonim Alter, who spent most of his life as a successful businessman and not as a Torah scholar, may have added to this stereotype. In any case, the Gur Hasidim, like other Hasidic sects, have gone to great lengths to prove that wisdom does not reside only in Misnaged yeshivot, and that a Gur Hasid can devote himself to Torah study as well as anyone else. Lengthening a young man's period of yeshiva study past his twenties has become an accepted phenomenon among the Gurs, and its implications will be examined further on.

The history of Gur Hasidism has been written by its men, so it focuses on the most prominent of them. Hasidic theology and its political struggles are not what interest us here, however.

The varieties of Gur Hasidic life to be found in this description are restricted to the community I visited, although I will continually try to link this to the experience of all haredim in Israel. It should be noted, however, that many Gur Hasidim from Tel Aviv and Jerusalem repeatedly requested that I make clear that the phenomena I describe in this book do not typify Gur life in other communities and are applicable only to the place I studied—"the Development."

The Development

The establishment of the Development was the result of a new and revolutionary concept articulated by the late admor, Rebbe Simha Bonim. It

had two purposes. The first was entirely pragmatic—it was intended to provide a solution to the housing problem created by high apartment prices in
Jerusalem and Bene Brak and to stop the conspicuous consumption that
was starting to become the norm in the Hasidic community. The second
was the expression of a conviction that Gur Hasidim should be dispersed
throughout the country. There they would establish contact with a diverse
population and establish nuclei of haredi settlement in secular areas. This
was accomplished by forbidding a newly married couple to live in an apartment larger than 75 square meters. In addition, no major changes or reno-
vations were to be made in the apartment before the young couple moved
in. A limit was placed on the number of guests that could be invited to
weddings. The ceremony itself was to be conducted with just the family
present, with a reception for guests thereafter. The young couple would be
required to live in their first apartment for five years before they could
leave the outlying areas for the center of the country.

Sixty years after having come to Israel, the Gur Hasidim (who were
best known as urban merchants, many of whom had large holdings) left the
confines of the large cities. This was neither an easy nor a simple matter.
The move to the developments was at first seen as a kind of deportation,
an exile outside the bounds of Jewish settlement. The Hasidim viewed
the rebbe's orders as a temporary hardship, a trial to be endured. When the
project began, many couples spent their first five years trying to raise
the money necessary to return "home." Now many of them continue to
reside in the developments even after the "exile" runs its term.

The Development at the edge of Tel Aviv opened in 1975. The first
ten buildings were constructed at the far end of a neighborhood that had
grown out of one of the temporary immigrant camps of the 1950s. It is considered a disadvantaged area and was included in Project Renewal, Israel's
urban reconstruction project of the 1980s. The area falls within the Tel
Aviv jurisdiction, but its character is suburban, and it is composed of several low-quality housing projects. Most of these have a population defined
as secular, and they contain no schools or other institutions (other than
synagogues) connected to the religious establishment. One of the neighborhoods near the Hasidic village is made up mostly of middle-class families living in public housing projects renovated and enlarged by the residents. Most of the residents are Oriental Jews, whose families came to
Israel from North Africa or the Middle East. There lies the local ritual
bath, or mikveh, as well as many synagogues. A Gur yeshiva and several
other of the sect's places of study are located in this neighborhood, drawn
there years ago by low prices.

Candidates for residence in the Development have to pass the scrutiny
of a board appointed by Agudat Yisrael. In principle, any haredi couple can
apply to the selection committee, but the reality is that most of the residents are Gur Hasidim. The village contains only residences. There are no

synagogues, nursery schools, classrooms, ritual baths, or shopping centers.
The relative proximity to Bene Brak and to the adjacent older neighborhoods made the village merely a bedroom community, with its residents
making use of the services existing in the area, or in Bene Brak.

Each morning the parking lot between the buildings is filled with
minibuses taking pupils of all ages to schools in Tel Aviv and Bene Brak.
Ten years after the Development was built, the Tel Aviv bus company
decided to establish a bus line between the Development and Bene Brak,
running six times a day. One kindergarten originally meant for children in
the secular neighborhoods has turned into a nursery school for the Development's children, but the Development itself still has no other educational institution. The Hasidim do their shopping in the neighborhood
shopping center, where the merchants stock the products with the kashrut
certifications that the Gur families demand. There are those who do their
shopping in the Gur Hasidic shopping center in Bene Brak. The neighborhood medical clinic and well-baby center serve those residents of the
Development who wish to make use of them. The new neighborhood community center, built as part of the urban renewal program, allows the
Hasidim to use its facilities by prior arrangement (for lectures, assemblies,
classes, and so on, open only to residents of the Development). Each summer, the municipal pool next to the community center sets aside days for
separate male and female swimming, and the Gur Hasidim use the neighborhood's men's mikveh. Few Hasidic women use the women's mikveh
located near the Development. Most, for reasons of privacy, prefer to travel
to Ramat Gan, Tel Aviv, or Bene Brak.[8]

Some seven years after families moved into the first ten buildings, ten
similar ones were built; there are now 400 families living in the Development. The feeling that moving there is "going into exile" has not entirely
dissipated, but motivation has risen. Many families that lived in the Development ten years ago have moved to Bene Brak, and their places have
been taken by young couples. The Development's image as a forsaken
neighborhood lacking any character of its own has become a challenge for
its new residents. These couples, just recently married, are made up of
yeshiva students and graduates of the Beit Ya'akov women's teachers college. Considered "good material," they have filled the empty apartments
that had previously been rented out on a short-term basis. The outward
migration was halted, and there is now an attempt to give the place the
character of a permanent settlement. Yet even when the fifth admor's
granddaughter moved to the Development after her marriage, it did not
lead to the establishment of local institutions. She is, however, evidence
that its image is changing.

The sense of physical exile is stronger among the women.[9] They
remain in the Development throughout the day and feel unable to connect

with the area in which they live. About a quarter of the women have jobs outside the Development as teachers or as saleswomen in family businesses. For the rest, the stores in Bene Brak and downtown Jerusalem cannot serve as an excuse for meetings with other women. Going out into the public sphere (the yards around the buildings or the small playground at the edge of the Development) during the morning is a public declaration that "I don't have anything to do at home." As a result, the public space is deserted in the mornings. The women who stay at home take advantage of this time to prepare lunch and to do routine housework. From time to time, they relate, they are overcome by the need for the commotion of the city. When this happens, they take a bus to Bene Brak, take a walk down Rabbi Akiva Street, and return home. Some of them add that they come back appreciative of the Development's tranquility, its clean air, and its open spaces.

At the center of the adjacent neighborhood stands a Gur higher yeshiva.[10] It was built in the middle of the 1960s and is the sect's second most important place of study, after the Sefat Emet Yeshiva in Jerusalem. Its many students come from all over the country, and the few who work there live in the nearby Development. The secular residents of the neighborhood have become accustomed to the sight of the *avrechim*, the young scholars, in the street. The neighborhood synagogues, which have trouble gathering the necessary ten men for a prayer service, are often aided by the young students, who are sent at request on various missions. There are those who ask them to come to a mourner's house to help make up the quorum for the afternoon prayer. Sometimes they are asked to visit the schools before the High Holidays or to help a local boy learn the Torah portion he must read at his bar mitzvah. From time to time disputes break out, especially over the use of public property, such as the use of bomb shelters as study rooms for avrechim or the construction of an old-age home for Hasidim on the lot next to the yeshiva. In general these conflicts are resolved through the municipality's regular bureaucratic processes, and only a few times have conflicting interests led to violence.

In 1987, during the period when extremist haredim were burning bus stops to protest what they saw as the immodest advertisements on display there, some Torah scrolls were burned at the yeshiva. Members of the neighborhood councils swiftly condemned the crime; the yeshiva did not blame the neighborhood residents. Living in proximity to a secular community has created delicate points of contact between the Hasidim and the surrounding population, which everyone has an interest in preserving. Still, only a few individuals on each side have become friendly with families from the other community. This was why I was astounded by the relative openness evinced by Rivka Zilberstein during our conversation in the doctor's waiting room and, later, by the cooperation of other women. The information supplied to me by these women, whatever their status and social position, constitutes a significant segment of the data in this research project, data that I will present further on.

Informants and the Nature of Information

Social and cultural anthropology has a number of divisions, each producing scientific work very different from the others. Some anthropologists study institutional structures in various societies; others delve into the life cycle of individuals or of the sexes. Some researchers endeavor to show the link between ecological or economic data and the sociocultural structure, while others present the connection between culture and personality structure, or the "national character." Despite these differences, one activity is common to most researchers: field work. That is, a social anthropologist is someone who has at least once performed unmediated empirical research among members of a human group at the place in which that group conducts its life. This is the trademark of anthropology.

The central tools for gathering information in anthropological field work are the researchers and their subjects. When the work is written up, the talkers, the listeners, and the onlookers are supposed to become objects of study and understanding.[11] It follows, then, that every discussion of the reliability and validity of the material produced by field work is really a discussion of the researchers and their acquaintances. The history of the methodology of anthropology shows a clear inequality in the attention given to these two factors. On the one hand, there is a plentiful supply of information about the subjects; on the other hand, there is a dearth of information about the researchers themselves. Anthropological correspondents provide their readers with much detail on those who conveyed information to the researcher, but barely mention who listened to that information, experienced it, internalized it, deciphered, ordered, and recorded it. This part of the information, if revealed at all, is found generally in nonscientific works such as travel chronicles or adventure stories, as an epilogue to the scientific work, or as purely literary material.[12]

For many reasons, this imbalance became the hottest subject in anthropological methodology in the 1980s. Studies included critiques of the colonialist relation between the West and the Third World, the appearance of researchers from the Third World (which had always been the subject, rather than a producer, of anthropological research) in the scientific arena, post-modernist thinking that criticized the power and value structure, literary criticism on the representation of "the other" through the eyes of cultural centers, and the accession of a new generation in the academic world.[13]

The academic shakeup that modern anthropology has undergone no longer allows the production of knowledge to be taken for granted.

Researchers are required to address the process by which they produce their knowledge and to share this with their readers. They must demonstrate an awareness of their strengths and weaknesses; of their social and political position; of the methods by which their material was gathered, classified, and written; and of their academic and critical goals.

At its radical extreme, the new anthropology made the researcher the center of interest; generally, however, the focus is still on the subjects. There are those who argue that these providers of information are marginal people,[14] exceptional in their societies, who by force of their position (whether high or low) are able to approach the foreign researcher without any risk to themselves. If the informants are indeed unrepresentative of the "average person," there is good reason to examine the validity of the information they pass on and especially its contribution to the understanding of the society as a whole. In order to answer this question, I will describe some of the women with whose help I obtained information, and afterwards the social context in which I wished to find the information significant. This will allow an examination both of the issue of "marginality" as it affects reliability and validity, and of the process of obtaining the information.

Hannah, who agreed to allow an academic woman with an interest in haredi education into her home, became my central and most important informant. Every event began in her apartment—going to a class, to a wedding, to a walk in the yard with the children, or on a visit with neighbors. Only rarely did I visit the Development without stopping by at Hannah's. A deep and complex web of relations was spun between us, only parts of which are described in this study.

Hannah Zilberstein

Hannah was born in Bene Brak; her father was born in Hebron and her mother in Switzerland, both to Gur families. When her mother arrived in Israel after World War II, she was betrothed to Hannah's father. Despite his Hasidic background, Hannah's father had studied at a "Lithuanian" yeshiva during his youth. The couple had seven children, five boys and two girls. At home they spoke Hebrew, because her mother wished to gain a reasonable command of that language. Yiddish was a familiar sound to Hannah's ears, but she did not grow up fluent in it. Hannah studied at the Beit Ya'akov school in Bene Brak and at the Wolf teachers college, the city's most prestigious women's college. At that time both Hasidic and "Lithuanian" women studied there together, and Gur women did not attend a separate college, as they do today. Her father was not a scholar, and earned his living at manual labor. The family had economic problems (though no more so than their neighbors), but the children were allowed to continue their studies for as long as they wished and were never pressured to work to support the family. Hannah was very close to her sister, who was three years older. She has powerful memories of long conversations into the night, summer trips to the women's beach, and leisure time during vacations. It was Hannah's sister who taught her about menstruation and adolescence. She would also allow Hannah to remain in the room they shared to listen to conversations she had with her girlfriends. Their mother was distant and worked hard, devoting herself to housework and avoiding intimacy with her children.

Hannah was notably studious. She was an excellent student, scrupulous when it came to "values"[15] and active in the girls' youth movement.

During Hannah's childhood and adolescence, Bene Brak was the entire universe. Social, spiritual, and intellectual life was conducted on the familiar streets, in the Warsaw Park, and on the corners of streets named after Jewish sages and rabbis, such as Rabbi Akiva the Hazon Ish.

When it came time to find a suitable husband for Hannah, her sister and three of her brothers were already married. One of her brothers had drifted out of the haredi community, left his studies, enlisted in the army, and married a modern religious girl who did not cover her hair after her wedding. Her brothers' marriages, which did not link her family to any particularly respectable clan, and her other brother's "apostasy" reduced her own chances of being married to a scholarly prodigy—the most desirable of matches. But her good reputation, her determined studiousness, her social activities, and her behavior stood her in good stead and gave her the image of being a woman prepared to sacrifice many personal comforts for marriage to a devout and exacting Talmudic scholar.

Hannah was introduced to an avrech, "but nothing came of it"; neither he nor she were interested. The second avrech she was introduced to came from a respected Gur family. His father was a well-known figure in the Hasidic community, his uncle was a rich philanthropist, and all his sisters had made fine matches. Why was his family interested in having him marry Hannah of all people, a girl with no family connections, from a modest home?

The first match proposed to him had been in keeping with his family's status, a girl from a highly-placed Gur family. The two of them met once, and he agreed to the match. The parents proceeded to negotiate the terms of the marriage. Custom has it that the details of who will provide what for the young couple—at the wedding and thereafter—are agreed upon in advance. The young couple is not involved in the negotiations; all is left to the parents. In this case, the young avrech soon realized that his intended was making very specific demands, and was unwilling to forgo certain prerogatives (such as specifying the size of the dining room table, the quality of the furniture and accessories, and the value of the jewelry she was to receive). He knew that these demands, while not at all unusual in the haredi community, would put a great strain on his parents. He also realized that the bride's parents were supporting her demands and were not making any attempt to persuade her to compromise or moderate her requirements. The young man, who had already evidenced independence of mind by attending a "Lithuanian" yeshiva, insisted that his parents terminate the match. He knew very well what termination meant for his future. But he would not be moved, arguing that if the girl behaved that way before her wedding, there was no telling what she might do afterwards. The betrothal was annulled.

Hurt and disappointed, the avrech demanded that his parents and the matchmaker find him a brave, modest, and wise girl who would agree to follow him on his life's journey, a journey that would be fraught with economic and social difficulties. The matchmaker found Hannah.

When Hannah and Moshe met at her home (the accepted practice), the two sets of parents left them alone in the guest room so that they could conduct a brief conversation.

"Didn't you feel uncomfortable?" I asked her. "How was it?"

"Of course I felt uncomfortable, it's no simple thing to talk to a boy you don't know after so many years of them telling you not to talk to boys at all. I said almost nothing, mostly I listened and I answered a little bit. But he, even though he looked at the floor the whole time, was very much to the point. He asked me three questions:

'1. Are you prepared to speak only Yiddish at home?
'2. Are you willing to go to the Negev Desert with me and live on a farm?
'3. Are you willing to be the wife of a man who will devote his life to study?'

"I said yes to everything. I knew already from my parents that he was a boy who demanded a lot of himself, and I was willing. I told him that I didn't know Yiddish but that I was willing to learn. That's what was agreed on. When it came time to write out the conditions, his parents were already upset from having been burned once. I didn't ask for anything, nothing at all. My parents asked for very little, and the whole time his father had to encourage me to ask for things. He literally dragged me to stores, and would tell me, why take such a small table, I hope you'll have a large family, take more, take more.

"After that I met him once more at the engagement, and that was it. There he didn't raise his head either. His sister always jokes that under the wedding canopy he had to ask her if I was the bride, because he didn't recognize me."

So Hannah and Moshe Zilberstein's life together began. An unusual beginning, a history known to every member of the Gur community. Everyone knows about the young avrech who ran out on his respectable match on the eve of the wedding, broke his betrothal contract, returned the presents, and went off to find himself a brave and modest woman willing to accept his three conditions.

"How did he know, just by those three questions, that you were the right wife for him?"

Hannah's cheeks reddened. She gave me a look full of humor, and responded:

> Whoever was willing, ten years ago, to speak Yiddish at home, and to go live on an abandoned farm where they want to set up a little community of scholars not even from Gur, and who doesn't want a *ba'al-bayit*,[16] someone like that, you already know a lot more than three answers, and he knew.

Thus started the love that developed between Hannah and Moshe. On her first birthday as a married woman, three weeks after the wedding, her husband bought her the *Tsena Ur'ena*, a Yiddish translation of the Torah with commentaries and homilies intended especially for women. He wrote her a dedication on the first page: "To the modest Mrs. Hannah-Ida, who afflicts her soul with hard and dedicated labor. May you be like the Jewish women who have read this [book]."

Hannah and Moshe lived for a year in the Negev Desert, where their eldest daughter was born, until the project for a new community failed. Afterwards they moved to the new Development at the edge of Tel Aviv, among the first families to settle there. They had four more children. When I met Hannah she was the mother of five, and two more children were born during the course of my research. She had three boys and four girls in thirteen years of marriage.

Moshe Zilberstein persevered in his studies. During the period that I made most of my observations, he was attending a yeshiva in northern Israel that gathered together talented scholars who were willing to go far from home for the study of Torah. Moshe would leave home on Sunday morning and return on Thursday evening. He did not call during the week and asked Hannah, who had the yeshiva's phone number, not to call him, either. When he came home he would listen to her report of what had happened during the week and spend long hours with her. She would write down his comments and the tasks he set her for the coming week. Hannah would secrete this note in the kitchen drawer, and on occasion, before going to Bene Brak to run errands, would glance at it and jot down reactions and answers for the next conversation.

After their first year of marriage her husband returned one evening from the admor's house in Jerusalem and told her enthusiastically about the few words he had exchanged with the rebbe. That same night Moshe asked her to stop wearing a wig and to start covering her hair with a kerchief.[17] Hannah agreed. She put the wig in its round box, which she put away on top of the old closet in their bedroom. She has not worn it since. Hannah cut her hair very short, almost a crewcut, and began wrapping her small head in colorful kerchiefs. Under the cloth she wears a net that shapes her forehead and raises the kerchief a bit. In the Gur Development, among the women she mixes with, and among her old and new friends, Hannah is practically the only one to cover her head with a kerchief rather than with a wig. Her sister, mother, her husband's sisters, and her brothers' wives all wear wigs. Only among the Oriental women she taught once a week, and with her neighbor, an "exile" from Jerusalem's Mea She'arim neighborhood, was Hannah unexceptional. Everyone in the Development knew, however, that Hannah was "different."

I knew from the start that Hannah was different. That was our opening position. But it was only slowly that I learned what this difference meant for her and her family, the context in which that difference was expressed, and its implications for my work.

There were times when it seemed to me that we were essentially alike—as women in society, as wives, as mothers. There were times when it seemed to me that there was a deep chasm between us. Generally, however, our dialogues were a mixture of what united and separated us, such as the time when I was not able to come on Tuesday night as I had promised, and came the next morning instead.

It was the middle of August, during an unbearable heat wave. I couldn't bear the thought of putting on the airless garments that the visit demanded. I donned them slowly—a black-and-white checkered button-up blouse, a black cotton skirt, black nylon knee-length stockings, and black sandals. I considered whether to cover my hair with a black or a white kerchief. I decided on the white, an Arab *kuffiyeh* left over from scout hikes, tying it very tightly so that not a single curl would escape out from under it. I looked at myself in the mirror. This time I would not go in one of my loose-hanging dresses that were fine as far as modesty went, but that were not the right style. This time it would be something closer to what they wore. Were I to see someone like me on a haredi street, I'd know she was an outsider—but it would take a long, hard look. That Thursday night I wrote:

> To my surprise, I don't feel hot. I move more slowly, don't rush
> like I usually do, it's not so horrible. At the apartment door Hannah
> smiles at me, you're elegant today, she said. The children had just
> woken up, Sarah-Leah (9) was sent to Bene Brak by bus to bring
> chickens for the Sabbath, Binyomin-Yair (7) to the shopping
> center to bring fish; Shrulik (3) was still sleeping. They were at
> a bar mitzvah yesterday and got back late.

The children showed me their supplies for the coming school year. Tsiporale was going into first grade and had received a new pencil box.

Binyomin, on his return, showed me his books. This coming year he would
begin studying Talmud. Hannah joined the ruckus in the foyer, where I sat
with the children around a low table, two photo albums in hand.

> I was just straightening up some of the closets, and I found these
> photo albums. We don't take very many pictures, especially since
> the wedding it's been a lot less.

The first album was from the wedding. Hannah was in a wig, thin to
the point of being bony. Her husband looked like a boy, twenty-one years
old to her twenty. There are pictures of Hannah preparing for the wedding
at her parents' house, pictures of the ceremony, pictures from the Negev,
where they lived after the wedding.

> That was a wonderful time. We lived on the farm, with other young
> couples, the yeshiva was there on the farm. We had a little house of
> our own with a lawn, and Sarah-Leah was born there. Here's a
> picture of her naked on the lawn, she had this skin condition, my
> husband looked it up in some books and told me to have her lie in
> the sun naked.

There was a picture of him, of her husband, as a child in a haredi farm-
ing community in the northern Negev, sitting on his father's lap. The father
looked like an honorable and respectable Jew, while the child wore, like the
boys in tales of Eastern European Jewry, a black cap with a brim from which
cascaded blond sidelocks. There were pictures from her husband's *halaka* on
Mount Meiron—the customary Hasidic ceremony of a boy's first haircut, at
the age of three. Then, oddly out of order, came pictures of her in Purim
costumes—Hannah as Queen Esther, Hannah as a bride—and then a
chronological jump to Hannah as a counselor in a haredi youth movement.
"You had a good time," I observed. "You look really happy here with
the other counselors."

> That was a very special period. We'd go on trips all over the country,
> to seminars, we'd get to all kinds of far-off settlements to be counse-
> lors for girls, I had a really good time then. The whole period of high
> school and college was a wonderful period for all the girls.

The second album contains the pictures of the children, a few of each
child. My efforts to identify the children in the pictures was a source of
great entertainment to my audience.

Photographs are often attempts to memorialize something or to catch
and hold an instant of time. When I looked at the pictures of the Zilberstein family, I found that many of them were nearly identical to the
pictures in my family albums. I, too, have pictures of myself in nursery

school dressed as Queen Esther, sitting next to Hava Pinhas the ballet dancer and Dalia Shmerling the Dutch girl. The girls in Hannah's nursery school were very similar to my friends and me. But the pictures from later years reflected the difference. One of Hannah's teenage pictures shows her with her girlfriends from school on a trip, sitting on a bed. In my pictures there are girls, but also boys, and we are portrayed on the side of a mountain in the Judean wilderness or standing with rolled-up pants in a wadi. There's generally one bold boy hugging the girl next to him, and the general atmosphere in the pictures is one of uninhibitedness.

"Do you have pictures?" Tsiporale wanted to know. I was afraid that if I were to take them out of my wallet, the invisible abyss between us would become tangible. Tsiporale would see me without my head covered. She would see my sons without sidelocks, and my husband, who is not at all like her father. But in that moment of intimacy, I took out the snapshots. My Chapstick fell out, too; Tsiporale picked it up and looked at it suspiciously. Then she examined the few pictures I had with me.

"You're not dressed modestly," said the five-and-a-half-year-old. "That's not good. And you've got long fingers, that's forbidden, you have to have like me, short and black." She was examining her nails and had noticed they were dirty. "Take me for a drive in your car."

"I can't, your mother wouldn't let me."

"*Mama, mir kenen furen mit ir, mama?*" (Can we go for a drive with her, Mama?)

Hannah again tells them no, that they can't go for a drive with a woman, because a car is a "male accessory." Tsiporale settles for having me pick her up. Her plump cheeks are misleading; her lightness surprises me. This five-year-old girl weighs less than my three-year-old son.

"Stay with us always, okay, and if you go, I'll go with you, to your house, to see your children."

The right-hand pages of my journal remain empty. There, one professor taught me, one should write one's comments. I wrote on the right side that this visit was notable for both closeness and distance, for intensive moments of intimacy and brief insights of estrangement. I began to understand that the growing relation between me and Hannah and between me and her children would be complex. Problems could be expected, problems that would grow out of this confrontation between the closeness possible between us on a personal level and the distance gaping between us on the social and cultural level. But I also knew that this woman who had opened her house to me, who would later leave her baby in my care, whose laundry I took off the line and ironed, was a special woman. I hoped that together we could, even if just for a time, overcome that complexity.

The extent of the "differentness" of Hannah and her family within the social sphere in which they lived became clearer to me as I broadened my circle of acquaintances. They identified me as "Hannah's," but in her absence they approached me directly.

In early September, a few months after I began my project, I went downstairs with Hannah and little Sheina-Brocha to the public telephone. The telephone was usually surrounded by people waiting to use it, but now it was free. It turned out that it was out of order. Hannah's neighbor, Mrs. Lichtenbaum, suggested that Hannah come up to her apartment to make her call. I was left with the baby in my hands, and she hid her head deep in my shoulder. Mrs. Lichtenbaum, who had just come on the direct bus from Bene Brak with her small son, said to the young woman standing by her:

> *Kik,* look, the little one doesn't want to come into my arms, and she's already lying on her. And what Yiddish she speaks with her, really fine. That's the way it is when you go to Hannah—you see nice things, *sheine zachen.* I'm telling you, her children are really little people, *kleine menschelach.* They go by themselves on the bus to Bene Brak, go shopping, the less you look at them the fewer slaps on the cheek you have to give. There's nothing at home, no toys, no *schtikelech,* nothing, *gornisht.* They come down to me, I give them a little raspberry syrup, for them it's *a groise zach* [a big deal].

The young woman gave me a sidewards glance and responded:

> The question is whether it's for money or for ideology. Because I also don't think you should give children everything. I've got a neighbor here in the Development whose children have a house full of toys, everything's Leggo and Fisher-Price, you know, all the best. And I don't think that her children are any happier than mine. But the opposite isn't good, either. Children shouldn't know that there's no money at home or that they have to grow up without anything. And I also don't understand why she doesn't send her girls to the Gur Beit Ya'akov school. Why does she send them to that Yiddish school, what's it called? I saw her little one, the one in first grade, coming home on the 2:30 bus, your heart goes out to the girl, at the Gur school in first grade they come home at 12.

"Her husband," Mrs. Lichtenbaum added, "doesn't go exactly by Gur. He learned a little by the Lithuanians, and now he's in the north, he thinks that it's a good school, that the girls need the Yiddish. And she does what he says, like a righteous woman."

"Maybe it's a good school," the young woman said, "but the girls will be alone here, without girlfriends, everyone here is in the Gur school."

I recalled how Sarah-Leah, nine years old, had once run home crying from a game outside.

"They won't call me Sarah-Leah," she said. "They say I have to choose, Sarah or Leah."

The girls had been playing a game called "King of the Letters," in which the players have to advance towards one of the girls while calling out their names. They told her that it wasn't fair that she had a long name and that it gave her more time. Outside they're all called Sari, Hani, Tovi, Brachi, and so on. Only she is Sarah-Leah. She did not give in and came upstairs. Hannah praised her.

> That's your name, and you weren't given it without reason and
> it doesn't change for a game. There are girls that are called Tovi,
> and there are girls called Shoshana or Yocheved, and that makes
> a difference, too, doesn't it? You're not Sarah or Leah, you're
> Sarah-Leah.

Hannah answered her with a smile on her face. She always spoke with her children lightly and used a lot of humor to manage them. I never heard her scream at or offend them. I never saw her strike them. Even when she spoke sternly, she tried to explain herself so that the children's agreement would be expressed in a smile they returned to her. So she did when she compared the length of the names Tovi and Shoshana. Sarah-Leah ex-changed her tears for a little smile, but the sadness of being different, being made fun of, the knowledge that the girls outside were laughing at her old-fashioned name, remained. Both she and her sister Tsiporale often pre-ferred to stay in Bene Brak after school, going to eat at their grandmother's and spending the afternoon with one of their school friends. The fact that most of the girls in their class lived in Bene Brak, and that the daughters of the neighbors went to a different school, made it hard for them. For them, Hebrew was the language of the street, a play language, and they had a rea-sonable command of it. This created an interesting situation: their "holy" tongue, the language of study, was Yiddish. The secular, street language was the language of the Bible—Hebrew.

As I've noted, the uniqueness of the Zilberstein family in its environ-ment became clearer to me the better I became acquainted with other women. These women tried to take advantage of my closeness to Hannah to milk me for additional details of her family life, and wanted to hear what I thought of various Zilberstein habits. While Hannah was in the hospital after the birth of her sixth daughter, Mirale, Rabbanit (the wife of Rabbi) Yungerman came from Bene Brak to give a talk on the occasion of the upcoming High Holidays. At the end of the lecture I walked home with Ahuva, who lived in Hannah's building.

Ahuva took advantage of the pleasant evening and of Hannah's absence to stretch out our conversation. She described for me how she had found Hannah's house when she had gone to help Sarah-Leah get the place organized for her mother's return. She held forth on the neglect of the children's personal hygiene, on the untidiness of the apartment, and on

Hannah's acquiescence to her husband's every whim. Since I did not cooperate, and even tried from time to time to defend Hannah, the conversation took a different turn. It was clear to me that Ahuva, Hannah's next-
door neighbor; Mrs. Lichtenbaum, who was close to her in standards of
observance; and the young woman who did not know her personally had
all experienced Hannah's lifestyle as being different from theirs and from
the community's as a whole. Hannah herself, very much aware of her status in the Development, took advantage of her relationship with me to talk
about that situation.

> *Hannah:* You think that I don't know, that when I see a group of
> women downstairs by the fence, sitting and chatting, and I get close
> to them, I see that they suddenly fall silent. I know what they've
> been talking about, and I'm happy that I'm their reminder that they
> shouldn't be talking about that.

> *I:* It doesn't make you feel bad, being like a policeman for them, so
> that when they see you they behave like school children do when the
> teacher gets close to their table?

> *Hannah:* Bad? The opposite. I'm not saying it's always easy, and that
> I don't sometimes want to have idle conversation or gossip, but if I
> want to do that it's my problem and I've got to overcome my desire.
> But for them I'm a help, a reminder. For me it's sometimes even
> funny, really just like you say, they see the teacher coming and hide
> the note in their satchel.

> *I:* What bothers me, Hannah, is that if that's the situation, who is
> your friend, who can you talk to?

> *Hannah:* It bothers you? It bothers me! I don't have any real friends
> here. I have Rachel in Bene Brak, our husbands study together, and
> the girls are together at the Sarah Ba'ohel school. I have my friends
> from college, one or two, that I sometimes get together with, like the
> one who was here before my brother's wedding. You remember, the
> one who helped me make the dresses for the wedding? We've been
> friends for many years. I talk to her, to my sister, that's enough. How
> much time is there to talk, after all. Then there's Ahuva, who I'd go
> up to some times when my husband was up north. We even went up
> a few times together, if I remember correctly.

Hannah described social and psychological distress, and the lack of
real friends close by. Yet her uniqueness supplied her with social and personal compensations that did not exist in the lives of those around her.
    Before I had come to the Development, Hannah had taught a group of
ba'alot teshuva, newly-religious women, while her husband had worked

with their husbands at a small yeshiva they had set up in the neighborhood. When he went north he stopped this activity, but renewed it later
when he transferred his studies back to Tel Aviv. In the end a kind of
study hall or yeshiva was established, with her husband at its head. Hannah also revived her meetings with the women. They gathered once a week
in the homes of one of the students (all of whom were from Oriental families) and listened to Hannah give a lesson on Jewish law. They began with
the laws relating to family purity (concerning the prohibition of sexual
relations during and after a wife's menstrual period), and went on to the
laws of the Sabbath and of dining. They also studied some Bible. This
activity brought Hannah closer to the physical and human surroundings in
which the Development was located. She had "friends" whom she would
meet in the shopping center, on the bus, and in their homes. These were
friends that none of her neighbors knew or spoke to; they did not even
know anyone like them.

For example, the mother of one of the young men who studied under
her husband was a "witch" who had begun her career in Tunisia. People
went to her to solve medical, psychological, and business problems, and to
inquire into the future. She read cards and coffee grounds, and handed out
amulets and other charms. Her income was enough to support her family
well. When her son was well-advanced in his process of becoming observant, he asked Moshe Zilberstein whether his mother's business was not a
transgression of the Torah. Hannah and her husband visited the woman,
saw her in action, and spoke with her. Moshe then perused his books, consulted with others, and ruled that so long as she was not cursing people,
and so long as she was using her own special gifts rather than invoking
divine powers, she was permitted to remain in her profession, because she
was providing a service to other people. Moshe himself had more than
once consulted with Rabbi Abu-Hatzera of Be'ersheva, who was known as
a gifted mystic, scholar, and ascetic who never left his home.

In this way they were "privileged" to meet on a first-hand and intimate
basis people and phenomena that were outside the experience of the other
residents of the Development. Even without going as far as Be'ersheva or
witchcraft, the Zilberstein family had an advantage in making social contacts.

Three years before I began my research, the apartment above Hannah's had been occupied by a modern religious couple. The wife's father
was active in the National Religious Party, the political faction most
closely associated with the modern Zionist religious public, but he apparently also had contacts within Agudat Yisrael. Officially, the Development
had been built by Agudat Yisrael, and anyone who claimed to be strictly
observant could sign up. Only a small number registered to buy apartments;
many of these bought apartments as a long-term investment, for their children, and rented them out in the meantime. For this couple it had also

been a good deal. The wife covered her head with a kerchief (in the modern religious style, which leaves a bit of the hair exposed over the forehead); the husband wore a knitted *kipah* on his head, the badge of religious Zionists. They were the only family of their type in the Development. Hannah developed strong neighborly ties with the young woman; they would watch each other's children when necessary and frequently talked about routine matters, but Hannah would not eat in her house ("You know what?" she once said to me, "I could *almost* have eaten at Shula's house"). After Mirale was born, when I sat at the kitchen table one evening with Hannah, Shula came for a visit with her youngest daughter. Shula worked in an enrichment program, helping children with their homework at their homes. After leaving the Development for a "knitted-kipah" neighborhood in Kfar Saba, Shula's work would sometimes take her in Hannah's direction in the evening. For this visit she brought a present wrapped in department-store paper.

> *Shula:* You know, I didn't know what to buy. With a sixth child I'm sure there's already too much clothing, and I wanted something all the children would enjoy.
>
> *Hannah:* You really didn't have to, it's enough to see you after such a long time, and Ainat who's grown so much, really a little lady.

I didn't know the young woman who had come in, and as I sat across from her I tried to decipher her. My first assumption was that she was someone who had recently become religious. But as the conversation went on I realized that this was not the case. I knew that it would be hard for such a woman to enter any other house in the neighborhood, and I saw in her a variation on myself.

> *Shula:* In the end I bought them a board game, it's very nice. It's called "A Package Has Arrived," you have to pick up a package at the post office and there are all kinds of complications.

I knew the game. The picture on the box was by Israeli humorist Efraim Kishon and depicted a clean-shaven man. I also knew the cynical comments hidden in the "surprises," and I thought that the woman was completely off target. How could she give Hannah's children such a frivolous game with no content? Only someone who didn't know her could do such a thing, and even then it would be considered impolite and inconsiderate. If I had not known a single religious family, and I had to bring a present for our first meeting, I wouldn't have dreamed of bringing "A Package Has Arrived."

Shula: It's no problem if you want to exchange it, go to the shopping center, there are lots of things for children there, I'm sure you'll find something.

Hannah does not open presents in front of the children. She waits until evening, examines what they contain by herself, consults with her husband if necessary, and then decides to allow or prohibit them.

When Shula left, I began to laugh.

I: Hannah, who brought your children "A Package Has Arrived"?

Hannah gave the background, and asked if I was familiar with the game.

I: Sure I'm familiar with it, I had it when I was a little girl, but I'm really astounded, someone who's your next-door neighbor for five years brings you a thing like that. I'm from outside, I've been here only half a year, but I wouldn't dare, it's really not appropriate, it's nothing close to what your children are used to. Not only that, it's something you'd never allow them to play with.

Hannah: That's your advantage, that you're from the outside, you understand? She, for instance, took driving lessons. She knows what I think about women that drive, and she comes to me and asks me to watch her little one when she has a lesson.

I: But I'm sure you did watch her. [I took a gamble and Hannah blushed.]

Hannah: Yes, that's right, I watched her. First, it's not the girl's fault. Second, if that was what she wanted, then I in any case did *her* a favor. But my neighbors told me that I shouldn't have watched her children if she was learning to drive, and none of them were her friend like I was. When it comes down to it, they were all pretty happy when they moved out—they didn't fit in.

The Zilbersteins' ability to break out of the normal frameworks of the Gur Hasidim and to meet Jews with lifestyles different than theirs made them all the more unique among those they resembled. They were radicals in the haredi community, the only ones who had authentic encounters with other segments of Israeli society. Apparently paradoxically, their "radicalism" made their openness possible. What was permitted them was forbidden to others. Their strictness of observance gave them freedom to be exceptional. Hannah wouldn't drive with me in my car, but she had a friend with a car. Hannah wouldn't go to a hotel in Safed or Arad for a vacation, but she had acquaintances from whom she could hear about far places and other customs, in Northern Africa, in Yemen, and at kibbutzim. The range of her knowledge and imagination was much greater than those of the other women in the Development. Hannah's three neighbors, who agreed to drive with me in my car, would laugh at the sight of my car parked by their building while Hannah and I went to wait for the bus to Bene Brak. These were the same neighbors who had criticized Shula and who had advised Hannah to refrain from giving her any assistance while she learned to drive.

Hannah's ability to navigate between the accepted prohibitions and restrictions and those that she and her husband imposed on themselves was without a doubt part of the image she fashioned for herself. She was unpredictable even among her neighbors, and she presented them with aspects of certain problems that they would never have considered on their own. She responded in an unconventional way and constructed her arguments so that she came out fortifying the religious framework as a whole, but at the same time somehow calling into question how perfect their behavior was.

Once Malka, a ba'alat teshuva, and Hannah's upstairs neighbor Ahuva dropped in. They wanted to find out how they could help in the preparations for a *brit milah*, or circumcision ceremony, that another neighbor was to have the next day. The conversation turned to Malka's neighbors, who were also newly religious. In this case, the husband was Jewish and his wife had converted to Judaism.

Malka: Do you know what she said to me? That they have been trying so hard to bring up their children in their new customs, and as much as they try, when they finally think that they've gotten going in the right direction, new neighbors move in.

Ahuva: So, what's wrong with new neighbors, why does that bother them?

Malka: They listen to the radio all day, and they go to visit friends in the evening, just her and him, to see wedding videos. All kinds of things like that. That's all on top of what she says, but I'm not sure she saw the neighbor go out to the balcony in her nightgown to hang out the laundry, and the nightgown was revealing.

Ahuva: What, really? I heard about it from Brachi, but I didn't know that the radio was on all day and all that.

Malka: Look, I listen to the radio, too, I've got permission from my rabbi, but I listen to talk shows or classical music. But them, don't ask. In my opinion it's a real life-and-death case,[18] that family is hanging by a thread, and everything can succeed or fail because of the surroundings. What do you say, Hannah?

Hannah had listened to the conversation in silence. When Malka addressed her directly, knowing that Malka tends to exaggerate her stories and her tone of voice, she said:

First of all, let's not talk about life-and-death, let's watch our language. The new neighbors are religious, their custom I don't know, and aside from that they're Oriental and they have their own way. But why jump from that to a question of life-and-death. If the family of Edna the convert needs help, then we need to give her help, but not at the expense of another family, that maybe all it also needs is help.

Malka: Hannah, you don't know about this, in such cases everything can collapse. You feel strong so you talk that way. I know what I'm saying.

Hannah: You know what it is better than I do, I'm sure, but "life-and-death" is greater than both of us, let's be careful.

Even when women adhered to strict observance, Hannah could be unpredictable. In this case, Malka, a ba'alat teshuva, told Hannah about a family that did not obey the accepted mores. Knowing Hannah, she expected to be commended and encouraged to intervene. Hannah, however, did not accept unquestioningly Malka's description of reality. She did not equate exceptional behavior with negative behavior; its causes need to be examined. Second, the extreme term "life-and-death situation" is one that Hannah does not feel everyone can invoke, especially not Malka. Judging others and interpreting their actions in a positive or negative way cannot be done in the "street," in Hannah's opinion; these judgments are reserved for certain people, to whom she considers herself and her husband close. The emphasis that amateur judgment should be avoided, and the knowledge that such judgment takes place, transfers the right to make such judgments to a higher level. Hannah's modesty and self-effacement when faced with the term "life-and-death situation," which is "greater than both of us," only underline her superiority. Whereas every other woman in the neighborhood would have passed judgment, Hannah "the righteous" presented herself as one who is not fit to judge.

The women heard her response, lowered their glances, and fell silent.

I could tell much more about Hannah's uniqueness, about the special relationship between us, the way she understood and interpreted my visits to her house and neighborhood, how she conceived of the university and of scientific work, what she expected of me, and more. I hope that some of this will be conveyed to the reader during the course of the book.

Rachel Lichtenbaum

Rachel lives in the apartment below Hannah's. I saw her many times when she stopped by to borrow something, and in the stairwell. Rachel is a large woman who covers her head with a tightly-tied colored kerchief, and her legs with opaque black stockings. Her face is smooth, and her blue, smiling, warm eyes stand out. Among the Ashkenazi women in the neighborhood, she and Hannah were the only ones who covered their heads with kerchiefs rather than wigs.

Hannah told me that Rachel was a seamstress, and that she had an establishment in a small rented apartment in Bene Brak. Her husband was a proctor in the nearby Gur yeshiva, and they had three children—an older daughter who had just married, a son studying in a yeshiva in Tel Aviv, and a small boy who went to *heder*. There were not many women in the Development who were friendly to me. Most were suspicious, cold, or apathetic. Throughout my research, it was Hannah's few friends there, the ones I had first met when I began to visit, who became my friends as well. Others, with whom I became acquainted later, made it easier for me and gave me the feeling that I had broadened my circle of acquaintances, but to a certain extent remained no more than part of the community of women I met. Rachel the seamstress thought it was a positive phenomenon that someone who was not religious had found a way to meet religious women. She admired Hannah, felt close to her, and in many ways assumed that "Hannah knows what she is doing." Slowly, Rachel began to make gestures of friendship. The first time, on the day before the Purim holiday, she came up to Hannah's apartment with a package wrapped in aluminum foil and with a little smile on her lips.

> I saw your car down below, and I knew that the class is today and that you were coming. I wanted to give your children a little something for Purim. Have a *freiliche Pirim* [a happy Purim].

Rachel opened the package and revealed three pieces of chocolate molded in the shape of a guitar, a house, and a tree. Astounded by the gesture and by the quality of the artistry, I said to Rachel:

> You made that? Really, Mrs. Lichtenbaum, you shouldn't have gone to so much trouble for us.

> *Rachel:* I do it every Purim. When we were in America, I brought a few nice molds with me, but some have already gotten lost. My

daughter, Gittel, may she be healthy, does these very nice. Give them to your children and tell them it's from me. You can also bring them some time, maybe you can bring them for the Purim feast, it's very nice by us, really, why shouldn't you come with the children. Your oldest is just like my little jewel.

I did not bring my children to her home, even though they ate her chocolate with great delight. I did, however, get closer and closer to her. I went with her to the admor's grave on the Mount of Olives in Jerusalem, and afterwards we visited her family in Mea She'arim. I went with her to a Gur women's charity night and to a family celebration, and I visited her sewing shop in Bene Brak and her home in the Development.

Rachel Lichtenbaum, like Hannah, was an exceptional figure in the community. She had been born to parents who had come from Hungary to Israel after World War II and settled in Safed. Her father had once hosted in his home disciples of Rebbe Aharon, or Reb Ahrale, a charismatic and insular Hasidic leader, and soon after joined the sect. The family moved into an abandoned Arab house near Mea She'arim, in Jerusalem. There Rachel, her brothers, and her sisters grew up, children in Reb Ahrale's court.

Rachel's father was a scribe and a learned man, and Yiddish was the only language spoken in his house. Rachel attended Ha'eda Haharedit girls' school in Jerusalem, five days a week, four hours a day. At the age of eighteen she was betrothed to a young scholar from Reb Ahrale's Toldot Aharon yeshiva. Rachel's hair was shaven and replaced by a thin black kerchief, the badge of women from Ha'eda Haharedit. She lived close to her parents and married siblings, her life restricted to the small and familiar area of Mea She'arim, Geula, Batei Ungarin, and Shomrei Emunim, the old haredi neighborhoods of Jerusalem. Their first child was a girl, Gittel, and it looked as if another Jerusalem haredi family was headed for the routine life of that community. Then Rachel's husband began taking an interest in the Gur rebbe's court. On Friday nights he would avoid Reb Ahrale's tish, the ritual Hasidic meal on the eve of the Sabbath when disciples gather around their rebbe's table, and go to the Gur admor's tish instead. He studied the Gur sect's literature and in the end sent the Gur rebbe a message telling of his distress and asking for help. The admor met him and was convinced of his sincere desire to change allegiances; knowing how Reb Ahrale's Hasidim would react to the move, he decided to send Rachel and her husband out of the country. The family wandered from Belgium to London to Brooklyn, and then, after seven years of exile, they returned to Israel—but to Tel Aviv, not Jerusalem. Both their families ostracized them. The sharpest response came from Rachel's brother, who announced that as far as he was concerned she no longer existed. Despite this, a process of conciliation began when they returned to Israel. Slowly, over the course of painful encounters, Rachel and her husband began to see their families again.

Now Rachel makes a point of visiting her family and her husband's family from time to time. They, however, do not come to visit her in Tel Aviv. Most of them have never seen the city.

The Lichtenbaums were much better off financially than the Zilbersteins. Rachel's husband had a job and received a salary somewhat higher than the stipend for full-time Torah scholars. The major difference, however, was Rachel's work and the small number of children left at home. Rachel had earned a reputation as a fine seamstress who knew how to make elegant dresses for family celebrations and special events. In her small workshop in Bene Brak I saw expensive fabrics made of sparkling threads, embroidered with sequins. Her dresses were always complex affairs, with pleats, tucks, contrasts of color and pattern, and high, stiff collars. Rachel would display her handiwork proudly and explain the special difficulties of each creation, how she had dealt with a problem she had with a heavy woman, or the psychological problem presented by a woman who was prettier than her daughter (something that should not be emphasized at a wedding) or by the mothers of a groom and bride who each envied the other's dress.

While Rachel worked she listened to cassettes on a tape recorder. Some of the cassettes were Hasidic music, and some were lessons for women, borrowed from a charitable society.[19] Rachel returned home in the evening with her youngest son, who finished school at 6:00 P.M. She spent most of her time in Bene Brak. Her customers were there; sometimes women even came to her from Jerusalem. She bought all her supplies and equipment in Bene Brak, where she was familiar and respected. When her workload allowed it, she went to visit her daughter and grandchildren in Ashdod. For Rachel, the Development was a space to sleep and spend the Sabbath.

Her apartment was arranged in the same way as most of the others in the Development. In the middle of the living room stood a large dining-room table, with high-backed chairs arranged around it. The room's longest wall was lined with bookshelves, containing the house's treasured books and a display of pretty tableware. Opposite the bookshelves, next to the wall, was a couch, with an armchair to one side. The room was crowded with heavy furniture. The kitchen had been redone: wooden cupboards replaced the former green formica, and red-tinted tiles replaced the standard white. The small balcony off the kitchen was turned into a tiny workroom for Rachel, where she receives local customers who come to her home rather than to Bene Brak. (She tries to have the customers come when her husband is not home.) The other two rooms were bedrooms, one for her and her husband, and the second for the boy. When her daughter comes to visit, she receives the second bedroom and her brother sleeps in the living room.

The women at the Development call each other by their first names, with three exceptions who are invariably referred to by their family names. One is Mrs. Halberstam, sixty years old, who is Belgian by birth and who lives alone. The second is the elderly Mrs. Taub, who supervises the women who come to immerse themselves in the mikveh; she has lived in the Development with her husband since it was built. The third is Rachel, whom everyone calls Mrs. Lichtenbaum. I also called her this, even though she always made a point, when calling me on the telephone, of identifying herself as "Rachel." Many of Rachel Lichtenbaum's new neighbors had studied together with her daughter, Gittel. Rachel treated them as if they were her own girls, and they would call her "Gittel's mother." At public meetings, when a number of women gathered for a lesson, to see a play, or to listen to a guest lecturer, Rachel would sit in the first row alongside Mrs. Halberstam, Hannah Zilberstein, and Rivka (an Oriental mother of seven boys who, to everyone's great satisfaction, gave birth to a girl during the period of my research project), of whom she was especially fond. Rachel never sat among the young women.

My conversations with Rachel were conducted in her broken Hebrew and in my worse Yiddish. I generally asked her not to try to speak to me in Hebrew, and she was happy to speak Yiddish. At first many shades of meaning were lost on me, but when I sensed that I wasn't following her, I asked her to translate her words into Hebrew. For this reason Rachel acted as if my Yiddish were fluent, and did not hesitate to speak the language with me when we were with other women. The other women (most of whom lack a command of Yiddish) also thought I was fluent. My Yiddish conversations with Hannah's children in the yard displayed my limitations for all to hear, but this did not keep them from assuming that I knew what I did not know.

Rachel felt obligated to bring to my attention everything she thought might interest me. She supplied me with cassette recordings of lessons for women, invited me to Hasidic women's events, gave me a tour of Bene Brak, introduced me to her friends and to the lecturers who were invited to the Development. She became my second-best friend in the Development, another anchor in an uncertain, and sometimes inhospitable and hostile, sea.

Ahuva Graetz

I met Ahuva for the first time by the fuse box in the stairwell. Wearing a pink housecoat, clogs, and an offside kerchief, she had a screwdriver in hand and was trying to fix something. The first thing that caught my eye was that her face looked tired, as if she was ill. I went on and entered Hannah's apartment. A few minutes later she was knocking on the Zilbersteins' open door.

"Hannah, maybe you know what's going on with the light in the stairwell? As much as they fix it, it keeps getting broken again. My girls are afraid to come up. It's pitch black, and here I am with a horrible migraine and I really can't concentrate."

Hannah went out to her and Ahuva surveyed me quickly. When Hannah returned, I mentioned to her that the sight of a woman with a screwdriver trying to fix something always made me feel good. Hannah laughed, and we had a talk about "male" roles that haredi women assume because of their husbands' frequent absences from home for study or visits to the rebbe. My contribution to the conversation was information on women's roles in wartime.

> That poor Ahuva. Women's problems, you know. She has, thank God, five wonderful children, she's a woman with a model home, never lazy, spends the whole day with the vacuum, toils and works, but she's not 100 percent healthy. Ever since her miscarriage she's had no heart for anything. She so much wanted that pregnancy. They say there was some negligence by the doctors. She's a very good woman, always ready to help, I often ask her for help if I need someone to keep an eye on the children, even if I don't ask much, she's always ready to help. I even give her telephone number to my family so that if there's something urgent they can notify me [at the time Hannah had no telephone because her husband did not want one in their home. When telephones were installed in the project's new buildings, he gave in. The telephone was connected only a few hours a day, while the children were out, and for one hour in the evening] and she's always more than happy to give me the message.

My acquaintance with Ahuva became deeper after I went a few times with Hannah to visit her. Ahuva's husband worked in the evenings, and since at that time Hannah's husband studied at a distant yeshiva, both of them had free time after the children were in bed. Ahuva's apartment was exactly the opposite of Hannah's. During their ten years there, the Graetz family had made every possible change in the small apartment in order to turn it into comfortable living quarters for a family of seven. The foyer had been turned into a bedroom for the two older boys; the wall between the kitchen and living room had been removed, making these plus the dining room into one large space. The kitchen had been redone and equipped with the latest electric appliances. The living room ceiling was done in stucco. The balcony, previously separated from the living room by a glass door, had also been made part of the living space, and held the dining room table. The arrangement of the furniture was the customary one. There was a large teak bookcase, not overladen with books, parts of which were enclosed by glass doors protecting silver and glass implements, family pictures, the daughters' handiwork, elaborate ashtrays, and tableware for visitors. The house was always orderly and clean, and Ahuva would serve us, at our request, soft drinks or coffee. One of the Development's classes for women was held at Ahuva's home, and she was more than happy to turn her home into a meeting place.

As time passed, I also received her telephone number, and when I had to leave a message for Hannah with her, she and her children were gracious and efficient. A few times, when Hannah was not at home, I went up to Ahuva and spent the morning or afternoon with her.

These visits brought us closer together, and allowed me to get to know a woman whose husband worked rather than studied. At public events that Hannah refrained from or could not attend, I would use Ahuva as my guide.

Ahuva's children were always clean and neatly dressed. They were especially pretty children, I thought—as did the other women, I learned. Her girls had glittering black eyes and long, wavy black hair. Most of the children in the Development had light-colored eyes and hair and pale complexions. Ahuva's dark children stood out.

I noticed that Ahuva went about her home barefoot, without socks. One morning, when I dropped in unannounced, I saw her emerge from her bedroom, quickly tying her head scarf. This led me to believe that she, and perhaps others as well, removed their head coverings when they were home alone. But that is just a guess.

Ahuva revealed an aspect of life I could not encounter in Hannah's and Rachel's homes. Her hospitality gave me a chance to observe the family of a Gur working man.

Nava Zilber

I attended my first class at the end of the summer. It dealt with worms and insects, which must be removed from grains, flour, fruits, and vegetables before they can be eaten. After three months of observations I was being given the opportunity to witness a women's public activity. Thirty women sat in Bina's house and waited. Two young women, who came late and out of breath, mentioned Nava to me for the first time.

> Hi, Nava won't come today. She says there was a misunderstanding and that the class will be held only once every two weeks. She apologizes to everyone, we ran into her on the way here and we were surprised because we thought we were late. Then she explained the mistake to us.

Nava was a young woman of twenty-one, of average height; her face was clear and her cheeks had a natural blush. A member of the faculty at the teachers' college, she wore a short wig and glasses, behind which were blue-green eyes, small and darting. She had been born into a respected Gur family, and had married a young and promising avrech from another family of esteemed lineage.

Only a select few of the teachers' college graduates are offered positions as teachers there. Nava was a bright student. She had been blessed with exceptional speaking ability, and her great self-confidence was firmly based in her talents and her family background.

When I met her, she had been married for more than a year but still had no children. This allowed her to devote the greater part of her time to teaching at the college and to furthering her studies. Her lack of experience in child-rearing and as a housekeeper did not prevent her from expressing firm opinions on matters of kitchen and home. She was listened to politely and respectfully, even if she more than once sparked arguments at classes she attended. When she was a participant, rather than a teacher, Nava would pepper the speaker with penetrating questions, displaying her erudition and absolute self-confidence. Nava never took part in the women's backyard conversations because she had nothing to do there among the strollers and toddlers. Once, when she passed such a group that I was part of, she muttered "hello" under her breath to her collar and rushed on. Another time, when I was standing with Hannah's baby by Nava's building with a few other women, she came down dressed as if for a celebration.

She turned to Nehama, who was trying to interest me in buying car insurance from her husband, and greeted her while completely ignoring me.

Nava: I'm running to the six o'clock bus to Bene Brak.

Nehama: Why are you so dressed up?

Nava: I'm going to the Ginzberg wedding.

Nehama: Oh, right, that's today. Well, I hear only the best families have been invited, a real good match.

Nava: Yes, but don't forget that she's also one of my students.

Nehama: I'm sure that she would have invited you even if she weren't one of your students.

Nava did not answer, gave me a stern look, nodded goodbye to the group, and went on her way. Feeling that Nava was annoyed by my presence in the Development, I questioned Nehama.

I: Tell me, is she ignoring me deliberately?

Nehama: Who, Nava? That's the way she is. One day she can stand and talk with me just like that, like today, and another day she'll pass right by me without even saying hello. So how do you expect her to act with you?

I noted a few times in my field notebook that I would like to speak with her, to call her and set up a meeting. I asked Hannah whether Nava had ever asked her about me, expressing disapproval of my presence in the Development or any other opinion. Hannah said that Nava had not spoken to her, but that it was reasonable to suppose that she was not overjoyed about my presence. I shelved my plans to approach her. She might have responded positively; it may well be that she was waiting for me to call her—but she may have also left me empty-handed. I don't know. I did, however, track her attentively for two years. She gained weight steadily and I assumed that this had something to do with fertility treatments. If so, they were successful—after I left, I heard from Hannah that finally, *mazel tov*, she had had a baby girl.

Although I had not established primary contact with Nava, and felt that she would have liked to see me disappear from the Development, she taught me important things. Just as Ahuva represented the women married to working men, Nava represented the elite. When she stood before the women to introduce a lecturer who had come to give a class, when she did not raise her voice even when there was a commotion in the room, when she passed by her neighbors without noticing them, I learned what the haredi "aristocracy" was. Nava was an informant without speaking to me, an informant despite herself.

Malka Shamir

Malka Shamir became religious thirteen years before we met. She was the most senior of the ba'alot teshuva in the Development, and had lived there almost from its inception. At first Malka seemed to blend in with the other Gur women. She was large-bodied with an olive complexion and wore a wig. I noticed, however, that she did not dress elegantly like the other women and that her teeth were not cared for, making her seem older than she was. All three of the other ba'alot teshuva covered their heads with kerchiefs and came from Oriental families.

One evening I jotted the following in my field book: "Find out from Hannah whether Malka is a ba'alat teshuva." That same evening, after a Jewish law class at Bina Akerman's house, we took a slow walk home. On the way we met up with a group of women sitting on the steps of one of the buildings. Malka was among them, and she began talking to us. With an eye on me, she said:

"With those socks you look just like a *dosit*" (a mildly derogatory term for a religious woman).

The bluntness and quality of the remark were new to me. Up until then I had seen Malka only among other women; but her use of the term "dosit" made it clear that she had not been born into Gur.

Malka was a close friend of Hannah's. As an anomaly in the Development, and as a woman in need of friendship and aid, she found in Hannah both a confidante and a teacher. I later learned that Malka had advised Hannah not to take me in. She said that the academy and religion are incompatible, and that I was interested in research and not in religion. When Malka saw that Hannah would not go back and that making me religious was not the consideration that motivated her, Malka tried to approach me.

My conversations with Malka were a rest for both my tongue and my head. I could remove the "word processor" I kept in my mouth and return to my sharp Tel Aviv idiom and say things that I had been careful not to say in front of the other women. Malka, for her part, after thirteen years as a ba'alat teshuva, practiced on me the various accepted methods of conversing with candidates for the religious life—until she tired and changed tactics.

I learned little from her or from Hannah about her past. Malka grew up in the center of the country in a middle-class family. Her adolescence was normal, the usual high school experience of the end of the 1960s. Her attraction to the mystic led her into astrology, which she studied in depth in London. That overseas period was similar to those of other Israelis who went to Europe to glean what was left of the sixties, hoping therein to find the meaning of life. Then she met Gidon, now her husband. His spiritual condition was similar to hers, and together they discovered religion. Gidon is a guitarist and makes his living playing in a band that performs at haredi celebrations.

When I met her she had two boys and a baby girl. Her pregnancies did not come easily, and she was trying to close the birth gap between her and the other women, who had begun having children years before she did.

Of all the many women I met, and of the few who served as my direct informants, Malka was the easiest one for me to deal with. She was sharp-tongued and close to my way of thinking, understood my language, and sensed what I was experiencing. After trying unsuccessfully through seminars, cassette tapes, and social exchanges to get me on one or another track to religious Judaism, she understood that I was interested only in strengthening my links to the women of the Development.

Malka told me that a parenting class for women was beginning at the community center. The class was to be directed by a counselor from Bene Brak, and it would include ten women from the Development who would share their routine home-life problems. Malka intended to join and proposed that I do so also. I pounced on the opportunity, even though it was clear to me that the women would not easily agree to my presence. Malka promised to inquire into the matter for me and report back. Having already spent a year in the neighborhood, I took this as a kind of public test. Malka returned to me to report failure. The nine women who had already signed up for the group had to decide whether to accept me or another young woman who had asked to participate. During the discussion, Malka related, the women had argued that they were not interested in having someone with a different lifestyle in the group. I "didn't belong," they said. The counselor said that if I was interested, there were parenting groups for ba'alot teshuva in Bene Brak. Malka told the woman that they were missing a good chance to bring me closer to Judaism, and tried to make them feel responsible for that missed opportunity. The women were unfazed by the threat, and rejected our attempts to persuade them. We failed.

Malka's position in the Development, and her role as a ba'alat teshuva, appear in the section of Chapter 4 devoted to the newly-religious.

On the Outside Looking in

"My" Hannah (and this is also true of Rachel, Malka, and Nava) is a person from the "periphery." She is undoubtedly a full member of her society and very involved in what is going on within it. Nevertheless, social reality places her and her family on the edge of that society. This is not necessarily an inferior or inconsequential position. To a certain extent, Hannah and her family choose to live on the periphery, because they find that it gives them advantages that could not be had any other way (such as through a better economic position or superior social status). The periphery, as I see it, is not an existential state that detracts from the reliability of the materials drawn from it. In this matter I tend to accept the traditional anthropological approach that finds utility in the eccentric.

Hannah covered her hair with a kerchief, and this made me notice that all Gur women wear wigs. Hannah spoke Yiddish at home, and this led me to understand that Yiddish is a symbol of the stringent restrictions that the haredi community imposes on itself. I became attentive to the languages I heard around me, and thus came to realize that Hebrew was the language of most homes in the Development. The fact that I had studied Yiddish, and that I tried with all my power to speak it with the children outside and inside, enabled me to watch the various reactions of the other women. There were those who expressed regret at not knowing Yiddish, and at barely understanding even the Yiddish expressions and proverbs that have been adopted by modern Hebrew. There were others who saw my flaunting of my Yiddish (flaunting because Hannah's children knew Hebrew, and often preferred it in public) as an attempt to put myself into Hannah's category, to make myself into a kind of "deputy inspector." These women did not like that and kept their distance from me. There were women who admired my ability to become part of the family, and who made sure to tell me what they thought about the Zilbersteins' dogmatism. In Hannah's house, they would point out to me, there were no plants or ornaments. There were only the essentials: beds, dining table, chairs, and so on. Hannah's home was the archetype of the poor religious home as the secular might imagine it—dirty, unkempt, with bare and peeling

walls (which Hannah made futile attempts to paint)—a home that radi-
ated penury. Hannah's house served as a standard for decoding what I saw
in other homes. When I entered the home of another family in the neighborhood, I would immediately look for house plants, pictures, dolls, decorations, new furniture, electric appliances, labor-saving devices, and luxuries. In many homes all these were indeed plentiful. Initially I was
incredulous. The first house in which I saw an abundance of "superfluous"
items seemed like Sodom and Gomorrah to me; but then I saw another
home and another and many more, and I understood that it was Hannah's
home that was the exception.

Hannah does not dress herself or her children in anything in which
the color red is prominent. Red attracts the eye, she said, and is therefore
immodest. I assumed that Hannah based this practice on a provision of the
Shulkhan Arukh, the classic codification of Jewish law. Yet, after watching
other women, I came to see her position as an interesting measure of "hare-
dism." I saw many women wearing red in all its shades and variations.
Some wore colorful knits in which there was much red, and there were
those who wore red coats. Many girls wore red tights.

Hannah's observances, prohibitions, dispensations, and obligations
focused my attention on subjects that I doubt I would have encountered
any other way. From her life on the periphery I could see much more
clearly what was happening in the central arena. Hannah's and her family's
"marginality" derived, paradoxically, from their very insistence on strict
observance of certain principles. This punctiliousness becomes a deviation,
and helps the researcher ascertain these principles and the accepted limits
of their realization in the society under study.

If there is a common denominator in the social behavior of a group,
and if an anthropologist wishes to discover these limits of behavior, this is
a good place from which to begin.

Rachel Lichtenbaum, Malka Shamir, and Nava Zilber also became my
informants because they were exceptional. Ahuva Graetz, closer to "average," became closer to me as a result of good manners and neighborly relations with Hannah, and afterwards out of curiosity and friendship.
(Strangely enough, for me she was exceptional because of her "conven-
tionality," compared to the rest of my informants.)

Next to Hannah, Rachel Lichtenbaum was the second most haredi figure in the neighborhood. Her exceptional force, which presented a challenge
to the lives of other women, was mitigated because she came from outside.
Hannah was a regular woman from Bene Brak, from the Wolf Beit Ya'akov
teachers' college, who had become more haredi than the others. She was a
woman who had worn a wig during the early part of her marriage, and then
exchanged it for a kerchief; she had spoken Hebrew and exchanged that for
Yiddish; she sent her children to the Development's nursery school, but
afterwards transferred them to other educational institutions rather than

sending them to the same schools that the other children of the Development attended. Rachel had gone in the opposite direction. She had grown
up in Mea She'arim, had lived as the wife of one of Reb Ahrale's Hasidim,
and had worn a sheer black kerchief on her head. Now she lives in Tel
Aviv, works in Bene Brak, and wears a colored kerchief. Rachel's daughter,
who went to the Gur Beit Ya'akov teachers' college in Bene Brak, wears a
modern wig and speaks Hebrew with her husband even though Yiddish is
her mother tongue. At first glance, it would seem that Hannah and Rachel
meet at a single point, coming from different directions. The women
around them know this. Yet they criticize Hannah or take her seriously,
have reservations about her or admire her. Rachel they take lightly, as if
she were a character out of a story; it will be a generation before her
descendants become real Gur Hasidim. They see Rachel as living proof of
the correctness of the Gur sect: here is someone who was willing to pay a
high price to join them. Hannah is an ongoing challenge to the Gurs; she
is a living reminder that every paved road has alternate paths.

Nava Zilber, who was my "unwitting informant," was also a unique
woman in the Development. She stood out and attracted attention, and
that, after all, is what makes any given person prominent in her community.

I took notice of Nava because the way she taught and the way she
treated her neighbors, her fellow teachers at the college, and her students
expressed superiority. She was different from the other women not because
of the different path of advancement she had assumed (as was the case
with Hannah and her family) but because she was at the top of her society's normative ladder. My observations of her taught me how social superiority is created in a group in which status is not hidden, but flaunted. I
discovered the implications of the creation of such superiority for other
women, who appear to have accepted it as a given. It would seem that even
in a society where differences in social status are seldom open to challenge,
women are nevertheless expected to display collectivism, equality, and sol-
idarity with their sex. I understood that these expectations, whether uni-
versalistic or culturally constructed, give the women negative impressions
of those who flaunt their obvious superiority in public. I saw in the other
women's preoccupation with Nava's efforts to get pregnant an attempt to
interpret it as a punishment. Women in the society I studied were first and
foremost mothers. One who bases her existence on her pedigree, mind,
respected teaching position at the college, and learning will in the end
neglect the most important task, parenting, which knows no borders
between social classes.

When Nava finally became pregnant, the women were happy. On the
one hand, that happiness was only to be expected, since Nava had overcome her problems. Yet, on the other hand, her pregnancy was what joined
Nava to the most fundamental common denominator the women had: that
of giving birth. Pregnancy made Nava "one of the women."

In this case also, it was Nava's "marginality," her "otherness," that helped me as an investigator.

Malka Shamir, the ba'alat teshuva, was more than an exceptional figure from whom a researcher could learn. Ba'alei teshuva occupy a clear niche in the haredi community. For that community, they are the confirmation that the haredi view of the history of the Jewish religion is correct. They serve as mediators and agents between the religious and secular, and are often a source of satisfaction, curiosity, and amusement.[20]

During my time at the Development, women made various attempts to put me in contact with the ba'alot teshuva. Some of these attempts may have been related to their desire to turn me into one of them and, even more so, as a possible way of understanding why I was among them. This was also the way my family and friends sometimes wanted to explain my interest in the haredim. It was only logical that the four ba'alot teshuva who lived in the Development tried individually and collectively to assume a special role in my regard. In that gray area between the haredim and the secular we found that we had a common language.

Ahuva Graetz, the woman who lived one floor above Hannah, taught me much about the reality I did not see among the others. The undone housecoat and the kerchief tied in the morning at the sound of a knock on the door gave me a hint of how the women behaved when they were alone in their own homes. Ahuva's criticism of Hannah's relations with her husband, of the neglected state of the Zilberstein household, and of the expectations she had of her children showed me the accepted norms that I would not have been aware of had I not first become acquainted with what was different.

In addition to the "marginal" nature of the central figures I met who supplied me with information, there were also "marginal" events that made strong impressions on me. Anthropology's interest in these events, in rituals that everyone seems to have tired of, in public gatherings, in disputes, in social accidents, in drama, games, and slips of the tongue, is not coincidental.[21]

My field journal is full of descriptions of routine work days at the Development. This information is the basis for understanding every matter with which I chose to grapple. Yet, as one might expect, it was the special events—those that made a particular impression on me—that became the criteria that gave meaning to the day-to-day routine.

The exotic aspect of the event etched in my memory became an instrument for interpreting the normal and routine. On the macro level, anthropology has chosen to study groups that, in their universality, serve as examples of exceptional or marginal events in the society from which the researcher comes. Here also the discipline has aspired to use the results of research to understand what seems to be an accepted social and cultural order.

To state that my informants and I are marginal types, that the exceptional events impressed me more than anything else, and that some people see Gur Hasidic women as an eccentric, exotic, and marginal group is to say both everything and nothing.

The object is to describe what happened there, and to try to understand it.

Methodology

The event, the dialogue, and the content-analysis are the research tools used in this work. The event and the dialogue stem from the observation of the group under study, while the content-analysis offers a wider view of the social context of the group. These take the following forms: (1) documentation of public events, such as women's classes and gatherings, celebrations, plays, charity nights, and family meals; (2) transcription of conversations with the informants, including information imparted by all those taking part in the dialogue; and (3) content-analysis of a popular weekly periodical read by the group under study and by the haredi community at large.

At present, there is no dominant paradigm in anthropology, and this allows experimentation. There is currently a great tolerance of varied theoretical and practical approaches, and openness to defining new goals and areas of research. In such an atmosphere the anthropologist risks venturing on an untrodden road that leads to a dead end, or blazing a new trail.

Being There

By definition, anthropological research involves physically meeting the subjects of the study. Researchers leave their immediate social context and seek out others. Since anthropology deals with "social" subjects, researchers seek out public events at which they can make contact with people, and look for opportunities to converse with various individuals in the same society.

I met groups of women at classes on Jewish law, the book of Psalms, and Maimonides. One evening in the month of Tishrei (September–October), when the High Holidays were in full swing, I had the opportunity to be present at a large gathering, a "public event."

At 6:30 P.M. Sarah-Leah, Hannah's oldest daughter, called to notify me that that evening Rabbanit Yungerman would be coming to speak with the women on the occasion of the upcoming Yom Kippur holiday. The gathering would take place at 8:00 P.M. at the Libyan synagogue near the Development. Sarah-Leah informed me that her mother had returned home from the hospital on Friday with the new baby, who had been named

Mirale, after her father's great-grandmother. I arrived at their home at 7:30.

The apartment stank—the pungent odor of guavas pervaded it. I knew that Hannah's husband was home, and since I was used to his absence, I was tense. The voices coming from the balcony told me that he was sitting there studying. Hannah was in the kitchen preparing him a cup of coffee. No, she said, of course she couldn't come to the lecture. True, she was being helped by her mother, who would come daily for the ten days after the birth, but she preferred to finish up her work early, nurse Mirale, and go to bed.

On the way to the synagogue I encountered three men coming in the opposite direction. The path was too small for all of us. I stood aside, with my back to the wall, lowering my eyes and waiting for them to pass. I recalled how, a few weeks previously, a man had come up the stairwell towards me. I had been carrying a pile of books, which I was helping Hannah take to a bindery in Bene Brak. I remembered that then, also, I had backed into a corner of the landing, put down the books, and waited for him to pass.

I realized that I had adjusted to the haredi attitude toward the female presence, and that I was almost instinctively expressing this adjustment in encounters with haredi men in and out of the Development. I associated the memory on the stairwell with a third incident, this one on an El Al flight. I had found myself sitting next to a haredi man, who was squeezed into the center seat between me and another women, a proximity to the opposite sex that I knew any haredi man would find awkward. After take-off, I saw that there was a free seat in front of me, and I quickly moved. I had assumed an obligation to solve the discomfort I thought he felt.

Outside the synagogue, on a wooden bench, sat two young women whom I didn't know. I greeted them and they responded quietly. We waited, unsure whether the lecture would actually take place; it was 8:00 P.M. and we were the only ones there.

> They really do need to do something for the women about repentance, when it comes down to it what do we do for Yom Kippur, we're either at work or with the pots and pans. The men go to *selichot* [special prayers of repentance during the two weeks preceding Yom Kippur] and we don't have anything.

Her companion nodded her agreement and added with annoyance:

> At home I had so much to do that I didn't know where to start, and here I am sitting doing nothing, it's really aggravating.

In the meantime a few other women arrived, among them Brachi, Hannah's relative. She noticed me and smiled. They began to set the place up for the lecture. The lecture was supposed to be held on the synagogue's enclosed balcony, but it was dirty. One woman pushed the benches aside, another swept, another spread a tablecloth she had brought from home over the table in the center, behind which the rabbanit was to stand. All were worried that not enough women would come to hear the lecture, and that would be a disgrace.

In the meantime a truck driven by some Belzer Hasidim arrived, carrying live chickens for the *kaparot* ceremony. This ritual, performed before Yom Kippur, the Day of Atonement, involves symbolically transferring one's sins to a "scapegoat." All the women and children who had not yet performed this obligation took advantage of the opportunity and went out to the truck. I left the synagogue with Malka, the ba'alat teshuva, and we went, at her suggestion, to watch. A rare conglomeration of men, women, and children stood around the truck. The kaparot cost the equivalent of about $2. After the ceremony, the chickens return to the truck, to be taken to slaughter and then distributed to the poor or to yeshivot. The atmosphere is that of a carnival, not a religious ritual. The children run about, enjoying the rare encounter with animals. The mothers giggle as they hold the flapping chickens by the feet over the heads of their young daughters. The few fathers standing nearby see to their older sons, but do not perform the ceremony on themselves; apparently they had done so already elsewhere.

The partially lit parking lot is so close to my home. I stand and watch. The ceremony seems to me simultaneously ordinary and insane. It was like a rock video clip, at first surrealistic, but as it goes on the viewer gets into the story, and it begins to seem completely natural. Devorah, a member of the clique of Development women who grew up in Tel Aviv, jars me out of the video and calls me back to the synagogue, because the rabbanit's cab has just arrived. Rabbanit Yungerman had been Devorah's teacher at the teachers' college, and she had invited her in her capacity as coordinator of women's activities in the Development.

When we returned to the balcony, most of the benches were already filled up with women from the Development. A cursory survey of those present indicated that this audience was different from the one I was accustomed to seeing at the Jewish law classes I had attended. This was a large gathering of some sixty women, while a normal class was attended by ten to twenty women. Most of the women seemed to be between twenty and twenty-five years old, and most of them looked like newlyweds, well-dressed and in impeccable wigs. They knew each other, whispering among themselves in a way that indicated they were friendly and close. Devorah introduced the rabbanit. She was a pleasant-faced woman of about forty-five whose clear eyes could shoot a sharp glance. Her body was large, and her feet were swollen; she wore clumsy orthopedic shoes.

Every woman and every person must prepare themselves for Yom
Kippur. There should be no case in which a woman reaches Yom
Kippur unprepared, realizing that Yom Kippur has arrived only when
she opens up her prayer book. When I speak to you, I make the
following suggestion: take five minutes with yourself and think,
find something that meets these two conditions, which I quote from
Rabbi Deskel:

    1. Something that you feel you are absolutely fed up with.
That you are sick of and that you can't go on with, and that this is
something you've been sure of for a long time.
    2. That you think that, with heaven's help, you can abide by the
change and carry it out.

    It is best to accept these conditions, rather than to make a
big promise like "I promise to be all right from now on, to improve
everything, and to change." Even what seems like a small decision,
like to read *birkat hamazon* [the grace after meals] from the prayer
book or from a printed copy. Here I'm talking from personal
experience—that is something, too. It is an improvement, and a little
improvement, like the tide, raises the entire level of the home. You
can decide to improve your attitude towards the children, not to call
them names like *schlimazel* or *schlemiel*. Even if its just before Shabbat
and everything's falling out of your hands, and this one hasn't taken
a shower yet and that one hasn't gotten dressed, and you're standing
there with half of everything in your hands, and one of them gets you
mad because you've been telling him to do something for half an
hour. So you just blurt it out because it's hard, and then you go into
Shabbat with anger and nerves and a bad feeling for the child and for
you, what good is a Shabbat like that. You can decide to improve
relations with your parents, that's not easy. Or with the in-laws.
Your mother comes to visit once a week and she always has some
comment. Why isn't the child dressed warmly enough, and how have
you arranged the dishes, and why are you waiting with the drapes,
why haven't you sewn them already. And the anger and the words
are on your tongue, and you feel angry in your heart, what do I need
this visit for, that's supposed to help me but actually bothers me.
Here you can decide on an improvement. It's not just respect for your
parents, which we are commanded to have, it's also thinking of your
parents in an adult way. Think about their good intentions, their
concern. You're already mothers and you know what that is. Thank
God you have homes of your own, and your husbands, and you'll run
the house the way you see fit. It's just a visit, it will end and only the
feelings will remain. You can decide to hold back and that pays off,
believe me.

At the end of the lecture, which lasted about half an hour, the women rose and the rabbanit exited to the foyer, where she stood to take her leave of the women and wish them a *g'mar hatima tova*, the traditional Yom Kippur greeting. The women thanked her politely and respectfully for the lecture, and shook her outstretched hand. When it was my turn to stand before the Rabbanit, I found Rachel Lichtenbaum next to me. She apparently sensed my awkwardness, and came to my rescue.

"Please meet Rabbanit Yungerman. This is Mrs. El-Or, who has come to us to learn. She's a guest of the Zilberstein family's and works at the university."

I mumbled a g'mar hatima tova and tried to explain myself in a few words. I thanked her for the interesting lecture and praised her eloquent Hebrew. She said modestly that her words came from the literature and from the sages, and that she was only an intermediary. She evinced an interest in my work, and Malka proclaimed from behind me:

"She's doing her doctorate."

Rachel tried out her knowledge of the world outside:

"It's with statistics, right?"

Rabbanit Yungerman looked at me and said with a smile:

"God has his own ways to bring Jews to him and to his Torah. Some come from the university."

Thus she summed up our dialogue, allowed me to pass, to make way for the few women who remained behind me.

એ

This type of text, which comes out of "being there," is essential and important to anthropological research, no matter what school you belong to. First and foremost you have to be there, in the place you wish to learn about, among the people you wish to understand, with their daily affairs, in the midst of the acrid smell of the guavas, on the path too narrow to hold both men and women. To hear the Yom Kippur lecture, to see the kaparot ceremony, to rejoice at the ring of the informant's phone, to change clothes and go there. To lend your ear to what is said and to see as much as possible. To think that you are one of the crowd, and to hear Malka announce that you are "doing your doctorate." To assume that if you say that you are from the university that you are taken at your word, but still understand that there are those who think that God has taken you on a detour and that he means to bring you into orthodoxy through the academy. To return home in the evening, to sit down at the computer, and to tell everything that has happened, immediately.

Here it begins, and as it goes on it becomes, for a while, a way of life. This is not the absolute abandonment of your previous life in favor of another. You do not change homes; there are no long trips. You live both lives, and it is not easy. They separate and meet; there are mornings when you are one way, and different in the afternoon. At times I kept them separate, and at times I brought them together. Sometimes I listened, and sometimes I spoke.

On this evening, as on others, I arrived in accordance with information that something was to happen. Sometimes it was the regular weekly class in Jewish law, the Psalms, or Maimonides. Sometimes it was a celebration, a special gathering, a charity evening, or trips outside the Development. At all these events I played only a small active part. During the classes I almost never spoke. At lectures and assemblies I sat inconspicuously next to a woman I knew—I saw, I heard, I smelled, I breathed, and I remained silent. When it was possible (especially during classes) I took notes on the event, while everyone thought I was taking notes on the material.

At this Yom Kippur assembly two women chose to remove me from my anonymity and passivity and presented me to the lecturer. My otherness, my outsiderness, became an explicit subject of conversation. Rachel said, "She's from the university," and Malka said, "She's doing her doctorate." At other events I was part of the crowd, even if a little odd in my dress and my kerchief—watching, almost never getting involved, observing public events, social activities, ceremonies. I recorded what I saw from within the illusion of being a video camera, quoting what others said, very close to the original, recreating in writing situations as they happened, or so it seemed to me. These events, I learned, were the "meat" of my work, the real basis of my attempt to decipher the observed reality. Every piece of news I received about a coming public event make me rejoice. "Great!" I'd tell myself. "More material."

The Dialogue: Everyone Talking About Everything

Unlike public events, which I considered as "material" from the start, I originally saw my regular visits at Hannah's house as a mere necessity, a pipeline leading me to the real thing. Our long conversations and my observations of her daily life at first left me with a sense of disappointment, impatient "for something to happen already."

I learned slowly, especially after attending a number of public events, that my conversations with Hannah and the other women were much more than entry tickets to the public arena. I understood that talking in detail and at length clarified many sociocultural themes and cast light on what I saw in public. The dialogue that emerged was one of many voices, and allowed every aspect that was raised in discussion to be checked against other related themes. The opportunity to hear a melody being played on many instruments occurs not only in a public gathering. At such events social convention generally acts to conceal dissonance and emphasize harmony. In an ongoing, in-depth dialogue there is room for all tones of voice, and taking them all together allows one to see how complex the ethnographic production is—how shaky its foundation, and how far it is from the material produced by that imaginary video camera.

The "new ethnography" emphasizes the importance of the multiplicity of voices and the representation of reality, including its lack of harmony. This approach is of great use in dialogue, as a mediator between the oral and the written.[22] The difficulty in turning spoken texts into written ones and the need to make use of written material (ethnography) are at the foundation of the analysis.

Within the dialogue between me and Hannah, Rachel, Ahuva, Malka, and the others I could search for the sociological insights that could decipher the social events I observed. Dialogue should enable one to understand the quality of the observed event, and to use this understanding to decipher other events that at first seem to be familiar and self-evident. The multisided flow of the dialogue—the state in which all sides speak with each other and complex contents of the dialogue come from different levels of cultural and social expression—makes it the central mechanism of the methodology.

ॐ

Such a dialogue took place one summer evening in early September, and went on deep into the night. Taking part in this conversation between me and Hannah were her and my daily experiences, themes she passed on to me from her society and from other societies she had heard of, as well as themes I passed on to her from my society and other groups with whom I had met.

I arrived at Hannah's house at 7:30. I found a note on the door informing me that she had gone with the children to Degani Park. The park is a large one located in the neighborhood adjacent to the Development and serves all the neighborhoods in the area. I had received plants on Tu Beshevat, the tree-planting holiday, in this park when I was six years old, and I had clashed the cymbals when the kindergarten teacher gave the signal. My father would take me there when we had exhausted all other possibilities for play, and there I took my children when they did not nap in the afternoon. I decided to go by foot. It was the first time I walked the streets close to my home in the dress of a religious woman, wondering whether anyone would see me that way.

The park was almost empty. Daylight time ensured that it was still light between seven and eight in the evening. At the edge of the park, at the top of its incline, on a bench, I saw Hannah. Her children (except for Binyomin, who was in school until late and then went for prayers to the synagogue near the house) were playing on the grass. With her children were two little guests, the children of a friend who was attending a camp for women with large families (five children or more) sponsored by Agudat Yisrael. Hannah had gone to such a camp the previous week, and two of her children had stayed with these friends of theirs. Next to Hannah was a basket containing little cream cheese sandwiches, yogurt, and peeled cucumbers. The children ate eagerly, and from time to time came to Hannah for more. Hannah made sure that they threw their garbage into one of the park's many wastebaskets. She also told them not to play near the flowers and plants, explaining to them the importance of keeping the park in good condition. She had brought disposable plastic cups that could be filled at the drinking fountains, as well as a cup for the ritual hand washing required before eating bread. She returned the used cups to the basket. The children were in ecstasy, running through the open spaces, rolling down the grassy slope that formed a kind of natural amphitheater, ending in an empty pool with a platform above it. When a puppy running by alarmed them, they took cover next to us.

Hannah told me about the camp she had attended. The women had boarded at a yeshiva near Jerusalem, empty of its male students, who were home on a break.[23] The camp included tours of Jerusalem's Old City and its walls, a visit to the Western Wall and another to Rachel's tomb in Bethlehem. They heard several lectures, including one from a pediatrician, and another from an educator who counsels parents. She spoke about how to get through the summer vacation safely. Another lecture, given by a haredi woman who had immigrated recently from Russia, had made a strong impression on Hannah. The woman had shown them slides from Russia; Hannah thought it was a pretty country. The main part of the lecture was devoted to the things Jews there did in order to preserve their Judaism and to keep the commandments, despite the difficulties they faced from the authorities. Especially vivid for Hannah had been the description of immersion in an improvised mikveh containing ice-cold water, used by the speaker and her friends.

> When the woman entered the room, I wasn't especially enthusiastic. She was very elegant, with a blonde wig, and seemed very spoiled. When she began to talk I was amazed at her Hebrew—such a short time in Israel, and what Hebrew! She was fascinating, all the women were really overwhelmed. To be in Jerusalem, without the children, with four meals a day, and to hear about the suffering they endured in order to go to the mikveh, or in order to pray together. We learn to appreciate what we have here and to see how spoiled we are.

I had just gone with my students from a kibbutz college on a field trip to the Ramla prison. It was the first time I had visited a prison and I was bursting with impressions. I told Hannah about entering the cells, about the talk given by the warden, about the Druze deputy warden, and about the small, neat cells called "the Xs," where I met two infamous murderers, Rahamim Aharoni and Herzl Avitan. I told her who these two were, and noted that Avitan was actually a neighbor of ours, since his girlfriend and their son live not far from Degani Park. Hannah inquired about the crimes he had committed; I told her, leaving out the more gory details. Then I told her about the nearby Ma'asiahu jail, adjacent to the Ramla facility, where other convicted murderers told us, each one separately, that he had done none of the things of which he had been convicted. Hannah and I deliberated on crime and punishment, and on the character of a society that includes murderers and rapists. I felt a bit embarrassed, as if "my" society was responsible for these crimes, and for the way in which they and their deeds are treated.

When we returned to her home, Hannah managed to get the children ready for bed in the space of twenty minutes. We went into the small kitchen to drink a cup of coffee. Little Sheine-Brocha crawled between us restlessly until she fell asleep on the floor. Hannah let her be—it was a sweltering night and the floor was cool.

I took from my bag two final exams I had given to my students at the Tel Aviv University medical school. One was that of a modern religious student; the second belonged to a secular student. The question was:

"In serious illness, religious people generally consult simultaneously a doctor and a rabbi. How would you explain this, and what significance does this phenomenon have for the doctor's work?"

Hannah was impressed with the students' answers, and asked whether we had discussed the subject before the test. I told her that we had not discussed it directly, but that we had talked about how, in simple societies where popular medicine is practiced, people often consult both a "Western" doctor and a popular practitioner at the same time. I thought she would be insulted by the comparison, but she evinced a great interest and extolled simple societies for still not having been "spoiled." In her opinion, the search for the disease's meaning and the desire to know "why it happened to me" are signs of both moral and logical thinking, a desire that has been lost in modern, secular society. She explained her understanding of disease:

Hannah: If your child is sick before the age of thirteen, that's the parents' fault. That's why my husband doesn't understand how woman can talk about their children's illnesses in public. It's as if they're talking about their sins.

I: And what about epidemics, childhood diseases, and the like?

Hannah: That's also because of something. How is it, for example, that in the same house one child is sick and another one isn't? Or that the disease affects one family but not another? It's all in accordance with the magnitude of the sin. That's why they say, for instance, that when God wants to bring troubles on someone, he checks to see how much anguish it will cause those close to him, and decides accordingly. That's another reason to devote oneself to a lot of charity and good deeds, so that you have a lot of friends who can be references for God.

I told her about the Azanda (an African tribe studied by the British anthropologist Evans-Pritchard in 1937), and she exhibited much sympathy for their practice of witchcraft.

Their way of looking for the reason is, of course, a pagan way, and we have other ways like the Urim and Tumim, which we once had, or the rabbis and righteous men, or to keep it to yourself and pray and improve yourself.

Hannah then asked how I would write my dissertation, and whether it did not open the door to dishonesty and deception. What really interested her was how another society awarded titles, recognized knowledge, and bestowed respect and prestige.

At the time I was mulling over a possible transfer from Tel Aviv University to Bar-Ilan University, where the atmosphere is religious. I related the points for and against each institution. Hannah had a girlhood friend from Bene Brak who had gotten a clerical job at Bar-Ilan. She had met a young man there, and had fallen in love with him even though she was already married. She divorced her husband, but her relationship with the young man did not go well, either. Hannah was afraid that she might bump into the friend one day in Bene Brak. She had seen the woman's mother several times and had avoided her. They had been so close as children. "Bar-Ilan . . ." she said, "I don't know if that's more 'kosher' than Tel Aviv." I told her that I had already met the faculty member whom I wished to be my dissertation adviser. This professor, I told Hannah, had expressed concern that Hannah and the Development might close their doors to me before I finished my research. Hannah did not deny that this could happen, but added:

"Didn't you say that it might open some doors for you, too?"

The end of this long conversation was conducted in the stairwell. It was almost two in the morning.

The dialogue, which had begun that afternoon in Degani Park and which had continued into the night at Hannah's home, contained no less than thirteen levels of content and perspective. Conversation between two women embraced seven sociocultural states:

1. The park is the place that I went to during my childhood and adolescence with my father or with my friends.

2. The park was also a place I took my infant children to when I became a mother. My oldest son's sixth-grade-class party was held there, and the children in my younger son's kindergarten went there last Tu Beshevat, as I had in my childhood.
3. Hannah spends time in the park with her children. The two of us meet there and have our conversation. Hannah's children also play in the park with their friends, and learn to enjoy it and keep it clean.
4. Hannah tells me about a woman from Russia. She tells me things she heard from her about what happened there.
5. For Hannah, the themes of the story from Russia cast light on meaningful matters in her life here.
6. I introduce the fact that I teach at a college associated with kibbutzim—many of which subscribe to an antireligious ideology.
7. During our dialogue, I told Hannah about the lives of prisoners. The reality of prison deepens my understanding of existence outside the jail walls, and perhaps Hannah's as well.
8. What I saw in the prison clarified for me, and perhaps also for Hannah, important themes relating to her and my attitude towards crime, and social responsibility for it.
9. When we reached Hannah's home, I showed her exams from my students, and presented them to her as a teacher.
10. We spoke of me as a doctoral student.
11. Hannah gave her opinion about the academic world—in other words, she criticized my world.
12. We spoke about illnesses, and returned to the subject of reward and punishment for one's deeds. Hannah criticized herself in accordance with her own religious criteria.
13. Hannah criticized me as a mother, in accordance with criteria that are not mine.

The sociocultural spheres we moved in, and to which we alluded in the space of a single evening are:

1. the Jews in Russia
2. the haredi Jews in Israel
3. the kibbutzim
4. prisoners
5. the secular public
6. simple societies
7. the academic world: medical students, Ph.D. candidates, various universities

Directly touching on so many themes, both of us able to listen and speak, submitting all the information that entered the conversation to criticism—this yielded material that was qualitatively different from what was gathered in the previous event. I received indefinite information, multidirectional in terms of its flow between her and me, multilayered for each side (for her as a woman and a religious mother in her cultural nexus, and for me as a woman with my cultural nexus). There were many times when I thought that conversations of this type were the chaff of field work, part of the great amount of material that is not included in ethnography. After much time, when I could reflect on the many dialogues I had had, I could start seeing meaning in them. This meaning, even when unclear, became primary. I knew that this complex and multicultural state was closest to the reality I wished to understand. Only much later, when I organized my thoughts and put them in writing, did I realize that a large part of modern ethnographic literature has been written in a similar way. Maybe, I thought to myself, there really is something like a zeitgeist.

Content-Analysis

Other than the never-ending obligation to explain the dialogue and the experience in the cultural context, I felt a need to reach comprehensive social levels that the research field could not supply. My lack of knowledge of practices in haredi society in general (which I could correct slowly through reading) impelled me to search for an additional source of information that would cast light on the events I experienced. The women I met several times mentioned a magazine they read. Hearing that it had a large circulation among several levels of haredi society, I decided to subscribe. *Marveh Latsameh* began arriving in my mailbox once a week.

Marveh Latsameh is published by the Organization of Daughters of Israel and Haredi Youth in Israel. The magazine's cover identifies it as "a weekly magazine for counselors, parents, and educators, on doctrine, Halacha, and Agada. Complied and edited by Rabbi Yisrael Pollak. Address: The Mahane Haharedi Center, Bene Brak."

The magazine is printed on cheap paper. It contains no pictures except for those on its cover, and these always depict rabbis and righteous men (always men). The magazine contains some illustrations, mostly in conjunction with children's stories. The graphics remind one of a school newspaper or a periodical from the 1930s. The layout is confused and makes reading difficult. *Marveh Latsameh* is read by various haredi groups (unlike the daily newspapers, which haredim choose in accordance with their political affiliation: *Hamodia* representing Agudat Yisrael; *Yated Ne'eman*, the Lithuanians). The variety of articles and the letters to the editor indicate that its readers include Hasidim, Ashkenazi Misnagdim, Sepharadim, and ba'alei teshuva.

The magazine has a standard internal structure. It opens with an explanation of the weekly Torah portion, after which come the regular features: The Children's Page, The Creator's Wonders, Around the World, The Weekly Story, A Word to Parents, For the Young Woman, For the Girl, From the Proverbs, From One Woman to Another, For the Home-maker, For Your Health, a serialized story, and letters to the editor. A special, larger issue comes out before each holiday, containing the laws applying to the holiday, the customs of various groups, and special stories. Sometimes it contains articles on current events or epistles from important rabbis. Many articles are taken from other sources and are presented in translation or in condensed form, with the source given on the back cover. Most of the magazine's readers are women, children, and teenagers. The editor is said to be an enthusiast; he must be, for it is largely a one-man project. It has few regular writers, and some say that the bylines are pseudonyms for the editor himself.

I received the magazine for two years, reading and sorting through its contents. The material helped me understand the subjects that occupy the haredi public. It contained descriptions of secular society in Israel, of the non-Jewish world, of ecology, and of the universe. Although I was aware of the need to question how representative it is of haredi society in general, and how valid the conclusions drawn from it can be, I found it useful.

From the broad spectrum of behaviors I observed, out of the chaos of the data gleaned from multiple voices and the richness of the documentation, this study focuses on one subject. There is a transition from abundance to scarcity, from a social reality to analytic reality. This transition makes it necessary to forgo the description of a rich but incomprehensible reality in favor of parts that may be understood, and from which one may infer hypotheses on the less understood parts. In fact, this exercise is not unique to anthropology—it is characteristic of all types of scientific inquiry.[24]

When anthropologists began studying complex societies, the necessity of forgoing the whole became apparent. Up until then researchers were able to delude themselves into thinking that they were conducting comprehensive research. Their methods remain open to interdisciplinary negotiation.

It seems as if every anthropological study is a test case, because it generally discusses a single sociocultural group. In complex societies, researchers choose to focus on a field of interest or segment of society because of their inability to take in an entire group and an entire set of subjects.

In this case, I chose two foci from a rich social reality, which are really two aspects of the same thing: the paradox of women's education. The first is the axis that leads to understanding the existential state of the haredi communities in Israel, and the second is a specific case of this general subject, which illustrates the pattern of behavior and is explained by it. The events, dialogues, and press clips have been chosen from a mass of data in order to clarify these subjects, and to provide a foundation for the theoretical triangle (literacy, women, the haredi community) and to help decipher the research questions. The rest of the data contributes less to these goals, and will find their expression in other question to which they are more relevant.

Beyond ethnography (the data) and behavioral patterns (sorting and cataloging data) there is also theory (the interpretation of data). The greater part of the theory comes from the total insights that have already been obtained in the discipline, with another part deriving from the sociological imagination of the author of the work.[25] This is the incremental contribution of each study, for better or worse, for which the author is solely responsible.

Notes

1. Sepharadi Jews (those who came from the Islamic world) underwent different processes in their confrontation with the modern age and the establishment of the State of Israel. In terms of religion, most Sepharadi haredim identify with the Lithuanians, and in terms of politics, with the relatively new Shas Party, founded in 1981.

2. See Heilman 1992.

3. Ravitzky 1993.

4. Alfasi 5746 (1986). Most historical descriptions of the various Hasidic sects were written by the Hasidim themselves or by those close to them. I have found no independent historical study of the Gur Hasidim. My summary should be read in this light.

5. Agudat Shlomei Emunei Yisrael was founded in Poland in reaction to the establishment of Agudat Yisrael and the fear that Polish Hasidism would not be appropriately represented in the latter organization. Most of the members of Agudat Shlomei Emunei Yisrael were also members of Agudat Yisrael; a few groups that had refused to join Agudat Yisrael also were members.

6. The epistle appears in full in Alfasi 5746 (1986), p. 125.

7. Levy 5748 (1988), p. 42.

8. Devout Jewish couples are forbidden to have sexual relations during, and for a week after, the wife's menstrual period. Women are required to immerse themselves in a mikveh before resuming sexual relations.

9. A study by Yona Ginzburg (1988) of the new haredi town of Emanuel examined the mobility of haredi residents from crowded urban neighborhoods to more comfortable quarters in the West Bank. It also assessed their satisfaction with the ecological change. Ginzburg notes that the women, who spend most of their day at home, miss the bustle of the city, and say they need to "go into town" from time to time.

10. Education for boys and men encompasses the following institutions:

- Talmud Torah, or heder (elementary school).
- Lower yeshiva (secondary school).
- Higher yeshiva (institutions of higher education, in which boys study from the age of 16 or 17 until marriage).
- Kolel (institutions for married students, or avrechim). (Friedman 5751 [1991]).

11. For a discussion of the problem of presenting subjects (the researchers and their subjects) as objects (research tools and findings), see Schutz 1962.

12. On why the researcher's personal experiences while conducting anthropological study have been written in the form of nonacademic material or travel accounts, and on when and why the status of this material changed, see Shokied 1988; and Marcus and Fischer 1986.

13. Issues such as the status of the text as a scientific product representing the life reality of "others," the influence of the way it was produced (observation) on what was said in it, and the power relationships and the relations between the explicit or hidden interests of the researchers and their subjects were granted central importance in scientific discourse. Among the many works dealing with this issue, two books (Clifford and Marcus 1986; Marcus and Fischer 1986) and one comprehensive article (Sangren 1988) are especially noteworthy.

14. Indeed, if the informants do not represent the "average," there is good reason to test the validity, and especially the significance, of the information they provide. Shokied (1988) discusses this issue; it is further developed in Turner 1975; Frielich 1970; Pelto 1970; Ellen 1984.

15. Having good values (*midot tovot* in Hebrew) means having assimilated the expectations haredi society has of one as a female. These values relate to morals, and to the way in which a woman comprehends her position and presents it to the world. Midot tovot sometimes also includes inherent abilities that make it easier to educate her. A girl with good values is one who helps her mother at home, does not make demands of her parents, does what is required of her at school (though she may not necessarily be a bright, intelligent, or even good student), helps her friends, is involved in acts of charity at a level according to her age, and so on. These values develop as the girl becomes a woman. A woman of good values is one who helps others; who minimizes her own importance and her needs, including her economic needs; observes the rules of modesty; and in general accepts the established definitions of her position as a woman without doubting or deviating from them. Sometimes the phrase "a woman of good values" is used in the same way that society at large uses the phrase "a good girl"—i.e., a girl whose major virtue is that she does not stand out. While haredi society sees this image as a positive one, it may nevertheless sometimes express an acceptance of the fact that the woman in question aspires to nothing more—but at least her values are strong. ("Our Brachi might not be an outstanding student—but she's a girl with good values.")

16. Ba'al-bayit is the name given to a man who has left his studies and who earns his living in some craft or profession. The term carries certain connotations. On the one hand, it indicates failure—a man who could not make it as a scholar because of some intellectual or psychological reason, or because he gave in to family pressure. On the other hand, it implies a certain level of economic security. Additional adjectives can indicate significant wealth. The common use of the term ba'al-bayit, or its plural, ba'al-batim, must, of course, be examined in context. It is often used to express scorn, but sometimes the social discourse can grant it legitimacy and respect.

A yeshiva student receives a monthly stipend of between $300 and $700. The differential derives from the economic situation of the different yeshivot, as well as from the student's status and his position in the yeshiva. If a student has no other sources of income from his wife or family, he and his family will have to live off the stipend and the social security stipend he receives in accordance with the size of his family. In such a situation (which is that of the Zilbersteins), the family lives very close to penury.

17. Most observant married Jewish women cover their heads in public (although there are some in the modern orthodox community who do not, arguing

that it is not obligatory). In general, the fashion among modern orthodox women is to wear kerchiefs or hats; among the haredim (with the exception of the most extreme groups) most women wear wigs. Wigs are frequently denounced as immodest by many haredi religious leaders, but remain widespread. For more on this, see note 1 of Chapter 2; and Levy 5748 (1988), pp. 72–82.

18. The term Malka used is *pikuah nefesh*, a Jewish legal term denoting a situation in which someone's life is in danger. In such a case, a religious Jew is commanded to violate other laws in order to save a life.

19. These charitable societies, *gamahim* in Hebrew, are voluntary organizations that provide aid to those in need. There are both large public gamahim and small private ones. Many families in the haredi community take part in giving aid in various areas as part of their religious obligation to give to charity. Private gamahim may provide cassette libraries; pacifiers, diapers, formula, and other baby needs; medical equipment; school books; or tableware for celebrations. There are those that serve as lost-and-found departments, that provide aid to brides and orphans, that help children with their homework, and so on. So many gamahim have been established that in many communities it is difficult for families to find a niche for any new gamah.

20. The haredi community's attitudes towards ba'alei teshuva will be discussed in Chapter 4, in the section "Haredim and the Secular."

21. Most anthropologists agree that their informants are "marginal"; they also accept that exceptional events—rituals, celebrations, mourning periods, big disputes, violent incidents, and so on—are what fill most of the pages of their journals. The anthropological literature justifies the importance and significance of special events in understanding daily reality. See Van-Gennep 1908; Levi-Strauss 1964; Gluckman 1967; Van-Velsen 1967; Geertz 1973; and Turner 1975.

22. Dialogue generally indicates conversation between two individuals or two groups. Even in its nonscientific usage, however, it sometimes designates a conversation with many participants (for instance, "our dialogue with the Arabs"). In anthropology, the current use of the term emphasizes the fact that anthropologists do not just "listen" and their subjects do not just "speak," and that there is not just one voice in a cultural text. It is a conversation with many voices and many themes, including tension, internal contradictions, latent and blatant interests, as well as accord. See Marcus and Fischer 1986, pp. 67–69.

23. The break, called *bein hazemanim*, is a three-week period in the summer before Rosh Hashanah, between the school years. During these weeks the yeshivot are emptied of their regular students and are used for other activities. The bein hazemanim period is a hazardous one for young avrechim, who often amuse themselves by going on dangerous hikes in the wilderness or by engaging in hooliganism.

24. Yanai 1989.

25. "Sociological imagination" is the free and creative element added to the findings and feeding the theory. While this part is supposed to derive from the reality under study, its main strength is the researcher's ability to be "liberated" for a moment from that reality, in order better to decipher it; Mills 1959.

2

· · · ❧ · · ·

Educated and Ignorant

If we succeed in instilling in our girl students that the purpose of their studies is to aspire to emulate our matriarchs, who did not study, then we have succeeded in educating our daughters.

—*the late Rabbi Avraham Yosef Wolf*
Founder and Principal
Beit Ya'akov College for Girls, Bene Brak

Appropriating Knowledge:
The Emergence of Women's Education

Early November. At 8:30 P.M. it was already cool outside. Some forty women had gathered in the Libyan synagogue. The early arrivals had swept up the synagogue's closed-off balcony, furnished with old wooden benches and two tables. The smaller table was put at one end of the room, with a chair behind it. All was ready for Mrs. Nehama Vechter, a senior teacher at the Gur sect's Beit Ya'akov girls' college in Bene Brak, and a scion of some of the most highly-respected Gur families. The women in the room passed time waiting for her in two ways. One group, gathered in the center of the room, was made up of the newlyweds, those women who had been married during the previous year. These were dressed in new clothes bought for them in anticipation of their wedding, and they wore conventional but high-quality wigs.[1] They spoke loudly, giggling and cheerfully greeting one another. The source of the excitement, and the subject of the talk, was the installation of telephones in all the new homes. These women had studied together at colleges in Bene Brak, Tel Aviv, or Jerusalem. They had not yet forgotten what it was like to be a student, and here they were on the cold balcony of a synagogue that had turned into an improvised classroom. When the rabbanit arrived, they quickly sat down and became students once more.

Another group was scattered around the room, sitting on the wooden benches along the wall. These were the older women, who were in the first group of families to settle in the Development. Each of these women was about thirty years old, had been married for about ten years, and had between four and six children. They spoke quietly, in twos or threes, resting somewhat heavily on the benches after hours on their feet. Most of them had left their children at home after throwing together a quick supper, leaving the older ones with instructions for caring for the younger ones. Then they had changed clothes, perhaps replaced a kerchief with a wig, and had rushed off to hear the lecture. Some had left a plate of food waiting for their husband, who was at prayers, at a late class, or with a study partner he met with at night. There were those whose husbands worked and who had managed to eat supper with them. A few of these men had also gone out to a Talmud class meant for *ba'albatim*.

The religious education of Jewish women was institutionalized and organized only about seventy-five years ago. Jewish law exempts women from religious study, just as it exempts them from a range of other "positive" commandments (that is, commandments that require action, rather than abstention) that must be performed at specific times.[2] The law does not forbid women to study, and Jewish history has seen a number of women scholars. The issue of study for women has been publicly debated from time to time, as noted in a few documents, digests of Jewish law, and descriptions of differences of opinion. But the institutionalization of the "women's learning society" began only in 1917, and it is still thriving. It has been influenced largely by two phenomena that are external to women's scholarship. One is the state of haredi Judaism as a result of the significant changes in society at large (both Jewish and non-Jewish); the second is the state of male scholarship within Jewish society. These two factors mold the nature of women's scholarship with regard to its extent, its content, its realization in haredi society, its effect on the status of women, and women's role in the community. A methodical examination of the sociohistorical context in which women's education has been structured shows that when the threat to haredi society increased, and as the options for preserving itself as an orthodox community in a secular, pluralistic, and democratic society grew fewer, education for women became more popular. By this logic, when haredi society senses that it has good prospects for maintaining its orthodox life-style, the restrictions on women's education increase. The restrictions became more complicated structurally and practically once women's study began to be institutionalized.

The most significant change in the opportunity of women to study came in 1917. In that year the first Beit Ya'akov school was established in Krakow, Poland. The moving force behind the project was Sarah Schenirer (1883–1935).

The emancipation of European Jewry in the nineteenth century was seen by haredi Judaism as a spiritual holocaust that was a predecessor to the physical Holocaust of the twentieth century and the political holocaust of the establishment of the State of Israel.[3] It led to a significant decline in the centrality of religion in Jewish life. The opening of the ghetto gates, the more liberal attitudes of the surrounding population, and the opportunity for Jews to escape their traditional roles and partially integrate themselves into production, culture, and politics led many to abandon the ways of their parents. In some countries mandatory education was instituted for all citizens. Jewish education was recognized in some of these countries, but since traditional Jewish educational institutions served only boys, the girls had no choice but to attend non-Jewish institutions. In countries where Jewish education for boys was not recognized, the boys pursued Jewish studies in the heder at the end the school day.

It took only a few years for the young women of the Jewish middle and upper classes to become fluent in Russian, Polish, or German and to have trouble expressing themselves in Yiddish. They were better acquainted with the culture and history of their host countries than with that of the Jewish people, and their outward appearance (both their dress and their head coverings) became more and more like that of non-Jewish women. The haredi leadership was concerned by the reaction of parents, who evinced no real opposition to this development and considered it an incontrovertible fact. When Schenirer returned from Vienna, where she had lived during World War I, she launched an attempt to establish a haredi educational framework for women.[4] She began to teach the Torah, the Bible with Rashi's commentary, and so on. She was a seamstress; her circle of acquaintances was limited, made up mostly of her customers. She soon turned her energies to the education of young girls between the ages of seven and eighteen. The rabbinical establishment in Krakow and elsewhere gave their blessing to Schenirer's initiative, though there were opponents both among haredim and secularized Jews.

The fruits of the emancipation, the growing strength of Zionism, and the pre–World War II migration of Eastern European Jewry to the United States, Australia, and Palestine together created a real threat to orthodox society. This situation (which, from any viewpoint, constituted a state of emergency for orthodoxy) created the opportunity to initiate a fundamental change in the status of women. After much hesitation and with no little apprehension, the rabbinate realized that it did not have the power to oppose the innovations that Schenirer brought from Austria.

In Palestine as well—in the heart of Tel Aviv, the first Hebrew city, which more than anything else symbolized cultural renewal and the break with the "old yishuv," as the pre-Zionist Jewish community in Palestine was called—Rabbi Meir Scharanski established, with little means, the first Beit Ya'akov school in the Holy Land, in 1936.

After the establishment of eighty-seven Beit Ya'akov schools in Eastern Europe, serving some 10,000 girls, the third congress of Agudat Yisrael, held in Warsaw in 1929, approved the following decision:

> The assembly confirms that the Beit Ya'akov movement has proved that it is the only solution to the question of education for girls, which is a difficult and painful problem. The assembly recognizes that the foundation of the movement is the educated religious teacher.[5]

However, in order to compete with the public and Zionist schools, the Beit Ya'akov schools offered a generous helping of secular studies in addition to the religious studies. The girls studied Hebrew (even though the official language of instruction was Yiddish), as well as pedagogy, cooking, sewing, bookkeeping, business, accounting, and, in some of the schools, nursing.

World War II aborted the process through which Eastern European Judaism coped with the changes that had occurred around it. The war confronted Eastern European Jews with a cruel new reality. The great movement that had given pre-Holocaust women an opportunity to receive an education, which had been a kind of feminist revolution led by women for women (cooperating, since there was no other way, with the male establishment), changed direction.[6] Up until that time the qualitative threat to the existence of the orthodox Jewish community in Europe (which became more pluralist and democratic) would have aided this revolution. Haredi society had to give its attention to the cultural state of their women, because of the growing contact between it and its surroundings, which made change possible. The institutionalization of study for women came after the fact, as a response to the declining status of orthodoxy. Cultural competition and the opening of the cultural market forced the spiritual shepherds of the various communities to fight for the souls of their girls and women with the same weapons used by their opponents.

On the eve of World War II, in 1937, there were 250 Beit Ya'akov schools in Europe and the United States, in which 38,000 girls were studying. Beit Ya'akov became the central educational arm of the women of Agudat Yisrael. Two other movements were set up at the same time: Batya, for girls, and Benot Ha'aguda, for women, both of them ideological movements. These were designed to compete with the Zionist and other Jewish movements (such as the socialist-Yiddishist Bund) that were active in the Jewish communities of Eastern Europe, the United States, and Palestine.

After the Holocaust, haredi Judaism occupied itself with collecting its scattered pieces. Horribly depleted and deprived of the religious and scholarly institutions that had been destroyed in Europe, it tried to understand the catastrophe it had suffered and to reestablish itself physically and spiritually.[7]

The Beit Ya'akov institutions in Israel, which had until then tried to establish a cultural system that could face the challenge of Zionism (and especially the rival that was most similar to it, the religious-Zionist movement Mizrahi), now organized to absorb the refugees from the Holocaust.

However, many other movements also were demanding their share of the post-Holocaust wave of immigration, and orthodox society was probably the least organized of them. The other movements had their Youth Aliya institutions, their boarding schools, and large budgets. Agudat Yisrael, which was not a part of the Zionist establishment, got only crumbs.

Orthodox society's difficulties in the face of the Zionist renewal, the severe blow that the concept of the Diaspora had received in the Holocaust, and the adjustment problems of new haredi immigrants to Israel together created a significant threat to the society's existence. Most of the men worked to support their families, as did a minority of the grown women. Many haredi families were unable to find homes in orthodox neighborhoods, and were forced to live in mixed neighborhoods. The general feeling of weakness was expressed in the persistent attempt to strengthen education for women.

The anniversary book that was produced to mark the twenty-fifth year of the Scharansky girls' college in Tel Aviv contains important documentation of the character of that cultural struggle and its significance for women's scholarship. The subjects and questions that were raised, which were to become major public issues, are eye-openers for anyone who knows haredi society today. Teachers and educators had to consider issues such as the cinema, literature, military and voluntary national service, and whether women could spend an evening shopping or at a coffee house. These subjects are not even *raised* in haredi society today. Once haredi society was established, this process of self-examination ended because it was irrelevant. But from the 1950s through the 1970s, haredi society felt threatened. The values of the young Israeli society, the spirit of building and renewing the country, the army, and Israeli secularism were all closer to the gates of orthodoxy, and the haredim had to address them.

So, for instance, wrote Rivka Sharpherz in the anniversary book:

> "Glittering culture" includes within it the debased arts of cinema and literature. This is an ultra-modern culture, devoid of all content of any value, and its charm is in its shell, which has a counterfeit and false glitter that deludes and misleads. Debased literature is driven by appetites, nudity, and presumption. . . . This literature destroys our souls, strips man of everything, turns life into debauchery and lawlessness, into a life in which sex controls the human, and infernal laughter holds sway over divine wisdom. This malignant literature cries out to us with a great voice from the walls and store windows. It arouses, kills, breaks up families, and creates an abyss between one person and another.[8]

This invective implies that some haredim go to the cinema, read secular literature, and adopt elements of that "ultra-modern culture." If not, then why would haredi society try to discredit them and describe the cost of their actions on the personal, family, and community levels?

During this period, Beit Ya'akov sounds like a spiritual and social refuge that shelters its students and points them along the right way.

In her collected writings, Rachel Wolner, a teacher and teacher educator at the college, makes the following appeal to her students:

> You come to Beit Ya'akov to drink the limpid water of the spring of life, which has flowed for thousands of years from where it wells up at Sinai. In this holy place, which was built with the sanction of the worldly and divine courts, thousands upon thousands of precautions are taken to protect you at all times and at all hours, to gather churning waters like a liquid wall, so that you may pass on dry land within the mad flood that inundates every scrap of good like a destroying angel, may the Merciful One save us.
>
> While you are still at home, when you are getting ready to come for your day of studies, we dress you in a uniform whose colors were carefully chosen and every stitch and line of which was planned. We transport you in private buses to save you from sights, and put you in classrooms decorated with Biblical verses, commentaries, and legends.
>
> You begin your day here with prayer and continue by studying the Torah and the prophets, which are learned with holy reverence, "put off thy shoes from thy feet, for the place on which thou dost stand is holy ground." The paper would wear out and the pen would grow tired before we could finish relating the great investment made on Rosh Hodesh and holiday eves, study days and seminars, secular lessons and social activity, because each and every one of these, and each and every minute of these, and all of these together will imprint themselves on your souls, and will build your characters.
>
> While you are here, in this holy framework, would any of you even think, for instance, of going to eat lunch at the restaurant on Allenby Street [a reference to a restaurant with a kashrut certificate]? No, there is no one here, I am happy to say, who would drink a cup of coffee on the way home. Not because we warn you every day not to eat or drink on the way, in restaurants, we don't even consider doing any such thing, because we have absolutely no doubt that a soul that has absorbed all the impressions of prayer and the Torah lesson and the uniform and the Rosh Hodesh lecture must necessarily spurn lunch in a restaurant in the middle of the street. And whoever does not even think of drinking a cup of coffee in a coffee house will not consider Sherut Le'umi [voluntary non-military national service for religious girls]. Where would she drink her morning coffee and where would she eat lunch if not in a restaurant in a hospital or a laboratory or a border settlement?
>
> What, exactly, is Sherut Le'umi? Let's suppose that we are really naive and believe full-heartedly that this is service for the homeland. What do you want to do in the framework of Sherut Le'umi? To go to a hospital to help the elderly, to hand out food. Excuse me, if such a spirit of volunteerism beats within you, and your willingness to help the elderly leads you to the enlistment office, perhaps you would be prepared please to list the names of the elderly, lonely women who live in the five buildings around you and tell me about all you've done for them? How was it that this urge to help the elderly was dormant until you were of draft age, and then wondrously awakened on the eve of your enlistment in the

army? Why haven't you served the homeland up until now? Does only the enlistment office know old people in need of help?[9]

It would seem, then, that the social-cultural threat that was created on the eve of World War II created new possibilities for women's education. The content of this education was based on religious subjects, but threatening subjects from the competing culture were added. The same thing happened in the 1940s and 1950s in Israel. Beyond the religious and routine secular subjects (mathematics, nature, English, and so on), the educational act was fortified with anti-secular, anti-national, and contra-modern messages.

The dialectical process that contained the possibilities of integration, assimilation, or creation of a secular Jewish alternative caused orthodoxy to turn in on itself, to compete, and to create a kind of counterculture. This process heightened the need for women's education and determined its nature.

During the years in which fewer haredi males were studying, the number of women studying reached its maximum. This situation, in which a society allows women to be educated when it experiences a threat to its very existence, or when it is trying to contend with a significant change that has occurred within it, is not unique to orthodox Judaism. In such cases, education is seen as something that can preserve and change social conditions. This must be considered before returning to the details of the specific case of the women of the Development.

After this interlude I will return to the epigraph at the beginning of this chapter in order to discover whether the education of haredi women lives up to Rabbi Wolf's expectations, or whether, perhaps, their education allows them to develop in ways that he did not foresee and did not desire.

The Power of Literacy

The educational theme under examination in this work is literacy. Literacy is the meaning and significance of knowledge in its social context, a significance that may be elucidated by the following question:

Does the fact that a person, (national) group, or minority possesses a certain type of knowledge make social change and empowerment possible for that person or group? Illiterate societies that learn to read and write, a minority knowing only its tribal language that learns Spanish as well, a woman knowing only household crafts who learns computer programming, a factory worker who learns to operate a sophisticated piece of equipment—do these additional bits of knowledge change the social power structure in which these individuals and groups live?

The sociological significance of literacy is examined here in light of the possibilities it gives those who possess it to decipher the sociocultural structure of which they are part, and in light of their ability to reread it, criticize it, and change it.

Science's interest in literacy has been growing ever since the Enlightenment. The material gathered on this subject in recent years touches largely on developing societies (Third World countries), simple societies, ethnic minorities, qualitative minorities (such as women), and low-status groups in modern society. Three significant periods in Europe from the Middle Ages to the present day can be delineated.[10] At first, knowledge was the possession of a limited group, mostly under the aegis of the religious establishment. During the second era, the Enlightenment, a humanistic ideology of the dissemination of knowledge was formulated. Based on a faith in the eternity of knowledge, its moral purity, and its emancipatory power, and with the assistance of the printing press, the learned of that age tried to change the world. They assumed that people's ability to read and write and the publication of written material were the two ingredients necessary to bring about a social revolution. The third period is that of institutionalization, in which most of the responsibility for the dissemination of knowledge has been transferred to educational institutions, and education, modernization, and democracy have been linked ideologically. Western countries still see knowledge as a tool for advancing industrialization and military power, and for securing democratic and capitalist rule. The result has been a decline in the humanistic aspect characteristic of the previous period. This has been exchanged for a "liberal" approach—granting the public at large equal access to knowledge and rewarding those groups and individuals that succeed in taking advantage of this opportunity.[11]

At the end of World War II a new world order established itself. The old colonialism disappeared, and many countries won political independence. Control of culture and the economy was organized in a different way. At this point, the study of literacy took two directions that ran alongside each other: autonomous literacy and ideological literacy.[12]

Autonomous literacy was based on emancipatory thinking. The British anthropologist Jack Goody, who in the 1960s developed the study of literacy in anthropology, argued that it was the invention of writing that had turned prehistory into history, allowed the differentiation of the mystic and the logical, and offered the tools for the construction of critical thinking, rationalism, and abstraction. All the changes that take place during the transition from a nonliterate to a literate society are linear, and their direction is from the simple to the modern, from the absence of technology to the development of technology, from the actual to the abstract, and from the totalitarian to the democratic.[13]

The autonomous model thus sees the acquisition of knowledge as a process that leads to change. These changes can be individual and personal or sweeping and social, but in either case they take place in isolation from their social context and sometimes even in opposition to it. According to this approach, children who live in a tribe that possesses concrete and mystical thinking may learn abstract reasoning and Western logic.

Where there is political division, the schools can blur it. In a multi-ethnic society, a uniform education system can bring the ethnic groups closer together. This model is consistent with the functional approaches in sociology, which see institutions as components of the total social organism. The power of these institutions and the legitimacy granted them allow them to act contrary to the social reality in which they exist.

In accordance with this model, the Israeli educational system took upon itself to accomplish social changes in areas defined as problematic. The school systems associated with the different political camps were eliminated as a way of furthering national, rather than sectarian, values; the schools were also used to further goals such as ethnic integration, education for democracy, meetings between Jewish and Arab youth, and so on.

Ideological literacy diverts the emphasis from the reality of knowledge to its contextual significance. Instead of enumerating the people who know how to read and write, it concerns itself with the possibilities for using this knowledge. It breaks this concern down into several questions: What really happens when people are taught? What happens to curricula in the passage from book to student? Do two individuals, or two groups, derive identical benefit from the same teaching system?

The question, in short, is whether literacy helps blur class, sexual, ethnic, and racial divisions, or whether it reproduces them in other, complex ways.

Based on historical, psychological, and anthropological research, the supporters of the ideological model argue that the educational system in general and literacy in particular have been co-opted by society to preserve existing social conditions rather than to change them. They believe that it would be ridiculous to assume that educational institutions can be a tool for fundamental change in the society in which they themselves occupy a preferred place.[14]

This approach depicts a fairly inflexible social situation, founded on a conspiracy that affects the intentions and coordination of the activities of the various social institutions. The impression it conveys is that the ability of individuals to thwart the social institutions is small. Individuals work within sets of social goals that are identical to the ones in which they studied and in which their children will study. The programs they watch on television, the magazines they leaf through, the street posters, and many other things all work together to keep families in their places, and to allow them small-scale real changes that provide a false impression of significant change. The examples of individuals who broke free of their social system (and these are an insignificant minority whose actions generally are not prompted by knowledge) are cited erroneously as proof that "whoever wants to, succeeds."

Making the system more flexible and opening it up to changes in which literacy is expressed depend, therefore, on significant changes in other social areas as well. A society that defines the direction of change acts to change its economy, its culture, its housing, its health system, and its education. Only integrated activity that revises the context in which knowledge is acquired can reinstate the great hopes that Rousseau, Voltaire, and Diderot had for it.

Rabbi Wolf's words represent the expectations orthodoxy had of the education of its girls, and indicates that this education was considered a means to create a generation that would be socioculturally similar to its predecessor, i.e., not literate. This is the paradox to be put to the test. Is it possible, through literacy, to educate a group and individuals in such a way that they will culturally resemble a nonliterate group? And if so, how is it to be done, and in the case of Gur women, did it succeed?

A study by Margaret Bryant on the entry of women into university education during the second half of the nineteenth century in England showed that the reasons for study were not revolutionary.[15] Upper-class women, who until then had preserved their social status by way of money, lineage, and property, realized that it was now necessary to shore up their position with education. As a result, this education did not change the social structure in England—instead, it perpetuated that structure. Nevertheless, the women who studied had significant personal experiences that received social expression in art, literature, and political opinions.

Studies of American society show that it was not possible to restrain study by women once the process had begun. Paradoxically, this education acted contrary to its primary goals. If the intention had been that higher education for women would reinforce the values of submission and domesticity among women and produce good mothers for the young men of the American republic, education actually provided them with both the theoretical and practical means of criticizing and rebelling against these values.[16]

Other studies of this period, as well as those dealing with the nineteenth century, also show that education given to women in order to prevent any change in their status created new facts in American society. Women who studied longer married at a later age than those who studied less. Most of the students continued their professional work after their marriages, in fields such as geology, nursing, midwifery, translation, and bookkeeping. The more educated women had significantly fewer children than did those women who had not been educated. At the turn of the century, 22 percent of the women who continued their educations never married and developed professional careers. The education of the citizens' mothers ended up making them less motherly and fertile.

Up to this point the argument has been that external forces—the male world's obstruction of women and the status it assigned them—led to the institutionalization of women's education. Now we must look inward, to examine what happens to women from the moment they begin to study, and see if the second half of the dialectic argument, concerning society's imperviousness to women's education, receives expression in haredi society. We have seen that the threat to orthodoxy encouraged the education of women. Does the strengthening of orthodoxy restrain and repress this education? If so, how can this be done when women's education has already become a well-rooted phenomenon?

In the United States, the education of women so that they may emulate the behavior of the illiterate[17] led to results that the men had not anticipated. This study will examine whether this is also the situation in haredi society. It will attempt to determine whether women's education has changed their status, whether haredi women have accepted and are working to achieve Rabbi Wolf's aspirations for them, and whether there is social or personal disquiet among the Gur Hasidim that derives from this paradox of education for ignorance.

The public discourse of the haredi community reveals that there is in fact intensive involvement with the paradox of education for ignorance.

Marveh Latsameh reflects these doubts. Of the one hundred issues I examined during the years 1986–1987, twenty mentioned, dealt with, or discussed the problem of education for girls and women. Two of them were almost entirely devoted to this subject.[18]

Lehathila or B'de'avad

The fact that women's education was founded and developed as a result of necessities imposed from outside continues to threaten its very existence. Ideologically, this education is seen as something that was permitted only a posteriori, or in Talmudic terminology *b'de'avad*, i.e., a decision that reflected an existing reality. This is the opposite of an a priori, or *lehathila*, decision (one that is meant to mandate a new reality rather than retroactively sanction something that has already happened). The haredi establishment and the public understand that women's education is an inseparable part of their lives today, but neither of them ceases to examine its essence and its intentions.

The Question Remains Open

In issue number 45 (1986) *Marveh Latsameh* printed verbatim a long letter from Rabbi Shmuel Halevy Vazner, the head of the Zikhron Meir religious court, under the headline "On the Prohibition Against Teaching Girls Commentators on the Torah in Depth." I present it here in abridged form (emphasis in the original):

With regard to the bounds of Torah study for women, even though the matter is elucidated in Maimonides . . . and in the *Shulkhan Arukh* . . . I will nevertheless not abstain from expressing my humble opinion. *It the nature of women that they cannot attain and understand the true point of the Torah, and as a result they trivialize the Torah's intentions.*

Here is the language of Maimonides and the *Shulkhan Arukh*. . . . "A woman who studies Torah receives [divine] reward, but even though she is rewarded the sages ordered that a man not teach his daughter Torah because the minds of most women are not focused on study and they trivialize the words of the Torah." In my humble opinion, in saying that one who teaches his daughter Torah is as if he is teaching her triviality, the sages were referring to the oral law [the Talmud].

Rabbi Hame'iri said on the tractate *Sota*, page 21—"'as if he is teaching her triviality'—the sages wished to say that . . . she acquires some cunning, but her mind is not able to understand it properly, but she thinks she attained it and peals like a bell to show off her wisdom to everyone." As a result Hame'iri defined the prohibition on study with a wonderful explanation—that by filling her with things that by nature are beyond her attainments, and her mind is not adequate for understanding them fully, but the woman believes that she has understood them and shows off this curtailed knowledge of hers, which produces distorted judgment. Hame'iri concludes with the following language (*Sota*, chapter 3): *"They said that it is better to burn words of Torah rather than to give them to women, which means that it is an insult to the Torah that it be subject to the judgment of women."*

Know that this is a simple matter, that the prohibition applies not only to a father teaching his daughter or that a school is forbidden to teach women the Oral Law, but that a woman is also forbidden to teach herself privately, even if she is sure that she is one of the minority not in the category of being taught trivialities. But, if after the fact, it turns out that she has a good mind and is not like the majority of women who trivialize the Torah, then she receives her reward as one who does something without being commanded to do so.

. . . There is no sanction for teaching women the Bible with the commentators and those who go into depth, but [one may teach it] with those who simplify it with the ethical lessons of our sages or with legal rulings. . . . Even these simplified things are better taught orally and not from a book.

. . . In light of the reality of our time it is difficult to teach without a book, so one should take care to study only what touches on the simple meaning of the Bible, ethics, and laws, and not to go into depth.

. . . I know that most girls' schools in our generation do not obey this and go beyond the bounds of the law. I once told the great rabbinical educator, the late Rabbi Avraham Yosef Wolf, that the Torah is eternal and if they said it is like teaching them triviality they meant it for all generations, and even if it is justified by "violating His Torah for His sake," that is, if not for this the women would be doing even worse things, in any case rest assured . . . that the bad that comes of it will come out in the end, and the rulings of the Torah and its restrictions will never change.

. . . Since the great righteous men of all generations treated the subject of schools for girls in accordance with the state of the generation and saw in them an important rectification, it is now difficult to insist that they not study.

Rabbi Vazner's letter is followed by a summary in simpler language, without the halachic terminology and citations. The inclusion of a summary reflects the magazine editor's assumption that women and young readers are unable to decipher a letter from a great rabbi. The women may not be able to understand the abbreviations that are a characteristic of rabbinic style, and the rabbinic syntax, so different from everyday language, is liable to be misunderstood. A document written by a man, a Torah scholar, must be rewritten so that women can understand it.

According to the sages, Rabbi Vazner says, women were not commanded to study Torah for genetic reasons. Women are made in such a way that their brains are unable to absorb Torah and in-depth interpretations of it. Only a few select women are capable of studying Torah (and even they cannot do it at the usual pace) and to internalize it properly. All other women make negative use of the little they have acquired, and as a result become deceitful and arrogant. The story of Bruria, one of the few female scholars mentioned in the Talmud, shows that even she, who thought herself one of the exceptional unfrivolous women, was unable to resist the sexual temptation her husband presented to her, betrayed him, and was sentenced to death. Given the state of our generation, Torah scholars of our day have ruled that it is better for women to study than for them to be doing even worse. Rabbi Vazner does not see this as sufficient justification for Torah study by women. The Torah and its rulings are eternal, he says, and if the sages once said that women trivialize the Torah, this judgment of theirs is valid in all generations. Sooner or later, the future will prove that they were right.

Yet, in the meantime, women are studying. Not only do they listen to oral lessons, they study the holy books themselves. The latter part of the letter is devoted to what material should be taught to women in this undesirable state of affairs.

Rabbi Vazner's letter recalls another one written by the admor from Klausenberg in 1973. This letter also found its way into the pages of *Marveh Latsameh*, issue 56:

> I am amazed, but I do not comprehend how anyone, even if he is as great as the cedars and reaches to the sky, may diverge in any manner from a clear ruling of the Talmud and *Shulkhan Arukh* and agreed upon by all those who rule in matters of law that a man not teach his daughter Torah because the minds of most women are not focused on learning, and anyone who teaches his daughter Torah is as if he is teaching her triviality, and how is it possible God forbid to make triviality into a fence around holy faith and abstinence. . . .

The letter cites all the rabbis who addressed the subject of study for women, and the books for women written in recent generations, such as the *Tsena Ur'ena*, *Menorat Hama'or*, and *Poke'ah Ivrim*.

The admor argues that the sages never considered opening schools for girls. Although he praises the Hafetz Haim (whose ruling allowing women to study because of "changed times" became the major justification of schools for women), he still does not understand how the Hafetz Haim came to the decision that he did. If we follow his example, others will come and use the same argument to permit women to do other things, on the grounds that times have changed. He has heard rumors that haredi girls' schools teach books that delve into the depths of the Torah, and even purely kabalistic books, to women who may well be in the unclean days of their menstrual cycle.

He concludes:

> We must cry out against Jewish women studying philosophy or kabala, especially when they are in their period of impurity and flow, and especially when young men teach them; this is the truth of the Torah and all the winds of the world will not move the truth from its place.

In printing these letters, *Marveh Latsameh* presents one extreme side of the paradox of women's learning. Rabbis and spiritual leaders challenge the change that has occurred in education for Jewish girls. The legitimacy granted by the Hafetz Haim to girls' schools because of changing times is questioned. The writers are skeptical of the material being taught and how it is being taught, and even if they understand that there is no way back now, they believe that the future will prove that a mistake has been made.

In the same magazine, sometimes in the same issue, there is also material that presents the other side of the paradox.

Support for Women's Study of the Torah

The magazine's editor, Yisrael Pollak, is an enthusiastic defender of women's education, citing the authority of great Torah scholars.

> In recent years the trend towards deepening women's education, of bringing it more in line with what men learn, has been especially noticeable. The Jewish people's great scholars have seen this trend as of supreme importance, especially as a trend in women's education. I have heard from the admor of Klausenburg, who once faced a difficult budgetary question and some of his disciples were going to close a girls' Yiddish nursery school opened under his auspices. The rebbe preferred to close the Talmud Torah for boys and leave the girls' nursery school alone. From this we learn what supreme importance the righteous men of our generation attach to the education of girls. . . .[19]

The same admor whose letter had been printed in a different issue as a declaration of the dangers inherent in women's education is quoted here as though he had recommended closing a boys' school in order to preserve a nursery school for girls.

In the wake of the quoted letter, a reader named E. Tal sent a letter to the editor in which he argued:

> Thank God a new generation of Beit Ya'akov graduates has grown up, and they have raised up a great and glorious generation. They know what laboring in the Torah is, and the great sages of Israel have ruled that the rules applying to the daughters of Torah scholars apply to graduates of Beit Ya'akov.[20]

The rule applying to her may be that of the daughter of a Torah scholar and not that of a Torah scholar himself, but the graduates of the elite educational system for haredi women have turned this into a meaningful status. They know what labor in the Torah is (meaning they can appreciate their husbands' studies). They can raise up a glorious generation of male scholars, whose wives appreciate them (and do not goad them to go out to work for the family's welfare).

Challengers Versus Supporters: The Magnitude of the Paradox

Haredi life takes place between these two poles—homage and praise of women scholars, and warnings that they are a danger. The relevance of study by females is not to be discovered in these extreme positions, which belong to minorities. *Marveh Latsameh's* message on women's education is a complex one. Various correspondents—teachers, rabbis, mothers, fathers, and writers—present the paradox of scholarship in its full scope and at all its levels. One of the magazine's writers quotes a letter from a mother who was reprimanded for having kept her daughter out of school one day.

> Aren't different domains being distorted here? Haven't our ways of thinking become warped? Isn't Beit Ya'akov different in its mission and its purpose from public schools? Isn't our main role to educate our daughters to be, first and foremost, kosher, good Jewish mothers? Do we not need to demand of them, morning and evening, that the home, the Jewish home, stands over all else? Isn't it the supreme value that we should aspire to? And if interests of the home and the school clash, should they not be taught that the home certainly is not an impediment or factor that interferes with school? Since, in any case, the home is, when it comes down to it, the goal? And when a child observes really, actively, the command of honoring his parents? Isn't it the role of the school to encourage this and not, God forbid, to weaken his hand? Can it be that only in her lessons on Judaism is a girl required to know what the concept of honoring one's parents means? Just to get a grade on her report card? Have our concepts not been distorted???
> . . . Yesterday my husband lost a day from his kolel. . . . Will he lose two? After Miri I have three big sons. We actually considered whether to have them take turns at home. But my husband argued that with boys there is an explicit matter of forsaking Torah study, and that it would be best for us to prove to them from the time they were small that their

Torah study is more important to us than anything else and that we do
not interfere with it. . . .[21]

Mrs. Even's letter, signed "A Frustrated Mother," raises a fundamental
problem in the haredi community's attitude towards education for girls.
The girls help out with the housework from a young age. They do the
shopping, look after their younger siblings in the afternoons, and take an
active part in the cleaning and upkeep of the home. Their absence from
home in the morning has become an incontrovertible fact (in Ha'eda
Haharedit in Jerusalem the girls do not study on Fridays, freeing them to
help prepare for the Sabbath, and their school day is shorter than that at
Beit Ya'akov). In the afternoons the girls spend from one to three hours
doing homework. The result is that their chores must be fit into the little
free time that they have. The priorities in the haredi home have been
reversed: first school and homework, afterwards helping around the house.
The school's teachers and administrators pressure the parents to respect
this order of priorities. In a community in which the teachers, principal,
and parents all belong to the same overlapping, compact social circles, it is
hard not to act according to the opinion of the majority. A mother who
keeps her oldest daughter home for a few days to help care for a sick family member is subject to sharp criticism. Despite this, as the correspondent
knows, most of the girls who graduate from Beit Ya'akov, including the two
years of post-secondary studies, will not make use of the knowledge they
have gained—not outside their own households, at any rate. It is clear to
her that most of them will not get jobs, but will assume the roles of wife
and mother. This means that the school educates the girls in values whose
practical application at an early stage is unacceptable to the system. Mrs.
Even's frustration as a mother is an outgrowth of this acute contradiction.
She knows that every woman who reads the article will find that it
expresses the very real predicament they face, a reflection of a fundamental dilemma in the education of haredi women.

The teacher embodies this paradox in the most obvious way. She is a
wife and mother, a graduate of the haredi educational system, works outside her home, and was chosen for her job from among hundreds of candidates. In addition to the problems familiar to any teacher, she must also
cope with the pressures growing out of the contradictions present in her
own life, as well as the lives of her students and their parents. The magazine has devoted a special column to this, called "This Teacher." The articles that appear weekly in this column discuss the problems of female education from the point of view of the female educator. One example:

"This teacher doesn't teach anything! The girl just isn't learning! She
doesn't do her homework! And you know why? Because there isn't any
homework!" So lamented one mother to the neighbor on the balcony
across the way.

"That's very interesting!" responded the neighbor across the way. "In my daughter's class it's just the opposite, the teacher loads the girls down with so much difficult homework that the girl is always pale, upset, can't help at home, all the time homework and more homework. So I ask you, where's the education that a teacher should be giving, are high standards the only thing she thinks of?"

And I, who was busy the whole time taking the clean and dry laundry off the clotheslines, sighed wearily. I didn't have the strength to reply, because I had just returned from a tiring day of work . . .[22]

The criticism is not directed only at the quantity of the studies; it touches on their quality as well. Another teacher told of her impressions after visiting the house of a friend:

During one of my visits to my friend I met her daughter. . . . I asked her to show me her notebooks, and she ran happily to bring her satchel. It was a paragon of neatness, with all her supplies standing like soldiers at inspection. When she took out her notebooks I was delighted by the variety of the covers, what a rainbow of colors. . . . Each heading was highlighted and emphasized with bold letters, strong color, and wavy handwriting, under which were several colored lines, and truly artistic decorations. . . . Pasted in the notebooks were many mimeographs, arithmetic tables, and so on. There was nothing to do but to shake her hand and wish her success in the future. . . . But when I began to examine her I was astounded to hear garbled answers. They bore no relation at all to the wonderful appearance of the notebook: we learned that a long time ago. . . . That's in the mimeograph. . . . We haven't gone over that enough and haven't had a test yet. . . . Do students really attain more comprehensive, deeper, and better knowledge by the new methods? . . . The evidence is that in boys' heder classes, where boys are given the basics of reading according to a method that has been passed down from olden days in the spirit of ancient Israel, the achievements are better, more fundamental. In boys' classes the percentage of children who do not read well at the end of the first year is much lower than in the girls' classes. . . .[23]

The two passages quoted above represent part of the haredi community's criticism of the educational system for girls. The latter passage compares it to the educational system for boys. Girls studying at Beit Ya'akov carry heavy satchels full of carefully decorated notebooks. The boys who study in the heder generally don't have notebooks at all. The literacy achieved in these two educational institutions is very different, and even if one compares only reading and arithmetic, as the writer in the magazine did, one discovers that the girls' achievements are inferior.

The writer blames the adoption of modern methods alien to the spirit of the Jewish people, and her proof is that the old methods, still used with boys, bring better results. The girls' schools are more open to extra-haredi influences, and, the writer believes, the community pays a double price for this: a decline in the quality of education and being uprooted from its sources.

The outside influence is expressed not only in how the study is accomplished, but also in the content. A story about a ba'alei teshuva couple contains the following section:

> One note infuriated Avital—she was asked to sign a form to be returned
> to school, on which she would authorize or oppose the inclusion of an
> electricity class during school hours. Avital waited impatiently for Moshe
> to return from the kolel. After supper she showed him the note, expect-
> ing a sharp reaction. "Of course," he said calmly, "it can't possibly be. Put
> down that you're opposed—I imagine that all the parents will oppose it.
> . . . How can they teach electronics in a Beit Ya'akov school?"
>   Only a few days later Avital received another note, in which she was
> asked to pay a certain sum to fund the electricity class, since most of the
> parents had expressed their support . . . ![24]

Varied use is made of stories of ba'alei teshuva. In this case, the point of view of Avital and her husband Moshe is presented to provide a new vantage point from which to examine the material being studied. The electricity lesson, accepted by a majority of the parents without reservation, was seen by Avital and her husband as something that a Beit Ya'akov school would obviously not include in its curriculum. Their amazement and the anger expressed by the mother when she goes to see the principal help the haredi reader stop and examine what has actually happened in the educational system for girls as it absorbs nontraditional subjects. This story began a debate that is still echoing in the haredi community; it is still not clear how it will end. In the next chapter of this story, which appeared as a serial in the magazine, Avital's daughter returns from school and relates:

> "A drama class!" the six-year-old said loudly. . . . "Do you know what that
> is, Mommy? You put on plays, and in the play you dress up in costumes
> like . . . on Purim and there are parts, it's so nice!" But Avital was no
> longer listening to the child. She felt her head spinning and collapsed
> into the first chair that came her way.

The reaction to Avital's story was not long in coming. A few issues later the magazine printed a letter from a reader, Emunah Schmidt.

> In my opinion, in the recent chapters of the story Avital is getting carried
> away by a worrisome and inexplicable extremism. I do not understand,
> what does she (or the author) find wrong with lessons like electricity or
> drama for girls? As long as the classes are given in the appropriate spirit
> by appropriate teachers, they also can be used to teach good values and
> reverence of heaven. Isn't that true? In the electricity class—through
> making a light bulb shine and becoming acquainted with electrical phe-
> nomena—she will be led to marvel at what the creator has done, in the
> spirit of the blessings "how myriad are your deeds" and "he who shared his
> spirit with flesh and blood." In the drama class it is possible to work on
> plays from the world of the Bible and of the sages. . . . And if we are

speaking of older girls where a drama class has no place, it still cannot possibly be the author's (or others') opinion that the girls will delve into the Torah alone and will work solely as teachers (so as to support their husbands studying at kolel). Why can't a haredi girl study computers as well, and electricity and typing with a word processor. I know one haredi woman who works successfully typing material (kosher, of course) in her home—and from this makes a respectable living while fully complying with "the King's daughter's honor lies within" [a Talmudic saying understood to mean that a Jewish woman earns respect by occupying herself within her home]. . . . In my opinion, the mother and teacher imbued with pride in our heritage have nothing to be ashamed of and no one to fear. On the contrary—the girls will enter the "grove of the Torah" in these classes and emerge from them strengthened in their spirit and in their view of the world in the spirit of ancient Israel.

The voice of the discourse on women's education, as it appears in the magazine, testifies to the extent and depth of the problem. A haredi woman attends school from the age of five to the age of twenty. After her marriage, she continues to go to evening classes held in her neighborhood. What is the purpose of these studies?

The selections presented above would seem to show that this is not at all clear. In the face of the institutionalization, the expansion, and the expanding influence of the Beit Ya'akov institutions, the schools' clients begin to wonder whether the education they provide is really necessary. A 1986 issue of the magazine (where most of the writers are women) presents its readers with an old debate, raising once again fundamental, primal questions regarding women's education. Why are such basic questions being asked now of all times, when the schools are growing, the curricula expanding, the school day lengthening, and the number of students multiplying? Along with the fundamental questions come ancillary questions: What should the girls study? What are they forbidden to study? What are they incapable of studying? What is the order of priorities among home, family, and study? To what extent can material from the outside world be included in the curriculum? To what extent can teaching methods be changed and "innovative and modern" methods adopted?

But the main question, which links the subject of women's scholarship with the state of haredi society today, is the question of the relevance of the studies to the way the haredi community is now organized. This is a community that has chosen to be a "learning men's society," and it has been shaped by its qualitative struggle with secular Judaism (and even more so with other religious groups), and issues such as government handouts and delayed enlistment in the army.[25] This choice, which was based on economic prosperity, brought about poverty. Many men draw out their years of study, and families lacking any additional help live on social security payments. Women who want to help support the family have trouble finding work in teaching, the only field for which they have been trained.

Almost all haredi women study to become teachers, yet only a fraction of them are hired by the educational system and get to enjoy the prestige associated with the profession. The others search for work in other fields. But when they find work they face a problem, as relates another letter to *Marveh Latsameh*, signed "Writing in sorrow—Anonymous."

> To put it simply: the problem is work for the graduates of the various haredi teachers' colleges in the country. It is no secret that the number of teaching jobs available is shrinking at a dizzying pace. Along with this, the number of graduates of the colleges is growing (and may it grow even more). This creates a situation in which many girls (and among them good and reverent ones who have been successful at their studies) are forced out of the teaching framework. They face a difficult and acute problem—what to do? Where to go? It is a bitter and difficult time, full of hesitations and doubts. . . .
>
> What remains is the possibility of secretarial work. But unfortunately, as if their sorrow and bitterness and tears were not sufficient, haredi society comes and slaps them in the face. They are not "enthusiastic" about a girl who does clerical work, especially if she works in a secular place, to the extent that these matters make girls put off establishing a holy home in Israel with a Torah scholar, because of outdated ideas on this subject. . . .
>
> Why does external and surface sparkle blind our public? It is not just that girls are repelled by other work, outside the teaching profession. They are repelled because these are the conventions of the society in which we live. Society sees that as being of lesser worth, as lower status, as a mark of Cain indicating spiritual and mental weakness. . . .
>
> Were our colleges to shed all the external sparkle and all the superfluous studies and devote themselves more to actually imbuing spiritual values and to creating an appropriate framework for a variety of kinds of employment afterwards, would it all not be more modest, and much better in both content and practical purpose?[26]

A woman who wishes to work in something other than the few occupations considered legitimate (teaching, helping out in a family business, child care in her home, graphic or bookkeeping work at home) puts her good name at risk. Modesty, which serves as a brake against social process, is again endangered. Now, just at the time when men are devoting themselves to study and there is a need for an additional income, haredi society enlists itself to condemn alternative occupations and, as a result, prevents many women from working. The result is growing economic hardship, and public discourse presents "poverty" as a form of worship. No wonder, then, that women's education is suddenly called into question. Education contains the potential for change (the development of new careers for women) that is not wanted by haredi society today. Now, when it is feeling sure of its ability to maintain an orthodox way of life, haredi society has no interest in promoting those elements that allow women to challenge this success. In order to preserve the "learning men's society," study by women must be kept under control. The somewhat natural choice of an entirely scholarly society (among the men) is threatened by every bit of change. Since the "learning men's society" is considered an achievement, even a miracle,[27] social mechanisms are developed to defend it. Poverty is praised as a virtue, even a form of worship (an issue that will be discussed in detail in Chapter 4). Last but not least is the control of women's education, our subject. The threat against the haredi community, which led it to create the women's learning society, has been dispelled. Women's education has become institutionalized. The tension between the learning society and women's education is expressed in full force in *Marveh Latsameh*, a sample of which is represented in the last letter quoted. That letter received several responses in the same issue, but the most important of them came from the magazine's editor, who quoted the words of Rabbi Wolf that appear at the beginning of this chapter.

Notes

1. I classified the wigs as follows: the modest, the regular, and the impressive. "Modest" wigs are made of cheap synthetic materials, easily recognizable because a woman who wears one covers her entire head. Generally, women with low incomes wear such wigs. The "regular" wigs are made of a combination of synthetic and natural hair; they are modest in style. They are not long, they match the original hair color of their wearers, and they are simply styled. This is the type most often worn by Gur women. The third type are wigs with long hair styled in the latest fashion. Sometimes they are streaked and decorated with glittering pins. Orthodox women outside Israel (where there is more flexibility on issues of modesty) sometimes wear wigs and comb some of their natural hair over them, so that it is very hard to make out that it is a wig.

2. The sages of the Talmud determined that women were exempt from these commandments because they must be free to see to the needs of other family members.

3. The emancipation, the Holocaust, and Zionism are considered by the haredim to be a series of catastrophes or trials that the Jewish people have undergone in recent generations. There are, however, differing opinions on the links between these phenomena and the relative severity of each one. One example:

> From the period of the emancipation to World War I the framework was chipped away. The Jewish home received the first hard blow during World War I. Afterwards, during World War II, the Jewish framework received a horrible and mortal blow without parallel in human history. Then not only did the framework collapse entirely, but human standards in place from creation also collapsed and the principles of justice and morality were obliterated by Hitler may his name and his legions be cursed. Immediately after the physical world war came a harsh spiritual war without parallel in the form of our people in the land of Israel, with the establishment of the state and the secular takeover of our people in the land of Israel, with the intention of bringing our nation to collective national assimilation. (Yisrael Pollack, *Marveh Letsameh*, issue 28, 5746 [1986], p. 3)

4. Documents written by Schenirer, and others written about her, show that in 1914, during her time in Vienna, she met with Rabbi Dr. Flasch, who preached a spiritual reawakening through the enhancement of study for women. The influence of this rabbi (who was one of the "new" or modern rabbis of Germany and Austria), was later downplayed because of Schenirer's association with Agudat Yisrael, which was not interested in promoting such a rabbi. (Schenirer 5720 [1960])

5. Sharpstein 5701 (1941).

6. On the establishment of the Beit Ya'akov system in Europe for girls and women, and the sociological significance of this innovation, see Weissman 1976. On the Beit Ya'akov system's place in the Jewish educational system as a whole, see Sharpstein 5709 (1949).

7. Stengel 1981; Bauer 1982.

8. Zaritzki 5729 (1969), p. 310.

9. Wolner and Kaminer 5742 (1982).

10. Studies on the history of literacy include those of Freire 1985; Freire and Macedo 1987; Giroux 1983; Kaestle 1985; Bloch 1986.

11. On the institutionalization of literacy and education in Europe and the United States, and on the connection between this social process and the concept of "citizenship," see Meyer 1977; Meyer, Tyack et al 1979; Ramirez and Boli-Bonnet 1987.

12. This distinction was made by Street 1984.

13. Goody wrote much on literacy and the transition from simple to complex societies. His first book on this subject (1968) linked literacy and modernization, but in his later writings (1977, 1988) he modified this link by coining the term "restricted literacy," using it to argue that the liberating force of restricted literacy is contained in social forces. He believed that literacy should not be seen as a clear means of liberation from the existing social framework, unless the traditional networks allowed this change.

14. The following studies subscribe to this view of literacy: Bourdieu 1967; Dreeben 1968; Henry 1972; Bloch 1977, 1986; Apple 1979; Graff 1979; Street 1984; Giroux 1983; Freire 1985; Bourdieu and Passeron 1987; Freire and Macedo 1987; Stromquist 1992.

15. Bryant 1979.

16. On the development of education for women in North America and its social consequences, see Scott-Firor 1984; Kaestle 1985; Kerber 1980; Schwager 1987; Giroux and McLaren 1986. For the special way in which women experience the learning process, see Belenky and Clincy 1986.

17. "Illiteracy" as used here does not mean an absence of knowledge, but rather the opposite of literacy as a social state, since "objective" knowledge is not meaningful in this discussion. Illiteracy is, then, a pattern of behavior, presenting oneself as one who does not know, who does not penetrate areas of knowledge where one does not belong, who does not intend to make any social use of this knowledge.

On the significance of knowledge and ignorance as a socio-historical dimension, see Funkenstein and Steinsaltz 1987.

18. *Marveh Latsameh* devoted issues 26 and 45, 5746 (1986) to the subject of female education.

19. Yisrael Pollak, *Marveh Latsameh*, no. 26, 5746 (1986), p. 3.

20. E. Tal, *Marveh Latsameh*, no. 32, 5747 (1987), p. 7.

21. R. L. Even, *Marveh Latsameh*, no. 26, 5746 (1986), p. 20.

22. S. Kosner, *Marveh Latsameh*, no. 27, 5746 (1986), p. 19.

23. S. Friedman, *Marveh Latsameh*, no. 27, 5746 (1986), p. 20.

24. T. Dor, *Marveh Latsameh*, no. 36, 5746 (1986), p. 16.

25. The decision to foster a "learning men's society" and its implications on community life will be discussed at more length in Chapter 4. The subject was studied by Friedman 1986b; Heilman and Friedman 1991.

26. "Anonymous," *Marveh Latsameh*, no. 25, 5746 (1986), p. 17.

27. On the existence of the "learning men's society" as a miraculous phenomenon:

> It is impossible to ignore this dimension, which did not exist previously. A large portion of them realize that this is an astonishing, new phenomenon. Some call it "a miracle that has happened to us." It is a phenomenon that has no parallel in the history of the Jewish people, and it has many implications. This is the major center of gravity in the haredi community. (M. Friedman, *Ha'aretz*, "Judaism" supplement, Sivan 5749 [June 1989])

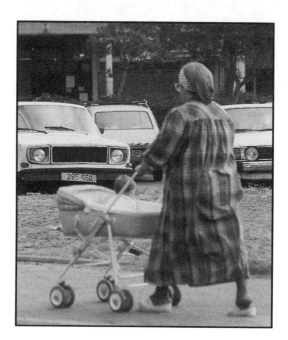

3

· · · ❧ · · ·

The Substantial
and the Practical

Women's education is the outcome of the tension between the changes taking place outside the orthodox community and its internal durability. The "learning men's society" applied a double standard to its own development. It is essential to put the paradox of women's education, as well as the other paradoxes described below, into this perspective. I believe that entering and escaping social paradoxical cycles are a pattern of behavior characteristic of Israeli orthodoxy, an existential strategy, and a means of creating social boundaries. But to do this, I must first describe the paradoxical component of women's education—both its nature and its dynamic.

The study of the social significance of scholarship among orthodox men shows that scholarship is the most significant expression of their Judaism.[1] The situation among women is similar. Women once learned to be kosher Jewish wives and mothers within the ghetto walls, in their mother's houses, and alongside their grandmothers. Today they must learn this in school. When the cultural market around them offers educational alternatives, orthodoxy constructs an educational framework that is, in its external form, a school, but its goal—at least, its declared goal—is to duplicate the Jewish mother's home in Poland.

How is that done, and does it succeed?

In attempting to answer the "how" question, anthropology has a certain advantage. The unmediated observations it conducts of social processes allow a close tracking of the "how."

During my period in the Development, I took part in several study groups, all intended for married women (sometimes the older daughters of one of the women would take part, but these exceptional cases were not accepted sympathetically). Unfortunately, I was unable to conduct observations in the schools, so the literacy under discussion here is that of married women alone.

One framework was a class in Jewish law. These lessons were taught by women from the Development on a voluntary basis.[2] The second framework was a year-long course on the book of Psalms, taught by teachers from

Bene Brak. The third (Rabbi Wolf's class on Maimonides) was held in the home of one of the teachers from Bene Brak. In addition to attending these classes, I also sat in on a broad spectrum of women's study groups held inside and outside the Development, but these were single events rather than regular frameworks.

On the basis of these observations, and in light of the insights collected by the social study of literacy, it seems to me that the women's education I observed strives to pragmatize the social reality and emphasize its material side. Women's education generates an ongoing translation of complex problems into simple actions. It levels questions of morality, faith, and justice into instructions for action in daily life.

Women's education simultaneously creates a social meaning of the world and confirms it. Studies of literacy among underprivileged classes have shown that there is inconsistency between the practical daily reality and the curriculum based in part on abstract thinking. This inconsistency has led to student failure, to aggression, and to withdrawal from the educational system.[3]

In an experiment, Paulo Freire, who has conducted research on literacy and who served as Brazil's minister of education, tried to create, from a practical framework, abstract thinking somewhat detached from the world of action. Through this, he wished to provide a foundation for radical and critical literacy. He based his curriculum for the disadvantaged and the ignorant on the reality that was familiar to them, such as the lives of fishermen or agricultural laborers. Out of the experiences of this reality, he built a set of abstract concepts through which he was able to achieve two important things: students could decipher realities that were foreign to them, and they could leave their familiar reality and move toward a broader consciousness. This is how he claimed to resolve the inconsistency between the reality that is familiar to people and the curriculum they study.[4]

Among haredi women, the situation is reversed. In order to create consistency between the social situation (in which men wish to see women "ignorant") and the actual condition of these women (which is not at all one of ignorance), the axis of learning becomes a pragmatic one.

Fifteen women are seated in Bina's living room. On the table are glasses and bottles of cold water, relief for the hot summer evening. My eyes wander around the circle. All the living rooms in the Development seem to be similar. Here also is the large book case with its religious books and tableware. On the wall across from the book case hangs a needlework landscape, and next to it a photograph of the previous Gur rebbe, Rabbi Yisrael Alter. In an Israeli living room one generally expects to see house plants, family pictures, and various trinkets, but here there are none.

This class, devoted to the requirement that foods be inspected for worms and insects, was supposed to have started five minutes previously,

and Nava, the teacher, is usually punctual. The women carry on quiet conversations as they wait. One tells of a successful matchmaking enterprise,
another relates news from the Gur development in Hatzor Hagelilit, while
another compliments her neighbor's new sandals.

Suddenly Sheindi and Sari burst into the room, out of breath. Both of
them had just been married at the end of the Sefira period (the seven
weeks between the holidays of Passover and Shavuot).

Nava sends her regrets, but she thought that the class is every two
weeks. She didn't prepare herself for today.

The room stirs. The women are disappointed. One of them addresses
Bina, the hostess.

"So Bina, why don't you say something, otherwise this will have just
been an 'assembly of scorners' [moshav letsim, a gathering in which no
words of Torah have been spoken]. Convey us something from the college,
a lesson you gave the girls. We're counting on you."

Bina is taken by surprise and is unprepared. She is a serious young
woman, one of the few hired by the college as a part-time teacher after
completing her studies. After a minute of thought she turns to those present and asks:

"Okay, what do you prefer, something substantive or something
practical?"

This was the first class I had attended, and I wanted to learn. Something with substance, I wished to myself, let them ask for something with
substance.

"Practical!" the women all shouted. "Practical!"

Hannah smiled at me from across the room. She must have guessed
what I had been hoping.

Bina, a large woman, rose. She was haphazardly dressed and perspiring.
In a characteristic gesture, she straightened her wig in front and began.

This was how I became acquainted with a most significant dichotomy
in the lives of these women: the substantive versus the practical.

The two sides of this dichotomy will serve as a basis for surveying the
progress and content of the classes, as well as the way they were taught and
the social reality created by and reflected in them. The "substantive" and
"practical" lessons also bore on the success of education for ignorance.

While Bina's lesson was "practical," I would soon find "substance"
as well. During one of the classes on the Psalms, the teacher (a woman
of high Gur Hasidic lineage) mentioned that Rabbi Wolf conducted a
class at her house. Hannah said that she remembered him from the college, and that if I wanted substance, she was prepared to take me there.
We went.

"Substance" Classes

The Class on Maimonides' Eight Chapters

For the past ten years Rabbi Wolf has given a class at the home of Nehama Wachter (who taught the class on the Psalms at the Development). On the first Monday of every month a group of women gathers to hear a man of close to eighty teach. Rabbi Wolf was the brother of the founder and principal of the Wolf Beit Ya'akov college in Bene Brak, and in his youth in Germany he had kept company with educated secularists, Zionists, Reform Jews, and the like. Upon arriving in Israel he had drawn closer to Hasidic circles, and while he did not consider himself a part of them, he felt spiritually close to Hasidism. Before retiring, Rabbi Wolf served as the college's "foreign minister," charged with liaison with local government authorities and the Ministry of Education.

The rabbi entered the Wachter house at 9:00 P.M. sharp, circling the audience of women in the living room via the balcony before taking his place at the head of the table. His wife sat to his right, and the rest of the places close to him were filled by older women, the most senior participants in the class. The average age of those in attendance was much higher than that of the Development's women.

When Hannah and I came for the first time, we were welcomed warmly and commended for our initiative and effort. Hannah saw familiar faces among the women. One was a friend of her mother's, another the mother of a former college classmate, and a third the sister of a friend. All belonged to Gur, whether by birth or by marriage.

The Wachter home in Bene Brak was actually two apartments joined together. The living room was large and different from all the others I had seen. While the basic organization was the same, there were innovations. A large dining table occupied the center of the room, and by it stood another table (which, during meals where there were many guests, could serve as a women's table). A corner of the room had been set off by a screen and contained a writing table, telephone, and office equipment. The part of the room close to the balcony was the actual salon, and contained a few armchairs and a large couch. The room's longer wall was covered by an overloaded book case that also held a small number of silver implements. All the available seats in the room had been occupied, and several more chairs were brought in from the kitchen.

Rabbi Wolf, in a short "German" jacket (as opposed to a long Hasidic coat), was tall and had a wrinkled face, a white beard, and blue eyes with a soft expression. He surveyed those before him, opened a small book he held in his hand, and plunged immediately into the lesson. His Hebrew was fluent, modern, and had a slight German accent.

The structure of the lesson. Rabbi Wolf read a passage from the fifth chapter of Maimonides' *Eight Chapters*. Most of the women had copies of the book in their hands and followed him as he read. When he finished reading, the women laid the books down and did not refer to them thereafter. Two or three of them jotted down comments in notebooks; I later discovered that they were teachers at the college. After reading the selection, he focused on a subject that he believed was the central point of the selection, explained it, adding comments of his own and examining its significance for the present day.

There was no dialogue between him and the women during the lesson. He did not ask them questions (except for rhetorical ones), and did not, during the course of the lesson, ask for their reactions. The women sat in absolute silence, a few closing their eyes, other staring straight ahead, a few directing their gaze at him and listening intently. The lesson lasted for about forty-five minutes. He concluded it without any special closing or comment about the next meeting, rose from his chair, and returned as he had come, with the women rising in a show of respect.

A sample lesson

> And when he is engaged in the acquisition of wealth—the end purpose of his intention should be its acquisition, such that he produce it with virtues and that he use it for his bodily needs and to keep himself alive, until he realizes and knows from God what he may know. (*Eight Chapters*, Chapter 5)

Rabbi Wolf: Maimonides is known as an opponent of luxury. How can he say this when the Gemara says, "A beautiful wife, beautiful furnishings, and a beautiful house broaden a man's knowledge?" For this it is necessary to understand what "broaden" means. This is what the selection we have read addresses. Even a man who occupies himself with Torah study must interrupt his studies to see to material matters. Going out into the material is a deviation for the purpose of broadening the knowledge of study, spirituality. This break allows a person to return to his study with renewed energy. A doctor working hard and with responsibility must also rest from his work to occupy himself with something material, to restore his power and return to his difficult work. Sometimes this pause even brings about a breakthrough. Both in study and in action. But all this is true only if the intention is to do God's will. If the occupation with the material becomes the main thing, it does not broaden knowledge. The goal is to separate the body and the spirit, and this is a task that only a select few can achieve, the prophets among them. Others must aspire to it, and they need to take breaks from their study. The same with luxuries. By "broadening a man's knowledge," the Gemara meant not only in the material sense, but also that the material broadens the spiritual.

In our generation there are no prophets. Today, if a man were to say he is a prophet, others would conduct an inspection—what fringes does he wear, what prayer book does he pray from, who are his friends [the rabbi chuckles to himself, and the women smile], and that is why we have no prophets.

There never was and never will be another prophet like Moses, since if there were to be a greater prophet he would be able to demand a change in the Torah. There have been those who have not sinned and were not prophets, while Moses sinned and was the greatest of the prophets. A prophet's sin is subjective. Others can not even reach the place from which Moses sinned. The sin of great men is the sensitive decision between two possibilities, both of which seem at first to be desirable. How can one know which is the truly desirable?

What does a man need in order to be a prophet? First he needs the expressive virtues, which are mind, comprehension, wisdom, and so on. Afterwards he needs the values: character, morality, etc. Prophecy infuses the wise man who understands God's word, the hero—the man who conquers his passions, and the wealthy man— the man who is content with his portion.

On the matter of conquering one's passions and on the matter of the virtues, the Gemara suggests that those born under the sign of Mars (who are hot-tempered) become butchers or circumcisers, and then their bloodletting will be for good. David, for instance, sinned in that he did not conquer his passion for wars, and waged elective wars [wars of conquest] before completing his mandatory wars [wars of self-defense and of conquering the Holy Land]. His bloody hands kept him from being allowed to build the Temple.

This reminds me a bit of Ernest Yefet [the recently retired director-general of Israel's Bank Le'umi, whose extravagant benefits and pension package had generated much controversy]. What happens to a Jew who imitates the customs of the non-Jews, and who takes money for his judgment? [The room awakens, and the silence is broken with laughter.]

Even Moses, who overcame all the barriers between himself and the creator, was not privileged to see God's face. Why? God has said, "A man cannot see me and live." That is, you, too, are a soul [mind] in

matter. The mind is not separate from the matter, that is, it is
not possible for just the soul or the consciousness [the mind], which
are worthy of encountering the creator, to be privileged to see it.
With the mind comes matter, and the material being who sees the
creator dies.

ॐ

At the end of the lesson, Rabbi Wolf's wife waited for him by the door, and
they left together. After the women had eased themselves out of their
silent attention, Rabbanit Wachter rose and said:

As we are accustomed to do, at the end of the lesson one of us
conveys something. Today it will be Shifra.

Shifra rose. She was a part-time teacher at the Scharansky Beit
Ya'akov College in Tel Aviv. Younger than the rest of the participants, her
clothing was especially modest—a simple wig and outdated clothes. She
wore glasses and stooped as she stood, gripping a handful of tissues and
speaking in a nasal voice.

I read in *Hamodia* [the Agudat Yisrael daily newspaper] on Friday
about our whole thing in Iran, how the government got mixed up
there with the weapons. I thought to myself that that's the price we
pay when we're dependent on someone. We, thank God, go our own
way, and don't have to depend on others. But despite that we don't
always act independently. First of all, the way we dress. Women say
to themselves: "What will other people say?" Who decided for them,
who are they worrying about? They should dress their own way,
modestly. Also education. Once we educated in the traditional way
and today there are innovations. Some of the innovations, well,
okay. But a lot of them are superfluous, the way of ancient Israel is
the right way, and we don't have to look to see what others are
doing. Certainly not what the gentiles are doing. What that means
is that we're being enslaved to ways that aren't ours. For instance,
there's a fashion about names. Everyone's giving new names. At first
that sounds wonderful, but after a while it gets ridiculous, the names
get old and there's no point to them. I heard that there are people
who give names like Ron, Shahar, Lihi. A few years later it becomes
funny. We have our own names. They've always been good and they'll
always be good, because the truth does not go out of date, it is eternal.

It looked as if the women in the room were very much affected by the
young woman's words. They congratulated her and went up to her with

broad smiles on their faces, seconding the importance of what she had said.

"You spoke well, good for you, we really needed that, we have to hear that from time to time."

"You don't even know how right you are, if you could see what's going on in the stores in Bene Brak."

It sounded as if Rabbi Wolf's comments on the barriers between man and the creator, on the power of consciousness and the mind, and on the limitations the material places on the soul had all vanished. The authentic, troubling, immediate reality returned to the room. All the women understood Shifra. Not one had drowsed off. It sounded as if each one of them was personally affected by what she had said. Rabbanit Wachter shook the young woman's hand warmly and said:

> *Yishar ko'ah*, good for you, congratulations, you are so right. I remember that in my time the non-religious gave the name Yoram a lot, it was in fashion. A few days ago someone at the college told me that today the name means something like "dolt." Like schlemiel or schlimazel. But with us, Sarah is Sarah, Rivka is Rivka, Moishe is Moishe.

After rummaging through the pile of coats on the kitchen table, we went out into the cold street. On the way to the bus stop, after a few moments of silence, Hannah said to me:

> I have a horrible headache. I haven't made such an effort for a long time. I'm not used to learning the *yekke* [German, i.e., rationalist] way. When I was at college I was more used to it, he taught us a class or two there. Now it's different, I go only to classes taught by women.

"Did you enjoy it?" I asked.

> It's hard to say whether I enjoyed it. I know that you must have liked it, but I prefer traditional study. It's too much over my head. Hurry up so we don't miss the last bus to the Development.

Rabbi Wolf's class is a classic "substance lesson." His level of knowledge and his way of thinking shape his style of teaching. The choice of Maimonides as a text is, in and of itself, unconventional. The Hasidim, like most other Ashkenazi Jews, do not base their legal rulings on Maimonides. While parts of his compendium of Jewish law, the *Mishna Torah*, are studied in the women's college, it does not have the authoritative, unchallengeable status that the *Shukhan Arukh* has. Maimonides' major philosophical work, *Moreh Nevuhim* (The Guide for the Perplexed) is not studied by women at all, nor is it a book that people keep at home or refer to. The *Eight Chapters* is notable for its concision and clarity. It is an early work by Maimonides, containing most of the ideas he expressed more fully later. It is written in simpler language than his other works, and is a good introduction to his philosophy for the uninitiated.

Rabbi Wolf's class was entirely different from the other classes I will describe. Even in comparison to the "substance" classes given by Rabbanit Wachter and her sister on the book of Psalms, it was exceptional. Here the teacher was a man, and he was not part of the Gur community. The teachers of the other classes were Gur women, some from the Development itself, and two who came from Bene Brak, but all central figures in the Gur community. Rabbi Wolf stands outside. The school where his brother was once principal, and whose current principal is his nephew, serves women from different haredi groups. When a special Beit Ya'akov college for Gur women was established in Bene Brak in the mid-1970s, Gur women stopped enrolling at the Wolf college. Rabbi Wolf is nevertheless respected and appreciated, as the site of the lesson—the home of a high-placed Hasid—shows.

The scope of this teacher's knowledge was not like that of the women teachers, or even like that of other male haredi teachers. Rabbi Wolf's rich and unconventional past affected the character, content, and form of his lessons.

Rabbi Wolf touched also on psychology and Aristotelian and Platonic philosophy, and applied Maimonides to immediate problems in haredi life (the fear of accepting the standards of the non-Jews) and of the Jewish people as a whole (in the implicit suggestion that deviation from religion is liable to lead to economic predicaments like that of Bank Le'umi's Ernest Yefet). Rabbi Wolf did not choose passages from Maimonides' book that would make it easy for him to comment on subjects the women would consider relevant. There is no lack of such passages in Maimonides, who wrote of medicine, property, art, law, and many other subjects. Rabbi Wolf spoke of faith, reverence, the barriers between God and his creation, and the attributes of the prophets. The connections the rabbi made between study and practice were slight; practically the only reference to practical matters was the mention of Ernest Yefet and the example (itself taken from Maimonides) of the doctor's need for a break from his medical work. Rabbi Wolf lectured, rather than sermonized, telling no stories and offering no instruction in proper behavior. He spoke in a low, even voice, without pathos.

In light of what he said, it is reasonable to assume that the rabbi's intention was not to emphasize the practical and behavioral. The women, who told Bina they wanted to hear a "practical" lesson, would certainly have classified Rabbi Wolf's lesson as "substance." Hannah complained of a headache, and said that she was no longer used to this kind of class. Rabbi Wolf's class, by this data, is exceptional—but so are the women who come to hear him.

Malka Shamir, the ba'alat teshuva, had been present when I first heard of Rabbi Wolf's class. She turned to Rabbanit Wachter and asked if it would be possible for Rabbi Wolf to come to the Development every two or three months. An awkward silence fell over the women present, and Rabbanit Wachter explained to Malka, as if she were an obtuse little girl, that Rabbi Wolf was an elderly and venerable man and that it would not be possible. On the way out Malka mumbled under her breath that she didn't understand what the problem was; the women around her did not bother to explain her error to her.

The women attending the classes at the rabbanit's house were, on the average, about twenty years older than the women of the Development. They had coalesced over close to a decade, and attended the class devotedly. It was a self-selected group. The class was not appropriate for all women, like the women's classes in the Development, nor was it open to all Gur women in Bene Brak. The rabbanit had invited several acquaintances, and these in turn had brought others. The group's welcome of the newcomer determined whether the new participant was to be accepted or rejected. Hannah and I were well-received. Hannah's outwardly evident strictness of observance, the effort she had made to get from the Development to Bene Brak especially for the class, and her husband's standing in the Gur community had paved the way for us.

Rabbi Wolf's class was not meant for the public at large, and was thus held in a private home rather than a synagogue or school, as classes by other rabbis are. But even such a "substance" lesson for older women whose "harediness" is not open to doubt cannot be left at that. At the end of each meeting, they hear "a few words." One of the women gives an educational homily. Apparently, this talk has become the most meaningful part of the class for most of the women. Shifra's lesson, not the rabbi's, was in the air as the women left. It had touched the audience on an emotional level and brought them back to familiar events in their lives. The practical, in this case, was the substance that the young woman presented to the others. It was relevant to their social situation, and was therefore absorbed easily and pleasurably, even though it was critical. To the non-haredi outside observer, it is difficult to understand why the women went to such lengths to congratulate Shifra so warmly. What wisdom had she imparted? And why did they not discuss the rabbi's lesson? But a minute's thought supplied an answer: Shifra's lesson conveyed a message consistent with the women's worldview. It portrayed a world that was not congenial for them (by attacking their consumerism), but it also validated and confirmed that world. Her very brief remarks had the power to validate the formal lesson and at the same time call its realism into question. She took the women from the heights of abstraction and planted them on familiar ground. From the prophetic virtues Rabbi Wolf had spoken of, Shifra had distilled the haredi housewife's shopping list.

What seems to be an absurd juxtaposition of events seems entirely reasonable to the women involved. The ancient world of faith, the spirit of
Judaism, and Jewish philosophy are diverted into the vessels of reality that
they know first-hand. This type of education, which offers substance in a
container firmly planted in the foundations of reality, is effective. Such
education fashions a view of the world and, simultaneously, confirms it.
This is the case with regard to men's study as well, except that the two
views of the world—the male and the female—are different. This will
become clear as we proceed.

The Class on the Book of Psalms

The local women classified the class in the Psalms as a "substance" class,
and in that it resembled Rabbi Wolf's lectures on Maimonides. Yet the two
were distinct in several ways. The Psalms class was open to every interested
woman in the Development. It was given by women, and the target audience was women between the ages of twenty and thirty. These women
(with the exception of three ba'alot teshuva and one Sepharadi woman)
belonged to the Gur community and studied at Beit Ya'akov.

The class was held at the local Sepharadi synagogue, and between
thirty and fifty women attended. About one-quarter of them brought
copies of the Book of Psalms, a book that may be found in all religious
homes, and that is much read by women. Three or four women even
brought pen and paper to take notes. The class was taught in rotation by
Rabbanit Nehama Wachter and her sister, Rivka. These two women are,
like Rabbi Wolf, professional teachers.

A summary of two lessons given by Rabbanit Wachter (both on the
same passage), and a lesson taught by her sister, Rivka, provides a representative sample of the lessons I attended at the Development. The content and structure of the lessons will demonstrate the tension between the
"substantial" and the "practical." Through them I will continue to scruti-
nize the way in which abstract questions are leveled into problems of practical action, and elucidate the implications of this style of learning on the
way the women think and grasp the social reality in which they function.
To underscore this, the structure of this lesson will also be compared to
classes given to working men who do not study full-time.

Rabbanit Wachter's class. The floor was swept, the money for the rabbanit's
cab was collected, and Rabbanit Wachter entered and greeted us. Wearing
a simple woolen dress, a short wig, and low-heeled black loafers, she was a
heavy woman of average height, with a small face and glasses. She began:

Much has been said about study by women. Not long ago we all read
an entire debate about it in *Marveh Latsameh*. The conclusion was

that study by women is a positive thing, as long as it does not interfere with the husband's study and with keeping the home in order. Now, if we are to study, the question is what? Should we prefer laws or something else, like the Psalms? This book has and continues to belong to Jewish women through the generations, and we will study the Book of Psalms here every two weeks. There are those who have derided the Book of Psalms, saying it is a book for simple people. We all know the expression *tehilim-zager*, the poor man who makes his living reciting the Psalms for others. There is a story about a wealthy man who held a great celebration in his home and invited all the leading men in the town. In the middle of the feast a scholar was called on to say some words of Torah. Just as he was speaking, the town's tehilim-zager entered the room and interrupted the learned disputation that followed the rabbi's talk. The wealthy man heard this and had him kicked out. The poor man, humiliated, went on his way. The next day the scholar went to the wealthy man and reproached him. All words of wisdom are nothing next to someone reciting the Psalms with devotion. The wealthy man went to the tehilim-zager and apologized, and more than that—he held an additional banquet where the poor man was the guest of honor.

We women read the Psalms all the time, so why should we study them? So that we can devote ourselves to what is written in them.

Abraham our father discovered faith, and Moses our teacher gave us the Torah, and King David gave us repentance.

This is why King David beseeched in his introduction to the Book of Psalms, "May the words of my mouth be acceptable in thy sight." The Book of Psalms must be read in a special way. The Psalms must be said with intention and thought, so that they bring us to rise above ourselves, to be inspired, and to repent.

The Sanhedrin tractate of the Gemara tells how Nebuchadnezzar wished to denounce the praises of God in the Book of Psalms. An angel came and struck him on the mouth, and Nebuchadnezzar suddenly found himself praising the Psalms. What did Nebuchadnezzar wish to achieve? He wanted to show that God had created the world and then left it. That he had no interest in this world and is occupied with higher things. By doing this, Nebuchadnezzar wished to show that God does not take a personal interest in each of us. Since the Book of Psalms is all about God's personal interest in us, the king wished to attack it.

Rabbi Nachman of Birdechev said that Nebuchadnezzar wanted to show that people can do nothing to repeal God's decrees. David showed that prayer and high spirituality can annul divine retribution.

"To the victor, a Psalm of David." What does that mean, "victor," over whom are we victorious? [Rabbanit Wachter is making a play on the Hebrew word *minatse'ah*. Many Psalms open with the dedication *"laminatse'ah,"* "for the chief musician." But the word may also mean "for the victor."] When the children of Israel are victorious over the Creator, the Creator profits. When the Children of Israel lose to the Creator, he loses also.

So, after such a demanding introduction, how will we actually study, given that we are women?

We will be like poor people given permission to walk through the court of a king. We will gather up the leftover food, enjoy the splendor and beauty of the garden, pick up what we find in the courtyards. For this there is nothing better than to begin with the first verse of the first Psalm.

"Blessed is the man who does not walk in the counsel of the wicked, nor stands in the way of sinners, nor sits in the seat of scorners."

What are scorners? Those who are satisfied with themselves, even though they may believe and do not commit any transgressions, but the Torah and the commandments do not interest them. They are occupied with the matters of the body, with the immediate. How does that connect with our day and age? We, also, for instance, waste time. We read newspapers on the Sabbath, even *Hamodia,* and there are families who have turned the intermediate days of Sukkot and Pesah to days for vacation and idleness.

Mesilat Yisharim [a book of moral teachings] says of the scorner: "Laughter dislodges one from straight thinking." Scorn covers the body and shields it from reproof. All scorn is forbidden except for scorn of idol worship.

Every society and community has its own "assembly of scorners." Everyone knows where it is, and must avoid it. What about a women's assembly of scorners? It is no different. Except that men have been told to study Torah in order to escape scorn and idleness. And women? Should they speak of the Torah? Women can always find something to talk about. About bringing up the children, to exchange recipes, to speak of matters of health and the like.

Hannah suddenly interrupted and asked: "And if we mention something about the weekly Torah portion, is that a transgression? Even if we aren't commanded to, it's allowed."

The room was silent. The women waited to see how the discussion between the teacher and Hannah would go. The rabbanit responded: "Why say things that no one will do? You're sitting down by the fence, your 'jewels' are running between your legs, one climbs up and one falls down, here one is crying and here another one comes to say something to Mommy, and women will speak words of Torah?"

"If we think words of Torah we'll also speak them." Hannah's cheeks redden, perhaps a sign that she knows she has said something unconventional, that she has challenged the rabbanit.

"Even talk about material things is preparation for words of Torah, if that's your intention," interjected one of the women. "If you accept your role as a woman, then you have something to talk about, thank God, without getting caught up in slander, even without Torah. How to avoid yelling at the children, what to do with leftovers, the children's health problems, that sort of thing."

The rabbanit added: "That reminds me of a story about a woman who had had a particularly bad day. Everything went wrong for her. You know, we all have days like that. Her husband came home from the kolel in the evening and found her in the kitchen. He said to her: 'How jealous I am of you that everything you do is a *mitzvah*.' The woman looked at her hands and said, 'Every plate is another mitzvah?' Her voice had a kind of sadness in it, a little dismissive of herself. 'Yes!' her husband said, 'and what a mitzvah!' Those words of his gave her the strength to go on."

"To sum up the first verse," the rabbanit continued, "we see there that from it we learn not to be dragged along, not to be influenced, even if we are sure that we live in a good area, you always have to be on guard. Bad company, a child who does not choose his friends properly, all these carry us away. One needs a critical sense and backbone, one needs the strength sometimes to go against the current, or what you think the current is. You have to be strong. A slight turn can divert one to the edge of the abyss.

"I've decided not only to teach the Psalms. We'll make a custom of concluding each meeting with a law from *Hilkhot Beitah* [a collection of laws concerning the home]. I think it's always good to learn laws, and I will try to present laws that apply to our times."

Rabbanit Wachter chose to teach the laws of Rosh Hodesh, the first day of each new Jewish month. Rosh Hodesh has special meaning for women and children, and she selected several laws touching on what is permitted and what is desirable on this day.

Rivka's lesson. Rivka is nothing like her sister. She is tall and thin, slightly stooped, her expression sterner. On the evening in question, she wore a blue dress with pleats from the waist down. Over the dress was a black coat that she removed when she began to talk.

When we decided, my sister and I, to give this class in the Development, I was a little apprehensive. You ask why? Well, I know most of you—only yesterday you were devoted students at the college. My apprehension is of another kind. You, after all, live here in a little community. You all know each other. In the evening, when someone wants to go to the class, she'll think to herself: they already saw me today with this dress, how can I look that way in the evening, too, so you'll go change your dress. If that's what happens, then all the good things we have in the class will be worthless. So I've decided to begin by asking you to beware of that, and that the class not turn into an opportunity to show off. This Development should have a pure character—after all, this is why we have gathered together, so that it won't be like it is in Tel Aviv or even in Bene Brak. Take advantage of this place for good and not for bad.

"But his delight is in the Torah of the Lord, and in his Torah he meditates day and night" [Psalms 1:2]. Here we already get into the positive aspect, not what is forbidden but what should be. The subject here is that *study is like life.* And study is not by the power of the mind, because by that power we do not obtain knowledge. It is study by the power of self-abnegation. This is an important principle in Hasidism. A person negates his will and desire, with which he will not get far. Before whom will he negate himself? First, before God, and afterwards a student before his teacher, a wife before her husband. "And in his Torah he meditates day and night." This says that the Torah does not become part of life, but rather life becomes part of the Torah. It is what defines all our life. And what about woman? After all, she is not required to study. How does the Torah become hers?

First, not by study! Can they both study? They'll come back from morning prayers and there will be no breakfast, they'll return from the kolel, there will be no supper, the children will run around like orphans—Mommy's studying! [The women in the room giggle, and the teacher is smiling broadly herself.] Then how? If a woman gives up things she likes—clothes, jewelry, a wig, she makes the Torah hers. If a woman is satisfied with the minimum and manages her household wisely, she makes the Torah hers. For this reason, in the history of the Jewish people, great Torah scholars have grown up in homes in which the wife and mother devoted herself to the household, was modest in her needs, and allowed her husband and sons to devote their time to their studies without any cares.

Women may study if they have free time, that's true. You know, after all, that there are no women Hasidim, right? [laughter in the room] There are only daughters of Hasidim and wives of Hasidim.

Nava: What about study in the form of teaching? For instance, I have to teach something to my students. Is my study forbidden?

Rivka: Oh, I see that the law I've chosen for today is very appropriate, so let's turn to *Hilkhot Beitah,* to the chapter dealing with study by women.

Maimonides says: A woman who studies receives her reward, but not like a man, since he is commanded to study and she is not. Likewise, she is not to be taught a priori. If she studied and succeeded after the fact, it is to her credit. It was already said before him that "anyone who teaches his daughter Torah teaches her triviality," and "women are of slight mind."

There was commotion in the room and the discussion got out of Rivka's control. The women spoke with each other. Some of them were teachers at the college, others had just finished their studies, and the subject was one that touched them personally. She had upset them, that was clear. It was hard to overhear their comments from where I was sitting, but I was able to make out the reactions of the two closest to me.

> *Nava:* Everyone has to know their own limits, in accordance with the occupation she is studying for.
>
> *Sheindi (who had just graduated from the college and married):* That's easy for you to say, there are a lot who don't know.
>
> *Rivka reestablished order and said:* There are those who say that teaching girls today has priority over teaching boys, and in our Hasidism we emphasize for the most part the study of laws. We base ourselves on the Hafetz Haim, who saw the education of girls as an answer to troubles of our times, and we add that women's study can come only if it does not interfere with her primary roles.

At the end of the lesson many women remained in the room and continued the discussion Rivka had set off. Hannah approached me and said: "They gave you a lesson to order, didn't they? Exactly what interests you."

For a split second we could have been two anthropologists in the field.

As noted earlier, the Psalms class was given in the Development by teachers from outside. The teachers were from the Gur Hasidic community, as were most of the women of the Development, but the teachers were scions of important Gur families. Rabbanit Wachter and Rivka held senior positions in the Beit Ya'akov college in Bene Brak, the most important Gur women's college in central Israel. The two of them were asked to teach at the Development by two young residents who are also teachers, Ita and Bina. Ita told me that "it was about time to hear a class on a high level, a class that we can't convey ourselves." They approached women considered to be of high ability, and thought that Rabbanit Wachter and Rivka were obligated to the women of the Development, who had been sent into this nearby exile by the rebbe. The many previous attempts to turn the Development into a cultural center had failed.

To ascertain the major characteristics of women's scholarship, as well as its form, direction, and aims, it is worthwhile comparing this lesson in the Psalms to a lesson given to working men who do not study full-time.

The sociologist Shmuel Heilman described the structure of a Gemara (Talmud) class for men (in the Ashkenazi community):

1. The section to be studied (generally, in a special chant) is read by the *maggid shiur* (the teacher).
2. The the section is translated. Since the Gemara is bilingual (Aramaic and Hebrew), the text is translated into Hebrew or Yiddish.
3. The issue and solution discussed in the section are explained.
4. Discussion follows.[5]

The men gather for the class and wait for the teacher. When he arrives, the lesson begins. Among Gur women, the lesson begins with an introduction meant to grant validity to its occurrence ("Much has been said about study by women." "When we decided, my sister and I, to give this class . . ."). Remarks validating the act of study are scattered throughout the lesson. The teachers remind the women that study cannot come at the expense of housework, and that it is not like men's study ("Let us be like Ruth the Moabite," "How does the Torah become hers? First, not by study!"). The validation of the gathering is reinforced when the study of a law is added to every lesson. In other words, even though the class is of the "substance" type, the study of Torah, it cannot stand on its own. It must be accompanied by the external certification of rabbinic rulings, of the sages, or of the haredi press ("Not long ago we all read an entire debate about it in *Marveh Letsameh*"). The law from *Hilkhot Beitah* reinforces the validity of the gathering and brings it closer to the practical level.

Then the lesson itself begins.

In the men's classes, the section to be studied is read by the rabbi giving the lesson. The others follow along in their books. In the women's classes, the section is read by the teacher, and about a third of the women follow along in books they have brought from home. What do they read? Over the course of ten lessons, verses from the introductory chapter of the Book of Psalms and from three other psalms were studied:

1. The introduction: "May the words of my mouth be acceptable in thy sight."
2. "Blessed is the man who walks not in the counsel of the wicked, nor stands in the way of sinners, nor sits in the seat of scorners. But his delight is in the Torah of the Lord, and in his Torah he meditates day and night" (Psalms 1:1–2).
3. A Ma'alot poem (an opening to many of the Psalms songs). "In my distress I cried to the Lord and he heard me. Deliver my soul, O

Lord, from lying lips, from a deceitful tongue. . . . Sharp arrows of the mighty, with coals of the broom tree" (120:1–5).
4. A Ma'alot poem. "I will lift up my eyes to the hills. From whence comes my help?" (121:1).

Out of the 150 psalms in the Book of Psalms, nine nonconsecutive verses were studied. Even assuming that the pace of the study is reasonable, and that it is necessary to limit the amount of time spent on each verse, it is safe to conclude that the teachers intentionally chose these verses and not others. The teachers told their audience why they chose this book to study, but did not explain their decision to focus on specific verses. Heilman does not explain the process by which the subjects studied by men are chosen, but we know that men generally work their way through a particular tractate of Talmud, or an entire order. (The Talmud is divided into six "orders," or divisions of the law.)

At the men's lesson, the rabbi translates the text into a language understood by the students. The women read from the Bible in Hebrew and do not require translation.

Heilman believes that the most significant part of the men's class is the segment devoted to defining the issue under discussion after reading the text that contains it. This section of the class structures the reality of the written text, answering the question "What was actually said here?" This being the case, it is supposed to be open to negotiation, ideology, interests, interpretation, and so on. Heilman reports that, in fact, the group has only limited leeway for entering into a real dialogue with the teacher. The reason is that the teacher makes this stage, like the earlier ones, into a technical one: he presents himself as explaining what is "really" written in the text, not what he *thinks* is written.

The explanation stage is also the most important in the women's lesson. After reading the verse, the teacher moves straight into its explication; she does not initiate discussion, nor does she allow the women to propose their own interpretations of the text. The women did not seem displeased with this; they did not interrupt the teacher in order to advance their own interpretation, and it would seem that they were accustomed to this. The reaction to the few occasions when women expressed their own opinions shows that the teachers strive to present their interpretations as the "real" one. When they encountered a problem, they retreated. The example that follows does not come from the lesson described above; it is taken from another lesson but provides an interesting illustration of such an event.

When the women studied Psalm 121, they spent much time on the first verse, "I will lift up my eyes to the hills. From whence comes my help?" Rabbanit Wachter suggested three possible interpretations of the word "hills": the forefathers, the evil urge, and the righteous men of the generation. The women accepted the first and third as needing no elaboration—help from the forefathers and the generation's righteous men seemed logical to them. But they had difficulty with the second interpretation, which reverses the metaphor and portrays the hills as the evil urge that must be overcome and the Psalmist as praying for help to find his way over them. In this context the verse seemed unfathomable.

> *Miri:* How can we put the evil urge in the same category as the righteous and as our forefathers? It makes it sound as if, through the evil urge, we can reach good things, doesn't it?

The room's silence was broken, and the women whispered to one another.

> *Nehama:* I don't want to get into a discussion of the evil urge here, it's not the right place. What is important to understand from the three interpretations is that all of them remind man of his smallness in the face of the powerful and the great. This is so that he may feel his insignificance and his inferiority, and that he may grow from this. This is why the text uses the word *me'ayin*, from nothing, rather than *minayin*, from where.

Any discussion of abstract subjects or attempts by the women to interpret the passage in an abstract way were rejected by the teachers. Even when they themselves raised such subjects, they did not delve into them. Nehama Wachter, for instance, spoke of the introduction to the Book of Psalms. She described the intention of its author, the attitude of non-Jews to the book and its contents, and the book's esteem among the Jewish people over the generations. This introduction touched on many abstract matters that are at the foundation of Jewish philosophy, such as God's personal interest in man, the order of creation, the relation between heaven and earth, and other subjects.

These subjects were not developed and were in the air for only a few seconds. Nebuchadnezzar's denial of God's personal interest was solved with the blow the angel gave him on the mouth, as related in the Sanhedrin tractate. The issues presented by the text under study were not interpreted in a theoretical–philosophical way; instead, they were transferred to the level of practice, of sermonizing, and of reproof. When Rabbanit Wachter addressed the essence of prayer and supplication as understood by David, she did not speak at length on the significance of prayer. Instead, she told the women to walk on tiptoe in the grove of wisdom, and reminded them of the miserable tehilim-zager, who occupies, like them, an important place in Jewish ethics.

During the course of the lesson, the interpretations became ever more insistently simplistic. The following verse, "Blessed is the man who walks not in the counsel of the wicked, nor stands in the way of sinners, nor sits in the seat of scorners," was turned exclusively into a discussion of "the seat of scorners," especially in its female incarnation. From here the discussion turned to the issue of slander. Along with the lecturer's interpretation of the verse—the sole interpretation under consideration—there is a discussion of washing dishes, of exchanging recipes, of watching the children in the yard, and of having neighborly relations. It sometimes sounds as if all this comes straight out of the Book of Psalms. The verse "But his delight is in the Torah of the Lord, and in his Torah he meditates day and night" is interpreted to present the women with one and only one way for them to possess the Torah, and that is by not studying it. A woman who abstains from various pleasures (including study) achieves the same result she would achieve had she studied.

Hannah, and to a lesser extent Nava (who, like Hannah, is considered especially haredi), challenged this interpretation and set off a power struggle. Hannah, known for her piety, proposed that women speak words of Torah so as to avoid gossip and slander. She wanted to see women behave as *hevruta* (study partners), as the men did—at least those who were Torah scholars. Nehama could not repudiate the idea, because there is support for it in the sources, so she dismissed it as impractical. Women will not behave that way, so why propose that they do something that they cannot carry out? The disparity between ideas and social reality is invoked here, which only serves to perpetuate itself. The teacher's answer promoted the women's self-image as being unable to speak words of Torah, and also confirmed this reality.

In the men's lesson, the discussion stage follows the explanation; in Heilman's view it is the sociological event of interest (mostly because of the dramatic emphasis and the interrelationships created during it). During this stage the actor is the group or hevruta. Even though Heilman describes a layman's study group, led by a man who knows more than any of the participants, discussion is opened, and the students themselves confront the text. During the discussion, the knowledge of the participants comes into play, as does their familiarity with the material being studied, their worldview, and their understanding of their Jewishness. The social reality is clarified during their discussion; doubts are expressed, and redefined. The study room invokes a far-off historical reality that is connected with the reality of today. There are differences among the participants, the same differences raised thousands of years before in other places. In these classes, contradictions are resolved, as they have been resolved millions of other times. This social repetition of fundamental personal differences is the heart of the study process. It is the *lernen*.[6]

Such a process must be accomplished in a group. The discussion, disagreement, and agreement cannot occur if one studies alone. Definition of the social reality is a matter for the group.

The discussion among the men is a way of constructing social reality, or reproducing the culture, accomplished as a process of social negotiation. This dialogue is not open-ended; it cannot end in apostasy or heresy. The very structure of the lesson—the way it is managed, the reading, and the interpretation—and the very fact that the participants acquiesce to its structure and context all determine its outcome. Here also there is a plan of study that conforms to the social reality in which the students live. It is a picture of that reality; it is a solution to the problems inherent in it (the relations between Jews and non-Jews or secular Jews in a mixed society) and it is the confirmation of the picture that it presents. The process, content, and resulting portrayal of the social world conform to the men's status. There is a debate; there are conspicuous struggles for power. There is also discussion of abstract issues, and, most important, there is no need to justify the very act of study. Study is seen by the men as the pinnacle of Jewish existence, not as a hobby that must be fit into one's leisure hours (even if the students are not full-time Torah scholars).

No real discussion takes place in the women's lesson. When it breaks out, it is quickly suppressed by the teacher. No time is set aside for discussion. The high point of the lesson is not the social reality, reconfirmed by group discussion. Instead, it is the interpretation, preaching, and *ex cathedra* reproof of the teacher that confirm the social reality. The admonishment is the emotional and experiential part of the gathering. The teacher takes the verse under study, interprets it according to her needs, and paves the way to the emotions of morality preaching. In this way she manipulates it into the women's personal experience. She takes it from the biblical past, through the *midrashim* and Gemara, straight into the European exile and home to the Development.

The structure of such a lesson offers women a two-dimensional understanding of the reality in which they live. The *time dimension* takes them into the Jewish people's far-off and immediate past, where they find similarity between the problems that concern them in their daily life. Reading the Book of Psalms as a text dealing with the problems of back-fence gossip, submission to the husband's and family's will, and abstention from momentary pleasures is a kind of comfort. It makes the past meaningful and authentic, and it turns the present into a holy period in the historical continuum. The *space dimension* connects the women at the lesson to the haredi public as a whole. It grants meaning to their daily existence, against the background of others in the community. In this way, washing the dishes can be considered a mitzvah, and washing the clothes of a Torah scholar can be a way to possess the Torah.

Both the men's and the women's lessons reconstruct, strengthen, and confirm the social worldview. Both men and women engage in study that is a cultural performance. The difference, of course, lies in the types of portrayals of the world that are received, and in the implications these portrayals have for the life of the individual and the ability of the group to accomplish social change.

"Practical" Classes

Women define as "practical" classes those that touch directly on their daily lives as women, wives, and mothers. Any information that helps them to perform these roles is considered practical. By definition, then, a "practical" educational framework is compatible with social reality. Such a framework, which applies Jewish law to real situations in the lives of the women, is always concrete (that is, it portrays pictures that may be seen from the classroom window) and is directly connected with the lives of the students. It is, for this reason, effective.

The social reality in which the women live is not one-dimensional. They do not just wash dishes, change diapers, and prepare food for their husbands and children. Some of these women work as school and kindergarten teachers; others help out in family businesses. There are those who run small businesses in their homes, selling school supplies, sewing supplies, and the like. Some give private lessons to girls at the college, or work in the evenings at bookkeeping or typing. These account for about a quarter of the women. Others are housewives, but they also read books, mostly books on Jewish ethics, the lives of righteous men, and other religious matters. A minority reads fiction, largely in English, because the cultural distance makes it less threatening; they also read Hebrew literature that does not slander religion. They read *Hamodia*, and may read non-haredi newspapers as well. They walk through the streets around the Development and in the big cities, and encounter men and women who are not from their community.

Literacy helps one decipher extreme and complex situations, but it also provides a new paradox. The knowledge that women ask for and receive is supposed to help them construct their world as Jewish women (at the conservative pole) but as Jewish women in Israel at the beginning of the 1990s (at the dynamic pole). As a result, the "practical" classes reconstruct the image of the ignorant woman, and at the same time (paradoxically) help the educated woman who lives in Israel to shoulder all her responsibilities.

It took a long time before I was able to understand this phenomenon. I saw women who could express themselves astutely in certain situations, who demonstrated scholarly expertise, who were sharp-minded—and here they were asking their teachers to discuss yet again the same laws, to repeat the same familiar admonitions and interpretations at the classes they attended.

One evening, after I already had a first draft of my dissertation ready, I went to Bene Brak to meet with four women who did not live in the

Development. I presented them with my conclusions about the lessons, especially with regard to the "practical" lessons, and I reiterated my bewilderment. These women, all of whom held senior positions in the Gur community (some economic and some collegiate), laughed. Bracha said:

"Look, *from your point of view* you are right. It really is strange that smart adult women seek out such classes and say they came out of them 'strengthened.' *From our point of view* there is no other way."

That is, my point of view is that of my picture of the world, of the responsibilities and ideologies that I must confront. My point of view is perhaps the point of view of academic or male literacy, which has become *the* literacy for me. Their point of view is that of women who live in a world they have chosen to accept without questioning. They cannot resolve, confront, or liberate themselves from the problems, contradictions, and paradoxes it contains. These are facts for which an appropriate meaning must be found, one that will help the women live with them. In this way, just as they are overcoming the paradox of education for women in this age, they fall into a new paradox of education for ignorance. Educated women are taught to be ignorant, so that they may succeed in living as educated and ignorant.

When the educational arena is emptied of teachers and rabbis, the women remain alone. They initiate classes of their own on subjects that contain nothing new for them. When the women of the Development began to organize classes again (after 200 new young families came to live in the Development in its second stage), they did not look for courses in flower arrangement, French cooking, or sewing (among the courses available at the nearby community center, open to any interested woman). When the women "have a class," they "have Judaism." When women describe a good place to live, they specify that there be "a lot of classes for women" there. Like the Jewish town in Poland that had many study halls, the women's class is proof that the Jewish situation has been reproduced. Like the men described by sociologist Shmuel Heilman, the women also seek in their classes support for the complex situation in which they live.

Without guides, they choose the "practical" type of lesson. If the women's world of public literacy were a pharmacy, the women could take "substance" only with a doctor's (i.e., a rabbi's or teacher's) prescription. Over the counter, on their own responsibility, they take only the practical —but even that is not so simple, as will be shown by the three "practical" lessons that follow.

The Lesson on Worms

Nava showed up a week after the initial misunderstanding. At 9:00 P.M. I found eighteen women sitting in Bina's living room. All lived in the Development, most of them for only a year or two; others were from the first families to move in. With the exception of one fifty-year-old woman, the oldest women were thirty years old. The season was borderline between spring and summer, so the women were wearing light, new-looking dresses, styled in accordance with the accepted fashions. A few of the women wore light, shear nylon stockings and medium-heeled shoes; a few others arrived in slippers or clogs, some of the high-platformed type generally worn by older women. All, except for Hannah and me, wore short or medium-length wigs. The wigs, even if they were of the best kind, did not go beyond the bounds of "modest."

On the table in the center of the room stood a pitcher of cold water and a few glasses. Some of the women sat around the table; those who came later found room on the couch and on the extra chairs that had been made into a second row.

Nava greeted us and silence fell over the room:

It is written: "And you defiled your souls." Why is the letter alef missing? [Nava is explaining why the word for "defiled" is missing a letter as written in the Torah, making it look like the word for "foolish."] It is to show that eating impure food makes us foolish. Whoever takes care not to eat impure food is also taking care of her soul and mind. The proof is the intelligence of the Jews. Look, they're always saying that there's a "Jewish brain," and that's true, the non-Jews really are stupider. Today, unfortunately, there are Jews who do not avoid the impure and become stupider, but what's interesting is that whoever eats, God forbid, pork, commits a single transgression, but someone who eats the smallest fly commits six transgressions. Why? Because it's harder not to eat a little fly. But whoever watches out, God watches out for him. Heaven helps us. They say that our rebbe, long may he live, was once a guest at the Yoskovitz house for a Sabbath meal, and he did not want to touch the *cholent* [the stew traditionally eaten for lunch on the Sabbath]. Of course there was a great uproar, because everyone knows that in that house everything is as it should be, and it was a great insult to the hosts. They went and checked and ran around but he would not eat it. *Efes, shaiz shmekt nisht* [it just didn't smell right to him]. Afterwards, on Sunday, they checked it again and it turned out that they had cooked the cholent in a dairy pot. They say also that the late rebbe, the Rim, once did not want to eat meat. Everyone inquired and said it was all kosher, but he kept refusing. Afterwards it turned out that it was the meat of a first-born. Whoever watches himself, heaven helps him. Now you ask who in the home can screen the food. It has to be a reverent and earnest person. And a woman is more patient and can take her time. But even then you have to see if she is responsible, and after her bat mitzvah, and according to her character. When it comes to worms, as we will see, you need a lot of patience.

Worms that you can't see are permitted, because the Torah was given to human beings, but with the rest one must take caution. We will speak of how to examine for worms and how to take care in buying and storage. We'll also make note of foods in which there is a risk of worms, some that you all know and some that you would think there wouldn't be any worms in. Worms that have been ground up are considered insignificant, and that is permitted. But you must not grind them intentionally; first check and see if there are any, and then only if they were by chance ground up is it permitted.

The women giggled. Some were imagining ground-up worms in their food, and I heard exclamations of "ech," "pyu," "disgusting." The women sat close together and exchanged a few words with each other; occasionally they stopped Nava and challenged her.

A woman: Once I bought strawberries and I'm telling you, they were all full of these tiny black flies, I literally spent half an hour washing and washing but I couldn't get them out. I was afraid to throw them away because of *bal tashit* [the prohibition against throwing away food]. But I didn't know what to do. So that evening I asked my husband and he suggested that we put them in the refrigerator and then wash them again afterwards, and that really did help. Now I put them in the refrigerator first and then wash them.

Another woman: Yes, but then the flies in the refrigerator could get into something where you wouldn't suspect them, and then what would happen?

Hannah: I even put the flour and sugar and all those things that are suspect in the refrigerator, and then the worms can't develop—they told us that in college and that's what I saw at home, too.

A woman: Okay, but you can't keep the whole house in the refrigerator.

Another woman: The worst thing is the lettuce leaves, even over the fire and even in the light it's so hard to see all the worms.

Hannah: Right, and have you ever seen how they hide way inside cauliflower?

A woman: In cauliflower? Really? I never saw that. You're really scaring me, maybe it's better to fast, so many foods have worms and flies.

Bina: You haven't heard anything yet. Once in boiling soup I found little moths, and with onions, too, when you cut them—what kind of worm would want to live in an onion, but I've got news for you, in onions there are worms, too.

Nava (breaking in): We're studying now so that we can be careful, but I want to remind you that all foods were given to the human race so that we may enjoy them, and if the solution is not to buy and not to eat then we are making God sad, because he wants us to enjoy them.

Nava hands out some papers she has photocopied at the college, where she works. She asks for money to cover the expense. The paper is titled "The Prohibitions Against Insects and Worms according to *Kashrut Hamazon*, published by Davar, Jerusalem." The papers contain a summary of the laws, and also a list of foods and the types of insects common in them. At exactly 10:00 P.M. one of the women stood up. Nava thanked her for the reminder, and finished up the lesson.

At the next lesson, which was held at Yochi's house, the subject was what cautionary measures to take when buying food—where it was best to buy, what kashrut certifications could be trusted, what kinds of sifter should be used to sift flour, whether it was best to buy dried legumes by weight or in prepared packages, and the like. Nava was interrupted many times. The women were alert, and offered advice and anecdotes from their personal experience. Nava had been married only a year and still had no children, so when it came to practical advice, she allowed the other women to speak.

Hannah: It's not so simple. Once I sifted flour in a fine silk sifter and found nothing, but afterwards I found an even finer sifter and I was surprised to find two little flies.

A woman: But it would take you forever to use that sifter all the time, it's better to keep the flour in the refrigerator.

Shoshana: I really think that you can go every so often to that street in south Tel Aviv, what's it called . . . Levinsky. There everything is very fresh, they sell huge quantities every day, so there's no danger of spoilage. Because even at the Gur store not everything is always so fresh.

A woman: They say you can trust Rabbi Landau's certification with your eyes closed.

Varda: Don't trust anything with your eyes closed.

Hannah: Before our wedding I worked in my family's bakery, and I saw how Rabbi Landau's supervisors checked the flour. Believe me, none of you check your flour as well.

Many conversations were going on at once. After every comment spoken before the whole group, the women turned to their neighbors and talked quietly with them. A few minutes later, Nava took the floor again and focused the conversation.

Nava's introduction included an explication of the verse she first quoted—"and you defiled your souls." Despite the centrality of the verse, the teacher did not devote much time to it and did not go deeply into it. Even when she said that someone who eats pork commits a single transgression, while someone who eats a small fly commits six transgressions, she did not go into the point any further. The women accepted the verses as axioms for the practical discussion. They expressed no desire or demand to go deeper into the essence of the commandment, its roots, or its meaning. There was no preliminary discussion of the terms "impure" and "pure," no talk about the significance of kosher food. Such an opening, which would seem almost essential and certainly relevant for academic literacy or male study, was seen as superfluous in this context.

The women wished to bring the substance into their homes and kitchens. During these three meetings they frequently interrupted Nava to tell of their personal experiences and to listen to the advice given by others. Hannah, the oldest of those who attended regularly, and the most haredi of them, always set out the most extreme position. She was the one who recommended a second sifting, checking the cauliflower, and storing in the refrigerator. The young women did not challenge her. Sometimes they whispered among themselves or said that if that was the case, it would be easier just to give up the food in question.

The class on worms was to a certain extent a zoology and botany class as well. Nava tried to describe various kinds of pests that populate food. When she did this there would be a commotion and shouts of disgust. Haredi women have little contact with animals. There are no pets in their homes; they fear dogs and are repulsed by cats. They do not watch television or see movies or books with pictures that would give them any familiarity with the animal world. For them, the description of worms was a little like a trip to the zoo.

In the dynamic that was created among the women, no possible method of examining foods for pests was rejected. In other words, the methods were not subject to an unambiguous critical process. Notably, the main speakers were the older women who had from five to ten years of experience as housewives. The young newlyweds and the mothers of one or two children took less vocal a part in the discussion and often talked among themselves about what was being said in the central discussion. Hannah and Rachel, who were considered to be stricter on many matters, expressed extreme and rigorous opinions that at first elicited silence or astonishment, but afterwards led to private conversations among those present.

On the emotional level, the women exhibited a certain anxiety.

"I was afraid to throw it away, but I didn't know what to do." "In cauliflower, really?" "You're really frightening me." "You haven't heard anything yet." "But it would take you forever to use that sifter all the time." "Don't trust anything with your eyes closed." "Maybe it's better to fast."

Technical acts that the women performed mechanically were presented as criteria of their piety and their status as homemakers. This was a powerful combination. No one could take lightly a law or responsibility connected with her management of her home. So the flies in the lettuce and the worms in the cauliflower became monsters. The public dimension of the lesson required some of the women to testify that they acted properly (Hannah, Rachel), allowed others the opportunity to ask or remain silent, and reestablished the lines of behavior for them all. Malka Shamir, the ba'alat teshuva, did not participate. But during the afternoons, over the fences, she heard about the class. At the end of the third lesson, when we were on the way back to Hannah's house, we ran into her at her habitual place by the fence. She said:

> Hey, from what I heard from the girls, from today on you're going
> to stop eating lettuce, parsley, and cauliflower, and you're taking the
> onions out of the soup and won't buy strawberries in season.

Shoshana, Minda, Tsipi, and I laughed quietly. Hannah looked at Malka and responded, "Stop eating? God forbid, we just know what to watch out for." '

The class on worms ended after the third lesson. The discussion at the last lesson was mostly about continuing the meetings and what subjects should be discussed. Varda said that she thought they should have a lesson about gossip and slander. The women said that if she wanted one, she should prepare it. Varda retreated. Tsipi thought it would be good to learn laws of the Sabbath. She would be willing to prepare it, but she needed a little more time. The women raised no "substance" subjects. They did not suggest studying Bible, topics in ethics, Jewish philosophy, or Jewish history.

Varda's proposal that the women study the rules about gossip and slander would be repeated several times, but was never taken up. I believe that the women were reluctant to confront such a subject in a small and intimate community. Each time a unit was completed and gossip and slander were again suggested as topics, everyone agreed that it was an important subject, but no one was willing to prepare it. After Nava finished her three lessons on worms, Hannah took it upon herself to prepare a set of lessons on the laws of dining.

The Lessons on the Laws of Dining

The first lesson on the laws of dining was held in the middle of June, as had been decided at the end of the lessons on worms. Hannah, who had suggested the subject, was the teacher. Eleven women gathered at Ahuva Graetz's well-kept home. Sari and Hedvi, Ahuva's young daughters, were still awake and peeked out at us from the end of the hallway. Sari's hair was in two long braids, while little Hedvi's hair was full of coal-black curls. Ahuva asked them gently to go to their room. Pretty soon, she said, Daddy will come to say good night. The girls went to their room and Hannah began.

> The Torah contains no source for the washing of the hands before meals. The source is in the words of our sages, who say it dates from the reign of King Solomon and his court of law. Anyone who disobeys the laws of the sages is considered dead. Why did King Solomon decree the washing of hands? It began with the holiness of the priests, with the building of the Temple, during the time that terumot and ma'aserot [the tithes given to the priests, Levites, and the poor] were received. Then, to impress holiness on the people, the whole nation was commanded to wash hands, and so they prevented defiling acts with the priests. Solomon was unique among our sages in his wisdom, because unlike them he did not prohibit but permitted. He permitted anyone who had washed to come into contact with the priests.

Varda, who was called "Jerusalemite" because she came from that city, was considered an intelligent young woman. She was married to a successful avrech.

Varda: So what are we saying really, what's the connection between washing and impurity. I think you're bringing laws of impurity, and that, my husband told me, is not a subject for women.

Hannah: Do you think that didn't bother me? I studied by myself for the lesson—my husband isn't at home, so I sent my Binyomin downstairs with a note for Lichtenbaum, asking if he could answer a question for me. I thought, if someone like me sent a note to my husband, he would agree. And he in fact sent an answer with Binyomin that it was all right. I went down with two of the children. He listened to what I asked, and answered me while he looked at the bookshelves. [Hannah smiled and blushed.]

He in fact suggested not to go into that, but said, without going any further, that King Solomon wanted to accustom the people to the laws of purity, because up until then there hadn't been a Temple, only laws, and the people were not accustomed to it. Instead of telling only a part of them to keep the laws of purity, and then the priests would have had to keep separate from part of the people and not accept their tithes, he brought all the nation into the rule. That's what Lichtenbaum told me.

Varda accepted the answer and relaxed until her next question. Her questions caught my attention, and I began to observe her special role in the lesson's dynamic. In the meantime, Hannah continued to describe the source of hand washing. Towards the end of the lesson one of the women asked that the next meeting start a half-hour later, because it was hard for her to get organized.

Minda: My husband is willing to put the children to bed and also to give supper to our son who comes home late with him from evening prayers, but I'd still like it to be later. He wants me to go to classes, but I'd feel better if we made it a little later.

Varda: My husband asks at the synagogue if there is a class for me. Yes, yes, he finds out for me, because I never know if there's a lesson, or if it's been put off or canceled. He keeps up on it for me.

The next lesson began later, but not because Minda's request had been granted. Someone had heard that the Israeli women's magazine *La'isha* had printed an article on haredi women. According to rumor, the article said that haredi women bought their clothes in Paris, and that each of them had a $500 wig, and that they spent hours in beauty clinics.

Devorah, who styled wigs at home, had seen the magazine and reported:

She had her picture in the magazine in short sleeves and a denim skirt. She's divorced and her children were taken into a Gur heder just because of her father, who wanted to keep them, her father is a Gur Hasid. They went to one beauty parlor and spoke with whomever they met there and wrote about it in the magazine. Afterwards all the secular will say that those religious people are rich, and they just pretend to be poor so that the government will give them money.

Tsipi looked at me and asked: "So, what did they think about this article?"

I pretended as if I did not realize that the question had been put to me. A commotion of private conversations continued among the women, until Shoshana got up the courage to ask:

"Tami, you must have seen the article. What do you say?"

I said that I had run into it, but that it had not appeared in *La'isha* but in the women's supplement to the daily newspaper, *Yediot Aharonot.*

Anyone who knew anything about newspapers, I said, would know enough to put it in the proper perspective.

The written word, so strong in secular society, has immense power for haredi women. They feel that when someone has "written about them" that it means that they are again being stereotyped. They think (with no small measure of justice) that the next secular person they meet will cite the article as evidence against them. Even if my evasive answer did not satisfy or calm them, the women grew quiet and Hannah was able to begin.

> Today we will talk about hand-washing itself. It is a commandment that the sages gave us, yet the blessing we make that God commanded us to do it. What has he commanded us? It's from the sages, after all. But we base ourselves on the verse "Thou shalt not deviate from the sentence which they shall tell thee" [Deut. 17:11]. That is the basis for all the commandments that come from the sages.

Then Hannah explained how one washes the hands—with what water, with what vessel, before which meal, and so on. Even though all the women present had been washing their hands upon awaking and before meals even before they could turn on a faucet, Hannah was interrupted frequently. The women presented methods of washing that were different from what Hannah said was correct. They told how they washed, how their husbands washed, and how they saw it done in their parents' home. The most important comment, which held up the whole lesson, was on whether it was permitted to hold the vessel at a slant, so that it simultaneously filled up and poured water on the hands. On this issue no consensus was reached. Some of the women claimed that it was forbidden and that the filling of the cup should be halted while it was being emptied over the hands; the rest said it was permitted.

Miri: I never saw my husband do it that way.

Varda: My whole life I've seen my father hold the cup at a slant and wash from it—I can't even imagine any other way.

Hannah: I'm saying what I read in Pele Yo'etz [a digest of Jewish law], and of course I don't want to make rulings. That's what it says. Everyone should ask at home, that's why we learn, so we can know what to ask.

Tsipi: It's easy to say "no." The question is whether you can say "yes." That's the way it is with the Hasidim. What applies is what each one saw at home. Even if you don't know why, it's bigger than we are.

Hannah: I've already heard from the other side. My husband came home on Friday night from the synagogue and said that a few husbands had come up to him and asked what was going on at our class. So I want to be doubly careful. Each of you should ask at home.

There were four more meetings on the laws of dining. The subjects were the blessing over bread, the issue of what [rings, nail polish] is considered to prevent the complete washing of the hands, the quality of the water for washing, washing the hands while traveling or away from home, and the minimum amount of food over which a blessing should be recited. For each lesson, Hannah presented the appropriate law, its meaning, and examples from daily life connected to the law. The lessons lasted longer than anticipated because of the animated participation of some of the women. There were always comments, examples that conflicted with the ones Hannah presented, and challenges to the method she presented as standard. At the beginning of each meeting some of the women presented their husbands' reactions to the subjects discussed in the previous lesson. One entire lesson was devoted to answering a question raised by Orly, a ba'alat teshuva who lived in the Development.

> *Tsipi:* I checked with my husband about what you said, and he thinks that if your parents don't want to make a blessing on food except for bread that you shouldn't say anything to them. Embarrassing them is worse.

> *Hannah:* I remember one woman in Bene Brak who used to come to eat lunch with us every week. She was poor. My mother wouldn't ask her to make a blessing. After a long time, when she kept coming, my mother would ask her to repeat after her—*Baruch—Baruch—ata—ata*. So my sister and I used to call her "Baruch Baruch." We'd tell my mother, "Mommy, Baruch Baruch is here."

> *Orly:* But a week ago you said that it's the responsibility of the host, who is serving the meal, to see that everyone makes the blessing. So what's more important?

> *Hannah:* I can't tell you what's more important. All I can tell you is what we do. You should talk to your husband or whoever you need to talk to and decide.

(During the period of more than two years in which I was a frequent visitor to Hannah's house and ate many different kinds of meals there, she never once asked me to make a blessing.)

ॐ

Hannah, with her special and unconventional position in the community, presented the original legal precepts on which the specific laws under study were based. At times the lesson turned into an attempt to teach the sources of the laws, both those based on commandments from the sages and those based on explicit commandments in the Torah. The transition between the substantial and practical—that is, between the study of the law and the explanation of how to carry it out—was not easy. Hannah encountered resistance every time she went from the substance into the action derived from it. In contrast with the lessons on pests in foods, the discussions during Hannah's classes were not only over which of the women was a better or more observant housewife. Here there was a different struggle—over which of them were as observant as necessary. Hannah touched a deep and sensitive chord, so it was not at all surprising that it stirred even the husbands. It was not the subject that led to the agitation; it was Hannah's attempt to present only one custom as correct. All those present, except for the three ba'alot teshuva, came from Gur homes, and it is reasonable to assume that they were well-versed in ritual, including hand-washing and the blessing over bread. Yet there was no consensus in the room. The women did not question the necessity of washing their hands, but they did challenge the alternatives that Hannah presented as binding custom.

When one of the participants in the class on worms suggested that worms could be removed by washing or by hunting them down, there was no argument. The participants could accept one of the suggestions proposed or stick to their own custom. But at Hannah's class they seemed to feel that what they considered "true," unambiguous, and holy was under challenge. Judaism allows a wide variation of custom among its believers, and it has institutionalized ways of determining which customs are acceptable and which are not. Hannah presented (though with great caution) a single custom, making others doubt themselves. When it came to substance, Hannah was not part of the new literacy, but the discussion she led touched on a new type of literacy, a type that is not entirely legitimate for women. She delved into the subject and could no longer get out. She brought to the room the uncomfortable feeling that, when it comes down to it, every Jew has a different Judaism, and that in such cases, it is difficult to speak of an absolute truth.

Varda and Tsipi attacked her from their positions as literate women married to successful avrechim. They (and others) validated their defense tactics as follows:

I think you're bringing laws of impurity, and that, my *husband* told me, is not a subject for women.

My whole life I've seen my *father* . . .

I never saw my *husband* do it that way.

They said at *college* . . .

Apparently, Hannah also knew what she was getting into, and so made a point of saying that she was quoting from the literature, and that she had asked her neighbor, a proctor at the yeshiva, and her husband.

During the meetings the women made a point of mentioning that, despite the discomfort and the disputes rising out of the class, their husbands were following what went on in the classes and had consented to their participation.

"My husband is willing to put the children to bed"; "My husband asks at the synagogue if there is a class for me." The matter exploded somewhere between the power struggles that to a certain extent dramatized the paradox of studying for ignorance, and the approach to the male style of disputational study. Hannah retreated and did not strive to admonish or preach—as the teachers of the Psalms did, for instance. She left the question open. She herself was now wiser, as she testified:

> I won't give any more classes in the Development. It exhausted me. All those questions from the husbands. One makes one face, another makes another face—I'd rather teach the ba'alot teshuva in the next neighborhood—there they come to listen, not to lecture.

The last of the "practical" lessons was Tsipi's. As she had promised after the lesson on worms, she taught the laws of the Sabbath.

The Lessons on the Laws of the Sabbath

At the end of summer vacation, after a short break needed by the women to return their homes to a school footing, the class on the laws of the Sabbath began. This time seventeen women gathered at the home of Devorit, a Sepharadi ba'alat teshuva. Devorit came from a traditional family in the adjacent neighborhood. After her marriage, she and her husband decided to become more observant, so they moved into the Development. For the time being they lived in a rented apartment. Three young Sepharadi women had attended Hannah's classes on the laws of dining, as a result of their personal ties with Hannah. Sensing that they had been welcomed into the Gur women's framework, Devorit felt herself ready to invite the group to her home. The invitation was accepted warmly.

Tsipi was noticeably pregnant. A year ago she had married, she was teaching at the Gur Beit Ya'akov college in Bene Brak, and she was considered to be "a serious young woman." She spoke rapidly and tended to swallow her words. Enthusiastic and cheerful, she was always surrounded by her married friends from the college, who had come to live in the Development.

> As you know, we have decided to learn the laws of the Sabbath. Most of the girls here have graduated from the Beit Ya'akov college

and have grown up, thank God, in good homes. Everyone knows the laws of the Sabbath. So why study them anyway? It is said that whoever does not study can be sure that the Sabbath will not pass without a violation. But we do not study in order to make rulings, that's for men, and I want that to be clear, because it came up during Nava's class on worms and also during Hannah's class on the laws of dining. We are learning so that we will know what to ask.

Today we will talk about the basic actions forbidden on Shabbat. These were derived from the thirty-nine types of action described in the construction of the Ark of the Covenant. This derivation was made because in the Torah the description of how the Ark was built comes right next to the laws of the Sabbath. These labors were done in honor of the *Shekhina* [God's presence] and on Shabbat, when the Shekhina is with us, pervades us, there is no reason to do them. Each of these basic actions includes several other actions, that are borne from them.

Shoshi: What do you mean "borne"? Excuse me for interrupting, I've never heard that expression before, excuse me, what do you mean "borne from"?

Tsipi: I said that we're learning so that we can ask, so you can ask questions. You're correct. It is what comes out of the action, what is borne from it, connected to and similar to it. We'll begin with one of the basic acts: sorting. I'm teaching from my notebook on the laws of the Sabbath from college. Just as it was conveyed to me, I'm conveying it to you.

Minda: And if we saw differently at home?

Tsipi: In Hasidism, what you see at home is what you do. They say there's a little synagogue in Bene Brak where, when the avrechim enter, they bend over a bit. No one asks why, they just bend over. They think it's the custom of those Hasidim. What does it turn out to be? In Poland, in the synagogue they had there, there was a low entrance and they would bend over, so they continue to bend over here, too. That's the way it is.

The act of sorting is to separate food from refuse. If I want to take oranges out of a bowl and there are grapefruit there, too, the oranges are the food and the grapefruit are the refuse. You are permitted to take the oranges out of the bowl if you meet three conditions: food, by hand, immediately. That means that you take out what you want to eat, with your hand and not with an implement, and you eat it now and not later.

There was an uproar in the room. The women began talking among themselves, some quietly and some loudly. The point of contention was the word "refuse."

Rachel: What do you mean, "refuse"? Grapefruit aren't refuse, they're food, too. If you want to eat the grapefruit afterwards, and they're already refuse, how can you eat it?

Tsipi: If you want the grapefruit, then it's food, and whatever else is in the bowl is the refuse.

Rachel: I don't understand, how can it be food one time and refuse the next time. Why call it refuse?

The women try to solve the puzzle among themselves; the discussion takes place in an unorganized way between each woman and her neighbor, with those who think they have understood trying to explain.

Hannah: It's like the primary and the secondary. It's not hard to understand. Sometimes the primary thing can be the oranges, and other times it's the grapefruit.

Varda: So it can be, for instance, if you're eating fish, you take the meat off with your hands and leave the bones in your plate. I've seen people put the whole fish in their mouth and take the bones out of their mouth, what do you say about that?

Tsipi: Varda, what do you want from me, to give you an answer I have to think, and I don't want to think. Ask your husband what to do. I'm telling you what I learned, what they told me at college and what I wrote here in my notebook.

Malka, the ba'alat teshuva, throws me a little smile, as if to say, "Just look at them!" She says: "What's there to understand, what's so complicated about it? They're not saying that the grapefruit is refuse, and your example, Varda, isn't a good one, because the bones really are refuse that you throw away. Tsipi is talking about sorting, when you sort what you want from what you don't want. It's only *as if* at that moment that you want the oranges that the grapefruit are *like* refuse. It's not for real, it's as if."

The lesson was halted for ten minutes and the women continued to struggle with the practical definition of refuse and food, explaining, giving examples, trying to portray refuse in a positive context. It was very difficult for them to take in. They could not accept the word "refuse." When Tsipi finally managed to take control again, she went on to a different type of sorting.

When you eat watermelon, for instance, you really are taking refuse out of the food, and there it's like what Varda said, you put it all in your mouth and spit out the seeds.

Nava: On Friday, before Shabbat, if you have time, you can take out the seeds and cut it up and put it in a closed container, or you can buy the kind without seeds.

"Sure, take the seeds out for a family of ten," laughed Rivka.
Nava, who had been married for a year and was still not pregnant, blushed and fell silent.

Tsipi: Remember the main thing. In Hasidism we don't want to exhaust ourselves while we're eating. You have to obey the law but not go overboard. If you eat and enjoy, that's more to God's liking than if you lose your appetite over the laws.

Nehama: Why get yourself into trouble, you can have a Shabbat without watermelon.

Hannah: That's what you think? Then maybe we shouldn't study at all, so we won't get into trouble. Is that better?

Devorit rose and signaled Tsipi that it was 10:00 P.M. Tsipi promised to pick up where she left off next time. The next Tuesday, same time, same place.
In the two following lessons Tsipi insisted on order and the meetings went smoothly. In the middle of the last meeting the discussion centered on actions carried out by others (non-Jews or secular Jews). Tsipi emphasized that even if someone else performed the forbidden action, the action had been done and that was in and of itself contempt for the holiness of the Sabbath.

Varda: That brings us back again to the debate over the private generator and the battery and timer. I don't have the patience for that argument again. [Varda is referring to the dispute over whether religious Jews may use electricity from the electric company, which employs Jews on the Sabbath.]

Tsipi: That's not the argument, everyone acts according to their custom and both sides can cite authorities in their favor. We have our limitations, and we should get as little as possible into those things.

Yochi: Things you know there's a dispute about shouldn't be brought up. We're one group and there are enough things that are the same for all of us.

Tsipi: I don't want to cause a dispute. I said at the beginning that we're studying to know what to ask, not to make rulings for ourselves.

The lesson on the laws of the Sabbath led me to study women's literacy in the Gur community. I knew that the laws and precepts of the Sabbath were not an unfamiliar or marginal subject in their world. On the average, each of the women present had lived through 1,400 Sabbaths. Just as with the laws of dining and even the class on worms, the Sabbath was a familiar matter that they had already studied in other educational frameworks. Although questions had been raised during the lessons on other subjects, those voiced in this class were so insistent that they signalled the researcher that this was where the treasure was to be found.

At first it seemed to me that the women were unable to engage in pure cognitive thinking—that they could not draw parallels, think in the abstract, reach conclusions. When Tsipi asked that they think of fruit as refuse, there was an uproar. Even Malka thought that their ability to think was limited, and clarified the matter for them in a way that expressed a certain sense of superiority or scorn. But in fact the discussion in the room was about the issue of validity, about the need for and implications of abstract thinking, "substantial" thinking about the life of women.

Tsipi says: "I said at the beginning that we're studying to know what to ask, not to make rulings for ourselves."

"I'm teaching from my notebook on the laws of the Sabbath from the college. Just as it was conveyed to me, I'm conveying it to you."

"In Hasidism, what you see at home is what you do."

"What do you want from me, to give you an answer I have to think, and I don't want to think."

"Ask your husband what to do. I'm telling you what I learned, what they told me at college and what I wrote here in my notebook."

"I don't want to cause a dispute. I said at the beginning that we're studying to know what to ask, not to make rulings for ourselves."

She says this, and teaches, while the women say:

Nehama: Why get yourself into trouble.

Varda: That brings us back again to the debate over the private generator and the battery and timer. I don't have the patience for that argument again.

Hannah: Then maybe we shouldn't study at all, so we won't get into trouble. Is that better?

They say this, yet come to the class.

Women may now study "substance," but they are unsure whether to do so. This uncertainty is a product of the reality in which they live, and that they accept as a part of a package deal. The education that the women have received, and that they reproduce in the little free time that they have, is avowedly directed towards action and not towards thought. Kindergarten and school are supposed to teach girls how to behave. The best curriculum (quoted above from *Marveh Latsameh*) is one focused on behavioral instructions. The ideal woman is portrayed as being of good values, of simple faith, an exemplary mother and wife, benevolent. In the official educational frameworks, study for the purpose of inquiry and speculation, of understanding the source of the law, of delving into the various interpretations of the Bible, is considered negative and dangerous. Tsipi's answer to Varda during the class on the Sabbath sums this up: "Varda, what do you want from me? To give you an answer I have to think, and I don't want to think. Ask your husband."

Does Tsipi not want to think, or is she unable to think? Or maybe she thinks that she certainly can think, but if she thinks, she will change her perspective, will find her worldview challenged, will find herself questioning the social situation that she has accepted as axiomatic. If that is what Tsipi thinks, why in fact should she think? But the real question is, Is she capable of not thinking?

In all three of the classes described, the woman conveying the lesson declared that the class was not intended to make the women into arbiters of Jewish law. Not a single one of the women thinks to herself that after the lesson on the laws of the Sabbath she will be able to make decisions for herself. Even males who study do not presume to hand down rulings on legal issues; for that purpose there are rabbis and scholars. There are two other reasons for opening the meeting with the sentence "We are learning in order to know what to ask and not to know what to answer": (1) to emphasize to the audience that in this place, in this class, everyone subscribes to the reality in which it is not women's role to think, and (2) to approach the world of thinking and inquiry, notwithstanding reason 1.

The women's public pledge (to each other, and collectively to their community) is a ritual that upholds their community's definition of their status, yet simultaneously gives them the opportunity to refashion this definition. It is important to emphasize that this is not a pro forma statement that in fact allows them to do the forbidden. Declaring their intellectual limitations is not a cynical or conscious act meant to release them from their public obligations and to allow them to engage in forbidden activity. By emphasizing the limitations of their thinking and action, and by attempting to approach the boundaries that define these limitations, they give expression to the complexity of their existential state. The central axis of this existential state is a paradox, and it is the thread that winds through every segment of their lives. These haredi women, perhaps like all haredi women, live their lives in complete accord with their station, yet engage in unceasing attempts to comprehend this situation anew. The

great current of Jewish tradition, the structure of the Jewish religious community, and their conservative education sweep them along. Alongside
roars the river of modern times, of this place, and of the people around
them. And they try to keep their heads above water.

Through ethnography, anthropology attempts to describe the "how,"
i.e., how women try to correlate the system of study to a social state
through pragmatization, and how they use the curriculum to simultaneously create and validate their worldview. It may be that the lessons
described here answer this question. To clarify it further I will sum up the
essence of the social process that occurs during study, and its implications
for the status of the haredi woman.

Dual Literacy

The curriculum for women's study has been described as fitting the social
reality in which the women live. Status-wise, women who study are seen as
a group whose access to the society's important resources, such as decision-
making, political influence, and socioeconomic representation, is limited.
Unlike other similar groups, such as minorities, the lower classes, and ethnic groups, the social reality in which these women live does not nullify
their social status. Orthodoxy does not present the status of women as inferior, as in need of change or improvement. It is, rather, a "separate" status,
different and complementary to that of the men. The women, for their
part, accept this status a priori. As a result there is correlation between the
curriculum, which culturally describes and reproduces this status, and
the social reality.

I have already noted that studies of education and literacy made
among socially disadvantaged groups have found a large gap between the
curriculum and the social state of the students. This gap created tension
and alienation between the students and the curriculum, the teachers representing it, and the culture on which it is founded. In the case of study
among haredi women, there is integrated and coordinated action. The
women identify with the material under study and with the teachers (who
become objects of admiration and models to be imitated), and retroactively
reinforce their a priori acceptance of their social state. This, without a
doubt, is the ideal model for their education.

But this is complicated by the fact that they live within a Jewish society where the majority is not orthodox, and in a democratic country with
an open and competitive cultural market. It presents a challenge to the
ideal model.

Their actual, as opposed to idealized, study was observed in five classes
and is summarized below.

1. *The teacher*. All the classes were given by prominent figures in the community, people who belong to the "upper stratum" of religiosity. In three cases, this status was an institutionalized one: that of Rabbi Wolf, Rabbanit Wachter and her sister, and the young college teachers (Nava and Tsipi) married to promising avrechim. Hannah, who is not a teacher, won high status in the Development and the community as a whole because she is seen as being particularly observant. In such a case, any act of the reproduction of knowledge involving values and norms is carried out by central figures in the community identified with the content of the studies. There can be no study involving the presentation of conflicting contents, deviant personalities, or alternatives. If the community of women invites a woman teacher who does not fall into this definition, she would be a ba'alat teshuva (such as Alona Einstein, the wife of an Israeli rock star, who was invited to the adjacent neighborhood by a group of ba'alot teshuva), and in such a case only a small group of women from the Development go to hear her. The haredi women refrain from going on the grounds that they "have nothing to hear there." A new immigrant from Russia was invited to speak to an Agudat Yisrael–sponsored summer camp for mothers of large families. She was not a classic example of the type of teacher generally sought out for this audience, but she impressed them with her tale about life for Jews in her country of birth, and the lengths to which they went to keep the commandments. The women's learning society does not deliberate on its values by comparing them with those of other groups or (even in a didactic way) by confronting them with challenges. During their study, the women are exposed to positive examples meant to promote social reproduction without any circumvention or ingenuity.

2. *Validity*. The male teacher refers to the sources and to the comments of commentators and sages, but does not attribute his words to any external authority. He does not say, for instance, "They taught me at yeshiva that . . ."; "My father used to tell me that . . ."; or "My wife told me that . . .". He cites the sources to make his points, and uses them to explain or illuminate his teaching. The women, in contrast, make a point of citing the source of their knowledge: sages, judges, husbands, the *Pele Yo'etz* (Hannah), the teachings of home and college (Tsipi). This is done not to be informative, but to be sanctioned, to provide external validation for their words. In doing so, they accomplish three purposes:

   a. They present themselves as women who cannot themselves validate the knowledge they impart; they can only "convey" a lesson, not "give" one.
   b. They present the information they "convey" as absolute.
   c. They ascribe greater weight to the teachers of knowledge than to the knowledge itself.

Rabbi Wolf selects from the sources what he believes, to his under-standing, to be appropriate. The women who hear him sense that this is his personal interpretation, based on direct access to the material ("I have a horrible headache"; "I'm not used to learning the yekke way"). The women give the feeling that the teacher conveys the student the truth, that the material is factual rather than interpretational. This inclination has a great effect on pragmatization—education for action, not thought, a subject I will address presently.

3. *Material.* The two "substance" classes were given by external teach-ers. It would seem that when the women of the Development want to hear abstract lessons dealing with faith, values, or Jewish wisdom, they do not trust themselves. When they organize their own classes and they must choose a subject, they head directly for the laws, the practical. The incli-nation for practical education, which I have defined as education for igno-rance, recognizes the complexity of the world of substance for the women. What takes place in the room during a class, whether it deals with the abstract or the real, is an excellent expression of the women's awareness of the encounter between orthodoxy and all that is outside it.

4. *The women's reaction.* In order to understand the women's reaction, the reasons behind it, and its implications, it is necessary to remember that the women's "substance" lessons are associated with a "practical" comment (whether it is given by a woman after the rabbi has gone, or whether the teacher herself adds it at the end of the lesson). Besides the discussion of the laws themselves, the "practical" lessons include a varied and content-rich discourse that examines subjects such as the level of the women's observance and homemaking skills, differing traditions within the Gur community, and even (in camouflaged form) justifications for women's lit-eracy. The result is that the women (at the initiative of the teacher or at their own initiative) broadened the educational event that exists at one pole and stretch it towards the other. At first the impression is that prac-ticality reigns, i.e., that the "substance" lessons are always anchored with a "practical" addition that in turn becomes the center of the lesson and its main experience (such as Shifra's "few words" at Rabbi Wolf's lesson, or the laws taught by the sisters at the lesson on the Psalms). The descent from the level of values to the level of behavior does, in fact, bring the women much relief. They have been taught to aspire to the practical and the relevant, and to treat this norm like reflectors along a busy and dan-gerous road.

The sense of strength and gratification that they receive from the ser-monizing lessons on Jewish law grows out of routine and a longing for guid-ance. But the interesting thing is that in the lessons on laws that they organize on their own, there is a discussion of substance in matters that go beyond the program they have determined for themselves. In fact, the dis-cussion of these laws is not new to them. The teacher does not intend to "attack the law from a new direction," because this is not an acceptable program in haredi education; nor does she intend to lead an in-depth, disputational study of the law, in the style of Gemara study, because such study is forbidden for her and she is not to be trusted with it. In going over laws they know, the women seem to be conducting study on two levels. The first level is one that reproduces their social situation, a situation that they accept a priori, and gives it deeper meaning. They reproduce their culture in the same way that men at study do, but unlike them, when women are asked to think they drowse off, waking only for the section considered appropriate for them as Hasidic women. When the teacher speaks of the essence of faith, they do not follow the text. There is no discussion, no discourse, no raising of conflicting contents; the women accept their position in the community completely and passively.

On another level they are carrying out negotiations over their very existence. They examine themselves from outside. At the Psalms class there were some women who did not remain passive—they tested the boundary between the abstract and the practical. Nava asked up to what point they were allowed to stretch this boundary of inquiry and abstraction, in order to know how to teach others. Ita presented watching one's tongue as a form of divine worship by practical behavior. The borders of the substantial and the practical were raised for a contained and controlled discussion, but I could sense that the women in the room were experiencing a troubling complexity touching on their view of themselves. Whether or not it was comfortable for them to present themselves as ignorant, as "conveyers," as those who heard at home and so reported, they were confused, they thought, and sometimes they doubted.

When they remained among themselves, in lessons that took place in the Development, this other level came to the fore. The lesson on worms was at times a parody of the laws under study. The women stretched the confines of obeying the law to an extreme that revealed it as ridiculous. True, they were quick to relate how they solved various problems and showed off their talents as housewives, but the hysterical laughter at the description of the various kinds of worms, the comments about "so we'll stop eating strawberries" and "who needs cauliflower" sometimes overrode their ability to get the worms out of the onion or the maggots out of a package of flour. During the class on the laws of dining, the women conducted a penetrating discussion of the boundaries of the permitted and forbidden in women's literacy. The regular opening presented at all of the lessons, seeking legitimacy for women's studies in general, was broadened in this case into a real discussion. The dialogue between Hannah and Nava, the defenses each of them raised for their learning, and the slide into a debate over the value of tradition in Hasidism added a significant element of flexibility to this knowledge. Instead of knowledge presented as "objective" and "true," there was knowledge subjected to social interpretation and negotiation.

The lesson on the laws of the Sabbath could be stripped of the practical level to reveal that it really contained a discussion of the meaning of women's literacy. On the face of it, the discussion was about the major categories of actions forbidden on the Sabbath, but it included questions like: Why should I think? How do I know what I know? What kind of logic am I permitted to use, and what kind am I capable of using? What is the connection between what I know and what I can do? Such a discussion is not part of what the haredi woman accepts a priori. It is as close as this framework allows to confusion and doubt—close to academic literacy, male literacy, secular literacy.

The women maintain, therefore, a dual literacy. "Know-how literacy" is relevant to their existence as haredi women in what would seem to be a total and authoritative framework. This literacy supplies them with the information and tools they need to live in their world. "Knowledge literacy" is relevant to their lives as highly literate women, aware of what is going on around them inside their community and outside it as well, and partial partners in the social reality of Israel and the world. This literacy allows them, from time to time, to look at themselves and their society from a certain distance.

The constant movement between these two levels of literacy takes place in every educational event. It aids the integration of the meaningful but diverse realities they consistently confront, and allows them to decipher these realities and live within them in relative tranquility.

Women's literacy was promoted and institutionalized in the face of a threat to orthodoxy's very existence. Women study from the age of five to the age of twenty in institutional frameworks, and continue to be educated in informal frameworks from that age onward. They are literate. With the strengthening of orthodoxy and the fostering of the "learning society," their scholarship constitutes a threat to the desire to recreate the "isolationist" or "separatist" community that will be described below. This is a community that separates itself from others similar to it (such as other religious groups) and shapes itself to be the opposite of the secular Jewish community.

Women's education has become an irrevocable fact, so it is presented on an ideological level as "education for ignorance." But the ethnography reveals that the women use their literate ignorance as a conscious, emotional, and social means of living as educated Jewish women. In this way, this two-layered literacy allows women to live with the contradictions inherent in being educated and ignorant.

Notes

1. Sociologists who have written about the emphasis on study among Jewish men argue that the phenomenon should be understood as "making Judaism." Study

is more important as a social construction of Judaism than as an activity for the attainment of knowledge. See Heilman 1976, 1983, 1984; Helmreich 1982; Boyarin 1989.

2. It should be noted that the women of the Development spoke of "conveying" (*limsor*) a lesson rather than "giving" (*le'ha'avir*) a lesson. The use of "conveying" is significant—the teacher is seen as passing on the lesson, without making any changes in it. Just as the Avot tractate of the Mishna says that Moses conveyed the Torah to Joshua, who conveyed it on in a chain of succession until it reached the sages, so the teacher presents herself (and is accepted by her audience as someone who is) conveying knowledge rather than creating, improvising, or innovating it.

3. Many sociological and anthropological studies of education describe this phenomenon. Three examples are Dumont and Was 1967; Backs 1972; Mclaren 1989.

4. Freire and Macedo 1987; Heilman 1983.

5. In terms of program this is a comparison of two dissimilars—Gemara and Psalms. The comparison here is based on the ritual aspect and on the event's cultural configuration.

6. Heilman compares two types of study, which illuminate both the instances under discussion and the concept of literacy. "Learning" is a process of study to attain a certain piece of knowledge. Lernen (a Yiddish word) is study for the sake of study, and a reproduction of culture.

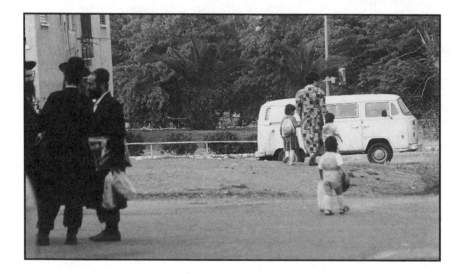

4

· · · ❧ · · ·

"Make Thy Way Straight Before Me"

Paradoxes and Social Boundaries

Literacy, women, and the haredi community in Israel are the three sides of this study's theoretical triangle. The connection between literacy and women stands at the center, with the haredi community connecting them. The linkage between literacy and women in haredi society is a paradoxical one: women are educated to maintain their ignorance. The sociological significance of this paradox in the community and among its women lies in the tension between the rich, varied, multifarious social reality of non-haredi Israeli culture of the 1980s and a community that is trying to remain homogeneous. The purpose of educating haredi women is to give them bodies of knowledge that will help them discern a single voice in the cacophony of modern society. As we have seen, however, the very act of gathering for study, even under these conditions, enables them to listen to a whole range of voices—even if they themselves continue to hum the desired tune. The haredim have constructed an educational system for women because there is no need to teach women, and the women have learned to be educated in ignorance in order to survive as educated women.

The educational process is supposed to grade a bumpy, potholed reality, making it smooth and easy to navigate. This exemplifies the way the haredi community deals with a whole range of paradoxes it faces: it strips them down into their individual components and compresses them into a single dimension. In the case of women's literacy, however, the way out of one paradox throws the community into another. The issue of women's literacy throws light on the social, conceptual, and value context of the haredi community as a whole and thus reveals other internal contradictions.

This model of behavior is not unique to the field of scholarship; it envelops the haredi community on all sides. This is because the haredi community, as a part of modern society, is open to outside stimuli that continually challenge it and force it into a constant reexamination of the content of its world. During the course of this reexamination, paradoxes

135

emerge that create incongruity between values and behavior that cannot be left unresolved.

As a result, the community creates social mechanisms to handle these challenges. From these it is possible to learn how the community constructs its social boundaries. The process of escaping the paradox can shed light on the symbolic, intellectual, and practical structure of the world of meanings in the society under study. This reveals the "social boundaries," which are not generally studied through the resolution of contradictions. I propose it as a new research method.

Two Worlds

Researchers who adopt a positivist approach[1] are interested in the functional question, How does the Jewish community succeed in preserving its separate existence when it has the option of assimilating into its surroundings? One wonders how medieval Jews were able to preserve their distinctiveness despite the restrictions, prohibitions, and persecutions they suffered; in this age the question is the reverse. Today one asks, How is it that the fall of the ghetto walls has not affected this part of Jewish society?[2]

These studies show that Jews who choose to maintain their orthodox lifestyle establish boundaries between themselves and their surroundings. They dress differently, preserve their own internal language, send their children to separate schools, eat different food, and so on. Deciphering this separatist existence leads to a study of the "social institutions": the family, the school, the synagogue, and the economic enterprises.

These studies, which assume the existence of social boundaries, set out to solve "the riddle of traditional existence within modernity" by recognizing the nature of the boundary and studying the way it is strengthened. According to them, orthodox Jews are in fact a unique phenomenon in modern society. In order to preserve their religion and the customs of their forefathers, while becoming a part of the economic and civil life of their surroundings, they create special tools for themselves. These tools allow them to control the extent of their approach to and distance from the surroundings, while exploiting to the maximum the link with this environment.

A Single But Complex World

The other trend in the study of social boundaries is based on a symbolic and phenomenological sociological approach,[3] and deals with the subject of social boundaries in a completely different way. The "social compound" in these studies is not a given whose character is to be studied, but rather a part of the unknown that the research is meant to discover. The questions that are raised include the following: Does a social boundary exist? How are cultural differences between one group of people and another created?

What are the social contents that fuel the act of constructing boundaries? How is it possible to discern the existence of a social boundary? What is the dynamic of moving, dismantling, eliminating, and recreating these boundaries?

This inevitably leads into the thematic world of the group under study: the way in which people work out the meaning of their social existence, how they arrange the phenomenal world, what their intersubjective interpretation of their experience of existence is, and what the implications are of this interpretation in their daily lives.

The three most prominent social researchers who have used this method in an attempt to understand Jewish uniqueness in the modern age are Shlomo Deshen, Shmuel Heilman, and Menachem Friedman.[4] For all intents and purposes, their conclusions nullify the contrast between conservative Jewish existence and the modern age, because in their opinions this authentic existence is a product of the modern age and does not contradict it. These studies do not treat the boundary between Jews and their surroundings as part of the social reality. Instead, they study the sociocultural causes of the formation of these boundaries. As a result, the phenomenon of the religious Jewish community in a secular society becomes one of the characteristics of the open society itself.

Friedman, for example, is not at all surprised by the existence of the haredi community within the modern fabric of life. On the contrary, he views the haredi community as one that acts within a free and open cultural market, which allows individuals and groups to choose their religious community. An examination of the history of the haredi community in Israel shows that its liberation from the public-at-large, which has chosen to be secular, turned the community into a religious elite. The boundaries constructed between it and its surroundings are part of the dynamic of modern society that allows individuals to choose the "religious package" they prefer. Friedman's view of the essence of these boundaries and the way they are established will be discussed in detail later. For now, it is important to remember that Friedman does not see the question of traditional existence within modernity as an interesting research question, but rather as a starting point. The relationship between the values that charge the thematic world of secular groups and the values of the haredi community is the key to understanding its existence.

Resolution of a Paradox and Construction of a Social Boundary

Presenting the option of belonging to the haredi community as one among an entire range of other possibilities in a competitive and open cultural market does not diminish the tension among these options.

Friedman does not wish to portray Israel as a pluralistic society in which each cultural segment can pursue its interests in cohabitation with other groups. The Jewish-Israeli instance is charged with practical, intellectual, and moral tension. This tension is not in the nature of a dilemma or conflict that may be settled or resolved. It is built in to the society in a circular way, and for this reason it is best described in terms of the dialectical and the paradoxical.

The haredi community interprets its existence in a way that contradicts the basic principles of the modern age, even though its interpretation is the product of that same age. In other words, haredi Jews are able to declare that they are different from modern society only because they are part of that society.

Many other paradoxes derive from this great paradox. What is the connection between these paradoxical situations and social boundaries?

The act of social interpretation of the phenomenal world is linked to each group's significant worlds of content. For instance, the Azanda tribe in Africa will interpret the drowning of a young man known to have been a good swimmer as an act of witchcraft. This tribe explains phenomena that have no other reasonable explanation as the result of witchcraft. Similarly, when five avrechim from a Gur yeshiva drowned in the Jordan River, the community explained the disaster with the instruments at its disposal. Since this community lives and functions alongside other communities that do not use or believe in these instruments, severe conflicts arose between its interpretation of the event and the interpretations of other groups (such as the Sea of Galilee Authority, the police, the secular bus driver who drove the boys to the river, the press). The Gur community's ideological and moral account of the disaster created a social compound that put them in opposition to all these other groups. The interpretations by different groups of specific situations reveal their thematic worlds and sustain the act of interpretation. The haredi community was forced to cope with many conflicts that arose between its internal thematic world and those of others, because of the double reality (orthodox-modern) in which it lives. The bus driver said that the avrechim did not know how to swim and entered the water in their heavy clothing. The Sea of Galilee Authority said that bathing was forbidden in the area in question, because of its proximity to a water pump that affects the river's level. A journalist reported that one of the avrechim drowned and that his friends drowned when they tried to save him, despite the bus driver's warnings. In the synagogues, the rabbis explained the event by saying, among other things, that God chooses to pick the purest fruit in the garden in order to waken his flock to repentance.

Living with conflicting interpretations disturbs haredi society, which believes that every phenomenon has a single true explanation. As a result, such a society must search for a way out of paradoxical situations. The anthropologist observing it cannot see the paradoxes, but lengthy observational work can easily locate sources of "interference," which bring about attempts to shake off and escape unsolvable situations. These points draw the observer's attention, just as a street fight or people gathering around a burning house may provide a key to understanding the lives of those involved. When one finally succeeds in pushing through the curious onlookers and observing what is occurring in the central arena, the paradox is generally illuminated.

Observation also allows the researcher to follow the way in which the community under study copes with the paradoxes (the primary and central one as well as those that derive from it). Such scrutiny may lead to the boundaries of the thematic world that structured and created the paradox (the "who's against whom" in the analogy of the street fight). The order of events in anthropological work is to observe energetic social action that catches the attention, attempt to reach the focus of the activity, define the activity as an act of escaping a paradox (in this case), follow the act of escaping, and learn the significant categories and central classification that have aided in this process of escape, or that were recreated and reshaped by the same process. If we return for a moment to the street fight, we can, perhaps, find out about the reasons behind the fight, what techniques each side uses to emerge from the fight in one piece, what each side hopes to achieve in this fight, how the audience is divided, and so on. The course of such work can reveal perceived social boundaries. By its very nature, the resolution of paradoxes is an unending business, and there will never be a real escape that demands touching on the causes, rather than the content, of the paradox. The more the group occupies itself with ongoing attempts to resolve the paradox it has encountered, the greater the distress the paradox will cause, in accordance with the paradoxical law of self-reference.[5]

How has the haredi community encountered its paradoxes, what mechanisms does it use to level and deal with them, and what new paradoxes does it create during this escape from them? I will try to answer these questions via four socially linked groups: Jews/gentiles, religious/secular, within the community, and men/women. Broadening the social spectrum to include these frameworks will allow me to locate the test case of the paradox of literacy in its broad context, and to present it as a part of a broader phenomenon. The emphasis will be placed, of course, on the way in which the community under study experiences the link between these groups, and the way in which it draws boundaries for itself between them.

Jews and Gentiles

A Goyeshe Pritsa (A Loose Gentile Woman)

6:00 P.M. Women and children gathered near one of the apartment buildings. The women, some of whom sat on the low fence, talked among themselves.

The children played on the adjacent lawn, on the sidewalk, and sometimes even in the parking lot. The summer was at its peak and the subject under discussion was the epidemic of diarrhea that had attacked the children of the Development. The young mothers, those who had no more than three children, traded advice and concern. The babies, who remained in their carriages, were rocked or left to their own devices. The toddlers came up to their mothers from time to time for one need or another. The afternoon routine.

Suddenly on the far side of the parking lot, a young woman pushing a stroller appeared. As she approached, the women saw that she was about twenty years old, dressed in very short pants and a thin sleeveless undershirt with no bra underneath. She had tanned, bare feet and short blond hair. The child in the stroller was about two years old and had black hair, and the girl pushed the stroller towards the women, who alternately looked at her and looked away in total silence. When she reached them, the girl spoke to one of the women in foreign-accented Hebrew and asked, "What time is it?" The woman answered quickly and quietly, and the girl went on her way, leaving the Development.

The silence was broken by a mother who had come to visit her daughter in the Development. She was holding a small grandchild in her arms.

"How does someone like that find her way here?"

"She's not from around here, don't you see that she's a gentile working for someone?" the daughter answered.

A Yiddishe Pritsa (A Loose Jewish Woman)

My second visit to the Zilberstein home took place just before the Passover holiday.

I was going up the stairs; the light in the stairwell was not working. I felt my way in the dark up to the second floor and knocked on the wide-open door. A girl of about five appeared and gave me a long stare. She was plump; her hair was honey-colored and was pulled tight into two ponytails. She was dressed in neat but old clothes.

"Is Mommy at home?"

"Yes. Mommy!"

Hannah appeared from one of the rooms, dressed in a robe buttoned down the front and stained around the waist. Her feet were in the crude clogs I remembered from our first meeting. Her fair face was covered with pimples and she stooped. She greeted me with a smile.

> Yes, yes, it's all right. Come, please, sit in the kitchen in the meantime, we haven't straightened up all the rooms, my daughters are on vacation for Pesah. This is Tsiporale, five years old, and this is Sarah-Leah, nine years old, and Sheine-Brocha is the one-year-old that you already met.

On the table were bread, margarine in paper wrapping, and white cheese. The girls sliced the bread on the table, not on a cutting board, and after washing their hands, they ate on the table, with no plates.

When Tsiporale finished eating, she began the blessing after meals, assisted by her mother when she had trouble. The girl never took her eyes off me, while her older sister grabbed a quick glance when she thought I wouldn't notice. When we got up from the table I heard Tsiporale whisper to her sister:

Zi is a pritsa? [Is she a loose woman? Pritsa literally means "prostitute," but is used more generally to mean "loose woman," and by implication, "secular woman."]

Nein, zi hat kurtsa har. [No, she has short hair.]

Hannah giggled and Sarah-Leah gave her sister a light shove with her elbow.

You understand, we don't allow the girls to have their hair loose, it's not modest. The younger one thought that you didn't have your hair covered, and the older one thinks it's a wig. They know that immodest women don't generally come to our house. The younger one doesn't understand yet.

I stood on the balcony by the washing machine that does ten loads a week, a small bench beside me. Tsiporale climbed up on it and stood close to me. She smiled, and slowly brought her hand up to my hair. When she was sure, she got down and turned again to her mother.

"Yo, yo, zi is a pritsa!" (Yes, yes, she is a loose woman!)

Hannah blushed and silenced the girl.

From then on I came to our meetings with my head covered, as her husband requested. Tsiporale continued to watch over me. She checked my nails, the color of my socks, and the collar of my dress. What I heard from her I saw in the eyes of many other women.

ॐ

In both cases described above an external figure entered the Development, a woman who, by appearances, obviously did not belong there. In the first case, a woman whose foreignness was apparent passed through a public space the women did not own. It was clear to those who saw her that she had gotten there by accident, that this was the first time she had passed through the Development, and that she had no prior intent of appearing before this public with whose sensitivities she was not acquainted. The women preferred to ignore the uninvited guest, satisfying their curiosity with stolen glances. They did not reproach her for her immodest dress and did not protest her intrusion into their territory. Their brief experience with life outside the completely religious neighborhoods that they had grown up in Bene Brak, Jerusalem, and central Tel Aviv had taught them to hold back when there was an exceptional event. The grandmother, who was a guest and who was older than the rest of the women, was the one who broke the conspiracy of silence with her question. The women preferred not to talk in detail about the event, and only the one woman who felt personal and community obligation towards her mother answered. Her answer showed that, for her part, despite the girl's rude violation of their space, the event was unimportant because the girl was not Jewish: "Don't you see that she's a gentile working for someone?"

The sight that presented itself to the woman was objectively exceptional. The girl's clothes would have drawn glances and comments in the non-haredi street as well. The women chose not to see it. The social meaning they gave to the phenomenon helped them ignore the visitor. The girl is not from here, no one here invited her, she is an error and a gentile. Anything further would interfere with the act of ignoring her existence, would call into question the hermetic and unique nature of the Development within its environment (which is problematic to begin with), and would bring to mind subjects that it would be best not to discuss.

The visual impression of the girl would be erased from memory the less she was spoken of. The grandmother, from the vantage point of her years and from the insularity of her home in Bene Brak, was not able to participate in the young women's conspiracy of silence. She may have seen this as her duty, or she may not have been able to hold back. For her, this objective anomaly had no situational justification. Her question, "How does *someone like that* find her way *here?*" carried a tone of accusation. It was as if she had said, "How can you allow something like that to happen under your noses, and how could you possibly have answered her question? Why isn't there among you even one who says something?"

The daughter chose to lend her support to the tactic of nullification. Her answer expressed her desire not to speak of the matter any further, and to present it as irrelevant. She is a gentile, she is in a social category for which we accept no responsibility, and with that, it would seem, the matter was closed.

A phenomenon that contradicts the accepted way of life in the immediate living space of a community creates an ambiguous situation. The women of the Development understand that they live in a place in which people dress in accordance with the rules of modesty. The appearance of a woman in shorts, who entered their neighborhood with no difficulty, threatens this interpretation of their social reality. The basic significance, the simple meaning of the event turns it into a complex state containing internal contradictions. If the women accept the event as an essential part of their lives, the primary interpretation will be negated and replaced by a new one:

In our Development, all the women are properly dressed, but on occasion women in improper dress pass through.

The very acceptance of such an interpretation is a paradoxical situation. As explained above, ambiguous situations that threaten a desired interpretation of reality in the haredi community are not easily accepted. Such situations are interpreted in a way that levels them, dismantles their complex meaning, and reinstates the one-dimensional picture to its central place in ideas and action.

Any normative anomaly that creates a paradox in the life of the community invites breakdown and interpretation that shape a revised understanding of reality. While the understanding that comes after the breakdown process strengthens the worldview that preceded the anomaly or contradiction, it also creates an expansion of the social reality that allows the event experienced to take the place assigned it in this reality. The place prepared for this problematic event changes from time to time, in accordance with the facts of the case (who has committed the act, where it was committed, who observed it, what its immediate and long-range implications are, and so on). The significance of the event, as part of reality, also determines what real actions must be taken with regard to it.

In this case the event was treated with "nontreatment"; the tactic chosen by the women was to ignore it. They categorized the girl as a gentile, someone lying beyond the haredi neighborhood, beyond the next neighborhood, beyond Israeli society, and outside the Jewish people. By placing the girl in such a remote category (even though she had just been under their nose), they saw the event as a nonevent. The immediate esthetic experience was as if it had not been. The women refused to accept responsibility for this behavioral anomaly by their homes. They did not gossip about it, did not complain about "immodest women" entering their neighborhoods, did not denounce the non-Jewish community for being inconsiderate of their sensitivities, and, of course, did not reprimand the girl herself, nor did they evict or threaten her. Their behavior reveals mechanisms for dealing with ambiguous situations, and points to the way in which they categorize the phenomenal world and create (with reference to the frameworks already created for them) social boundaries that allow their specific existence in a varied environment.

The second event is in many ways similar to the first. It also involved a conspicuous aberration from the local standards of modest dress. The mechanism that levels ambiguous situations that contain unsolvable contradictions was put into action. But the picture of reality that was received and the responsibility of the actors were different.

A woman enters one of the most strictly observant haredi houses in the neighborhood and is greeted with a smile by the mother of the family.

A young daughter, who is already familiar with some of the standards of behavior, yet still cannot grasp the flexibility they allow, is confused. She is faced with a contradiction that demands to be resolved. How can her mother, who always covers her hair with a kerchief (while other women in the neighborhood wear pretty wigs), welcome an adult woman whose hair is long and uncovered? Why has mother smiled at a woman who, were she seen on the bus to Bene Brak, would be referred to as a loose woman? How can it be that we girls are not allowed to wear our hair loose, and here at our breakfast table sits a woman whose hair touches her shoulders? Why does mother not reprimand her, why is she not told to leave, and how can it be that this loose woman knows some Yiddish?

Tsiporale travels to Bene Brak every day in a public bus. She sees many secular women dressed differently from the way she has been taught. She has her own view of why these women dress as they do. For her, it is quite simple—they are pritses. But the presence of such a pritsa in her home, and her mother's treatment of her, were for her a paradox that demanded a response.

What is permitted a gentile, and what is observed with revulsion in the surrounding Jewish community, does not apply to a Yiddish-speaking Jewish woman who enters a haredi home.

Tsiporale's older sister broke down the paradox by deciding I was not married (and therefore not required to cover my hair) or that my hair was actually a wig. Tsiporale's parents, who know the truth, tried to remove the paradox in a more absolute way, by asking me to come in the future with my hair covered.

The application of a group's norms of behavior and the society's expectation that these be accepted are selective. Officially, the normative requirements are known, as is the way in which these requirements change according to the actor, the action, and the context in which the behavior takes place. Anomalous events serve as an opportunity to examine simultaneously the merit of these expectations and, especially, the social categories that create a background for understanding them. In these two cases there was behavior that deviated from the Development's accepted standards of dress. The way in which each event was interpreted points to the way in which the observers wish to understand them: the perpetrator of the anomaly (gentile versus Jew), the nature of the anomaly (absolute lack of modesty versus lack of head covering), and the arena where the event occurred (public sphere versus private sphere).

These dichotomies help trace a picture of the world desired by the community and the behavioral precepts resulting from it. The division of the world into gentiles and Jews is a basic distinction that can be enlisted to justify abstaining from action. All the women know the significant difference between Jews and other people. These are categories that contain a multitude of meanings that they learned in their parents' homes and in their schools. To say that someone was a non-Jew was to remove that person from the circle of the community's social responsibility without any dispute. That same moment a boundary was drawn between the women sitting on the fence and the woman with the baby. The boundary gave meaning to each of the two areas it created, and allowed the women to abstain from reacting to the aberration. Such a boundary could not have been created between the haredi women and a secular Jewish woman. In my case, in order to continue my contacts with the Development I had to accept the norms of the place and cover my hair, in addition to wearing the modest clothing to which I had originally agreed.

Haredi Assumptions About Gentiles

Additional instructive data on the breakdown mechanism of the paradox that leads to making a distinction between Jews and gentiles, and a posteriori to the boundaries drawn between the two groups, may be gleaned from *Marveh Latsameh*. Being an Israeli magazine, matters concerning gentiles and the distinction between Jews and gentiles do not frequently appear; they come up only indirectly. Among the hundred issues I read, only ten dealt with this subject in one way or another, and these reveal two contradictory possibilities for understanding the relationship between Jews and gentiles. On the one hand, articles describe a permanent state of affairs in which the gentiles seek to destroy the Jewish people. At times, this is limited to expressions of animosity, to beatings, or to localized riots (in the Diaspora or in Israel); at times it is total: the Holocaust, pogroms, or wars against Israel. The gentiles' hatred of the Jews is presented in the magazine as axiomatic, needing no explanation, and independent of place or time. When necessary, the magazine recounts the sequence of events, but not their motivation. This is the case, for example, in a story the magazine printed about the Hafetz Haim, a non-Hasidic leader of haredi Judaism around the turn of the century:

> . . . and the Hafetz Haim continued enthusiastically: Here is proof for you, go out into the street and see how the non-Jewish boys and men gorge and guzzle—unlike the holy and pure Jewish children, whose mothers must always look after them and plead with them to eat just one more slice of bread, because the evil urge wants Jewish children to be weak so that they will not be able to learn the Torah in the future, but it wants non-Jewish boys to be strong and it entices them—eat and drink, gorge and guzzle, so that you will have the strength to hit and beat and kill Jewish people.[6]

In contrast, there are descriptions of harmonious and ideal relations between Jews and gentiles. Neither are these relations restricted to particular times or places, but many of the instances presented occurred 100–200 years ago in Eastern Europe. These stories and articles describe stable and reciprocal relations between Jews and gentiles. The gentiles left the Jews alone, provided them with physical protection, and allowed them to earn their living. The Jews in return gave the gentiles the benefit of their intellectual abilities and common sense in times of trouble. Both sides benefited from this symbiosis. The prelude to a story in one issue's "Children's Corner" related:

> In times past, the Jews lived in villages in peace and serenity with their non-Jewish neighbors. They had proper commercial relations and none envied the well-being of the other. There were borrowers and lenders and the borrowers paid back their debts at the agreed time and the friendly relations between them were not affected.[7]

Real life falls between these two poles: between the neverending desire of the gentiles to kill Jews on the one hand, and harmony and cooperation on the other. Every event combines these two poles into a single complex fabric that presents a challenge to this dichotomous worldview, and so demands a solution. An anomalous event can be any event that falls between them. Altruistic behavior by gentiles towards Jews contradicts the assumption that all gentiles want to destroy the Jewish people, while violation of the existential balance between Jew and gentile, the patron–protégé relationship, conflicts with the ideal image of the other pole. The children's story whose prelude I presented above describes a deviation from these ideal relations between Jew and gentile (emphasis added):

> Yet once there was an *exception*. An uncircumcised villager came to the home of a Jewish moneylender, bringing a string of pearls in exchange for which he asked for a loan of 25 gold coins until a given date upon which he would return the money and take back the pearls. The pearls, said the borrower, were the best of his wife's jewelry.
> The Jewish lender *was not suspicious* of the gentile. He accepted the necklace and gave the sum requested. A long time passed and the loan was not returned. The gentile did not come to return the money, nor did he come to get the necklace. What did the Jewish man do? He traveled to the city and took the necklace to an expert to have it examined. The expert gave the necklace a quick glance and stated categorically that the pearls were nothing but glass and that they were worth no more than a tiny number of copper coins.
> The Jewish man held his head in his hands and cried in despair: "I have been deceived! The borrower cheated me out of 25 gold coins. What shall I do now?"
> Suddenly he had an idea. The moneylender returned to the village and went to the inn, which was the habitual meeting place of the chronic drunks. He found a large band of them there. The Jewish man sat on a chair and pretended to be in despair, letting out sighs and groans. He attracted the attention of the drunken crew, who gathered around him and asked what catastrophe had befallen him.

The moneylender proceeded to tell them that he had received a necklace as a pledge from a certain gentile and that he had lost it. He pretended to be deathly afraid of what could happen when the gentile arrived to pay off his debt and receive his necklace back.

Word got back to the gentile, who resolved to extort compensation from the moneylender. He appeared, offering to pay off his debt, and demanding the return of his pledge.

> "I lost the necklace!" the Jewish man cried. "Why didn't you come at the time we agreed!" Finally he cried, "Pay back your debt and I will try to find the necklace!"
>
> The man gave him the money and the Jew put his hand in his pocket and drew out the "pearls."
>
> . . . So the Jewish man received his money back and returned the security to the borrower and returned to his home feeling a sense of relief. He had acted in accordance with the rule "deal crookedly with a crook" and had succeeded.

This story, meant for young children (it was printed in large letters, with the vowel marks that are omitted in adult material), begins with a prologue describing harmonious relations between gentiles and Jews. The "exception" to this state of affairs is the gentile, who cheats the honest Jewish moneylender. Because of the gentile's deception, the moneylender deceives him in turn, in order to get his money back. In the absence of real justice, the relatively weak position of the Jew among gentiles requires him to use methods justified in the text by the advice "deal crookedly with a crook." The gentile's stupidity, chronic drunkenness, and deceptiveness highlight the Jew's sharpness of mind and "unavoidable" artifice.

The idealized "real situation" presented at the beginning of the story can only describe the event as "exceptional." The progress of events and their conclusion serve to clarify, morally and practically, the actual system of relations between Jews and gentiles. All is tranquil; then a test case occurs. It reveals the true nature of each group, and shows that social reality is actually different from the state initially described. The child reading the story is meant to finish it with the feeling "You have chosen us": God has granted us tranquility in the exile, but he strews this life with tests. Yet he always provides his people with the necessary talents to face these tests.

The second element in this dichotomous attitude is the gentile's unrelenting desire to destroy the Jews. The magazine also recounts "exceptions" to this "objective" state, and these, too, seem to endanger the dichotomy. Yet, in fact, they are related in order to amplify the dichotomy. So, for instance, another story in *Marveh Latsameh* describes how the Japanese ambassador to Lithuania helped save Jews:

Senpo Sugihara was one of the righteous gentiles. Sugihara was an elderly man of 85. He lived in Japan. On the eve of World War II he was Japan's ambassador in Lithuania. . . . The Jews were looking for any way to save themselves and to flee Lithuania. Some went to the Dutch ambassador in Lithuania, and he suggested that the Jews flee to a group of islands in the Caribbean Sea that was Dutch colony. But the only way there was through Japan. Then Sugihara entered the picture—as a *divine messenger* he appeared to save the lives of Jews. . . . He gave transit visas through Japan to some 5,000 Jews, and so Sugihara became an *agent of divine providence* to save 5,000 Jews from death.[8]

The other side of Jewish-gentile relations is unrelenting persecution. This is never explained—it is a given. Just as God has created ideal situations in the exile, so he has also acted to embitter the lives of Jews, to the point of death. Neither of these is explored in the magazine story, nor is the question even raised. Both serve as fixed backgrounds to the relation of God to his creatures. Sugihara differed from his anti-Semitic colleagues, and his behavior raises questions about persecution and destruction. He risked his life to save Jews and that creates an ambiguous state that is solved and leveled into the unambiguity presented by the text. Sugihara was the agent of divine providence.

It is hard to believe that there any relationships between gentiles and Jews that have not been tried at some time during the course of Jewish history. Beyond the historical facts, which include testimonies of all types, there is also ideology and the utopian conception of these relations. The dichotomous attitudes described in the magazine reflect the recognition of the situation's complexity, and the way in which the haredim wish to decipher and understand it. The basic situation is ambiguous. The gentiles want to destroy the Jews, yet they also constitute the ideal sanctuary for the existence of pure and tranquil Jewish life. The paradox in this basic situation is solved by the catastrophe and the miracle. Reality does in fact include both components, but they do not cancel each other out. Every event that does not conform to either pole (and we may assume that this is the case for most events) becomes a miracle—such as the actions of the Japanese ambassador—or a catastrophe—such as the encounter with the gentile cheat. Miracles and catastrophes are not part of the social reality; they are God's work. The Japanese ambassador acted as an agent of divine providence and as the Creator's representative on earth. Gentiles are sent to abuse the Jews in order to test them (as in the story of the Hafetz Haim speaking of Jewish boys' lack of appetite and the need for them to eat so as to strengthen their urge to do good in its battle with the evil urge). In comparison with the gentiles, the intelligence of the chosen people is obvious, and this helps the weak Jew to use his cleverness to triumph over a gang of drunks. The spirituality of the weaker Jewish boys is contrasted with the hedonistic gorging and guzzling gentile boys. The Japanese gentile stands out among his anti-Semitic fellows, and all this is the result of God's intervention.

Real relationships with the gentiles cover the whole spectrum of possible behavior, from isolation to assimilation, from alienation to adoration, from cooperation to deportation, from annihilation to rehabilitation. Grasping that broad variety of relations, with its inconsistencies, is difficult for any type of consciousness, but is nearly inconceivable to the haredi community, which rejects the multifarious. This negation creates paradoxes that must find their solution in the framework of orthodoxy. It is this system of consciousness that creates the paradoxes, and is simultaneously obligated to find solutions for them. As a result, miracles and catastrophes become the center of experience in the links between Jews and gentiles. This is in order to deal with the two basic assumptions that are at the foundation of the paradox. These assumptions are polarized ones and cannot describe a continuum of social reality. Between the gentiles' established desire to destroy the Jewish people and their providing a comfortable environment for a rich Jewish experience, only the miracle and the catastrophe remain as concepts that can explain actual events between the two groups.

Where do these basic assumptions come from? I am unable to answer that interesting social question. Yet a description of the progress of life from the point of view of coping with such paradoxes sheds some light on the essence of these assumptions.

The classification of gentiles and Jews into different categories is clear; the quality and existential implications are less clear. Encounters between the two groups are rare in Israel. (Even contact with Palestinians, whether Israeli citizens or from the territories, is minimal.) When an encounter does occur, however, it may be dealt with as the women at Gur did in the incident mentioned above, by putting the non-Jew outside the system of obligations to which they are subject. The real, physical contact with the gentile woman was as if it had not occurred. The existence of gentiles in other places and in indeterminate Diaspora past is understood on the abstract, nonauthentic level. In such cases, gentiles enter the world picture (where the most notable things are the heights of miracle and the depths of catastrophe) as a fixed element.

The Religious and the Secular

The very notion of a cognitive distinction between different groups of Jews is problematic. According to Jewish law, anyone born to a Jewish mother or legally converted is Jewish. The haredi groups living in Israel know that they live among Jews, a majority of whom do not observe a large part of the commandments. This fact is the central dilemma of their lives. They know that in the not-so-distant past all Jews were similar, that all lived according to Jewish law. According to *Marveh Latsameh* editor Yisrael Pollak, three catastrophes have befallen the Jewish people since then: the Jewish Enlightenment, the Holocaust, and Zionism.

> From the period of the Jewish Enlightenment to World War I, the Jewish framework has been eroded. The Jewish home suffered its first heavy blow during World War I. Afterwards the Jewish framework suffered a horrible and mortal blow unlike any other in the history of mankind during World War II. Then, not only did the framework collapse completely, but human conventions dating from the six days of creation also collapsed. The very principles of justice and morality were obliterated by Hitler, may his name be expunged, and his troopers. Immediately after the physical world war came an incomparably harsh spiritual war in the form of our people in Israel, with the establishment of the state and the secular domination of our people in Israel, with the object of collectively assimilating our people as a nation.[9]

This spiritual war, Pollack says, is "incomparably harsh." It is conducted by Jews against Jews. In the State of Israel a special link has been created between the two parts of a single nation. The basis of this link between religious and secular Jews is a two-sided component of commonality and alienation. The various religious groups face a public that calls itself Jewish and is even defined as such by Jewish law, a public that speaks the language of the Bible, has as its days of commemoration and rest the traditional Jewish holidays, lives in the Holy Land, teaches its young people the Bible, Talmud, Jewish history, and Jewish heritage and culture. This public does not observe most of the commandments of Jewish law, and claims to be an alternative form of Jewish existence. Moreover, this secular public is the majority in the State of Israel.

These facts create a special situation for haredi groups. The people around them are brothers and renegades, partners and traitors, allies and enemies. These dichotomies create cognitive situations that seem at first to be impossible to maintain. Sometimes it seems that the haredim would actually prefer it if their brothers did not exist at all, or alternatively, that they lived in Brooklyn or Antwerp, where the matter is simpler. On the other hand, they experience the sense of partnership because of the very sharing of a daily social reality, and because of a heritage of collective responsibility that exists on an abstract level.

Life in Israel alongside Jews who do not observe the commandments causes many paradoxes for the haredim, and they for their part develop a variety of mechanisms to break the paradoxes down and give them meaning. This allows the haredim to proceed with their lives, constructing areas of unity and segregation.

The Religious and the Secular All Die Jewish

The second day of the month of Adar is the anniversary of the death of the fourth admor of the Gur dynasty, Rabbi Yisrael Alter, called the Beit Yisrael. During the course of the day the Gur Hasidim make the pilgrimage to his grave on the Mount of Olives; in the late morning two hours are set aside for women. Mrs. Lichtenbaum and I took the bus together from Bene Brak to Jerusalem. We planned to get to the cemetery with special transportation made available to the Hasidim, leaving from the gateway of the Sfat Emet Yeshiva in the Ge'ula neighborhood, where the current rebbe lives.

The bus driver's radio was on and was broadcasting live from John Demjanjuk's trial for the murder of thousands of Jews at Nazi death camps. The day we traveled the court was hearing the testimony of survivors of Treblinka. One of them, Yosef Cherny, testified in Yiddish. The passengers on the bus, some of whom abstain from listening to the radio at home, were attentive. The sound was familiar. A Jew speaking Yiddish, telling of atrocities. The noise of the bus made it hard to follow; people got on and off, the passengers chatted among themselves, but the witness continued to blare above us. He was there the whole time, and everyone seemed to sense that. When we got off at the Jerusalem central bus station and went through the underground passage to the local bus stops, we walked together with a group of women from Bene Brak whose destination was the same as ours.

Did you hear, Rachel, I had to translate some of it for my daughter, she doesn't understand Yiddish that well. What things, did you hear what he said? They would tell their dog, "Man, attack the dog," and he would jump on the Jew.

Mrs. Lichtenbaum gave me a look. She asked me:

Did you hear?
Yes, I've been listening from the beginning of the trial. Do you know that it's taking place here, across the way, at Binyanei Ha'uma across the road.
Did you hear, Shoshana, it's here, in that big building, there he's sitting, may his name be expunged.

The bus to Ge'ula came and ended the conversation and the emotional reunions of women who had not seen one another for a long time. Another bus brought us to the grave. When we reached the gas station across from the site, I recalled that a close friend of mine, Yair Svet, who had been killed during the Yom Kippur War, was also buried here. I also had dead on this mountain—Yair, and my grandfather's brother, who had been a Gur Hasid, and who, according to my mother, was buried at the entrance to the rebbe's burial cave.

Mrs. Lichtenbaum did not believe that we would find my uncle's grave. She said that many people say that they are buried alongside the rebbe, but you never find them. The convoy of women moved slowly; coming towards us was a group of women who had already finished their visit, and they nodded gravely at the new arrivals. Many women were trying to enter the "sanctuary" (the burial cave), and Rachel said we would have to push. One Hasid stood at a distance, shouting: *"Mach plats far di andere frau"* (Make room for other women). There was a grave that obstructed the entrance to the sanctuary. I glanced at it and there it was—Shraga Feibush Opatovski, my grandfather's brother. Mrs. Lichtenbaum was moved. When we left the crypt, she asked my Jewish name.

"Tamar."

"And your Jewish name?"

"Tamar, that's my name."

"And your mother?"

"Yona."

"That's not a name, either. Doesn't she have another name?"

"Yes, Tova."

Mrs. Lichtenbaum opened her Book of Psalms. The Psalms of supplication, petition, and thanks were her solace in times of trouble and her gratitude in times of joy. She blessed Tomer the daughter of Teiva, petitioned for me, taking advantage of the day in which the righteous man, the rebbe, was close to God and could intercede for his disciples.

We then went down to her husband's family's plot. By the grave of Rabbi Aharon, the founder of the Toldot Aharon sect, are buried her husband's mother and grandfather. She mentioned their names in her prayer. The names were the same as those of her son and granddaughter, and the tears in her eyes were for both the dead and the living. I descended to the military section and stood by Yair's grave. A standard army grave. Mrs. Lichtenbaum came slowly after me.

"This is the first time I've seen graves like these. I come here every year and I've never seen this place."

"This was a friend of my brother's. He was killed on Yom Kippur in the war. I liked him a lot. He was so huge, like one who could never die."

"How did he die?"

"He was killed on the Golan Heights during the first battles, when they were pushing back the Syrian advance."

"Why are there two of the same names here?"

"They're two brothers. One was killed in the Six Day War and the second in the Yom Kippur War."

"Oy vey." Rachel gave an ancient sigh. She looked at the flat graves, so secular to her, and looked at me as I stood there, staring silently. She again opened the Psalms and asked:

"His mother, your friend's mother, what was her name, and his father, what was his?"

Rachel Lichtenbaum stood there, the Book of Psalms in her hand, and prayed for Yair the son of Tsvi and Ruth Svet, whom she never knew.

"May they be our advocates in heaven," she said, wiping away her tears. "What are we worth, what is our fate, my father also took part in the Sinai campaign, what can I say, may they be our advocates. When you put a stone on a man [it is a Jewish custom to place a stone on a grave one visits] we're all Jews, there's no politics."

We had a view of all of Jerusalem from the Mount of Olives—including that far-off building where at that hour John Demjanjuk's trial continued.

ॐ

In Israel, Jews are buried in common cemeteries through the agency of the Hevra Kadisha, the burial society. On the anniversary of the Gur rebbe's death, several axes of loss and death met for Rachel and me: the Holocaust, Israel's wars, and family dead. In the same cemetery on the Mount of Olives, very close to one another, her dead and mine are buried. In the same city, not far away, the State of Israel chose to occupy itself with the death of many others for the purposes of education or heritage, or for other reasons. Yosef Cherny speaks Yiddish, does not know Hebrew, just like Rachel Lichtenbaum's parents. But he is not religious. My grandfather's brother was a respected Gur Hasid who had the privilege of being buried at the entrance to the rebbe's tomb, and I did not follow in his footsteps. The State of Israel was established before the Messiah's arrival, and its existence has been linked to wars and losses ever since. Mrs. Lichtenbaum grew up in Mea She'arim, among anti-Zionist Jews. But on the Mount of Olives, near the graves of her family, are buried Jews who died young because they were Jews and Zionists.

Is there any way out of this emotional and cognitive predicament? Is it possible to divide the dead into the "good" and the "bad"? Now, when they are deep under ground, after they have been given a Jewish burial, there is no point. In the face of this finality, there are no disputes. For Rachel Lichtenbaum they are all Jews, and on the grave of a Jew one recites Psalms.

The sense of partnership and of a shared single fate is characteristic of disasters. In such situations, the variety of human activity is blocked out, and only the consequences remain. There is no point in debating over the consequences; furthermore, it is possible to take advantage of the sensitivity

they create. This is what happened in the Development at the time of the
Habonim disaster.[10] The public storm set off by the tragedy did not rever-
berate in the Development. Unlike some other haredi groups, the residents
of the Development did not inspect *mezuzot* to find out whether the
twenty-two children "deserved" to be hit by a train. Nor did they accuse
the mayor of Petah Tikva of being responsible for the deaths because he
allowed cinemas to open on the Sabbath. The first reactions were, like in
the rest of the country, shock and sorrow. Radios, which are the community's selective link with the outside world, were left on, and this expressed
their sense of closeness with the victims. Radio was permitted because
"something happened."

> My husband came home from the kolel and told me to turn on the
> radio. I couldn't believe my ears, how did it happen, what happened
> there. Maybe the bus driver was in shock or was paralyzed, otherwise
> it's impossible to understand.
>
> I heard on the way home on the bus, and then when I got home I
> told my little girl to take the radio out so we could hear. What a
> catastrophe, what a catastrophe.
>
> I didn't know anything until I went downstairs with Shrulik in the
> afternoon. I don't turn on the radio just to listen, but now I'll listen
> to the news at eight o'clock.[11]

Some of the women who participated in the conversation pressed me
for additional details. My sense was that they were primarily interested in
the report I had seen on television the previous evening. When I had
added to their store of information, they escalated their expressions of
shock. At this point there were no discussions of reward and punishment;
they spoke only of the event itself.

> Really? They showed the parents, may God preserve us, what a
> tragedy, they sent the children on a trip in the morning, and what
> did they get back?
>
> What about the driver? Was she young? And the engine driver held
> his head in his hands and cried? May such things not happen to us.

When tragedy comes to Israel, the haredi community opens to the outside world. Sometimes the haredim exploit the tragedy to rebuke the secular for their failure to observe the commandments, but the women I knew
expressed only their sense of shared grief. At times like these it is possible
to narrow the gap between haredi and secular Jews. The haredim take
advantage of such opportunities because living in complete estrangement

from secular Jews is hard for most of them. The paradox created by the very
existence of Israel, in which there are those who observe the commandments and those who do not, creates a desire for contact. Distance, separation, suspicion, and contempt are put aside for the moment, and the
common daily reality becomes more significant. The radios are turned on.
The haredi community opens its channels of communication with the outside world it generally tries to avoid. The sights that the television brings,
which generally arouse revulsion, are sought out. The women wanted to
know how it "looked," wanted to experience the event with one more
sense. The boundaries that the entire community constructs and fortifies
become permeable. Jewish law commands that when a Jew's life is at stake,
the state of her soul is irrelevant; thus, disaster provides haredim with a
legitimate opportunity to make contact, to display sincere concern for the
public-at-large, to acknowledge a common experience, to belong to the
collective. The value and normative components of daily life are charged
in such a way that the social distance between the haredi community and
"the rest" grows smaller. The same is true of Israeli policemen, for instance.
The "Zionist" police, who are generally given a cold reception by the
haredi community and who are compared by them to gentile soldiers,
sometimes are portrayed as saviors. The following comes from the "Children's Corner" in *Marveh Latsameh*:

> The police promised to come at once. And in fact, a few minutes later,
> the police car's siren was heard. The car parked by the entrance to the
> school and uniformed policemen jumped out. They went with the prin-
> cipal towards the garbage cans.[12]

This reality is shared by all Israelis. The fear of bombs hidden in
garbage cans is common to haredi and secular children. Among the
haredim, the need for children to watch out for suspicious objects is put in
terms of a mitzvah ("Take therefore good heed to yourselves" [Deut. 4:15]).
The Zionist policemen in their uniforms leaped out of their car and
reached the site in just a few minutes. The story goes into great detail
about their efficiency, determination, and contribution to the public
safety. Similarly, a "suspicious object" was once found at a bus stop in the
Development. When I came in the evening the women were talking about
it. They praised the quick work of the police demolitionist and spoke with
admiration of his professionalism and his way of treating people.

> He thanked us for calling him, can you believe it? Instead of us
> thanking him. He said it was good that we had called him, even
> though it was just a bag that someone had forgotten. He said that we
> shouldn't hesitate to call them any time. He was so gracious, we were
> all impressed, a real hero.

The girl who called was astounded, she said that within five minutes after she put down the telephone he was already at the bus stop. He had all the equipment, and he took it very seriously. He must have a lot of calls like that every day, but he didn't take it lightly, he really sacrifices himself.

The Jewish people in general, and in particular the segment living in Israel, are considered in certain contexts to be a single public. The facts that lead to its division into various groups are fashioned by daily life into special criteria that sometimes make it possible to ignore the difference. In the face of tragedy, death, or danger the barriers fall—those same barriers in whose construction, at other times, so much effort is spent. The points of contact between the haredi community and secular Jews grow and make it possible to fashion the existing experience of commonality into the basic attitude of the community to its environment. Life together in a single country, life that has a price, is meaningful in ways that are not adequately expressed by the separation that exists on a daily basis. But these points of contact show another side in the context of other events.

How to Celebrate Independence Day

Just before Israel's Independence Day, *Marveh Latsameh* printed the following article:

> There are three approaches to Independence Day. The first is that it is a day of mourning and fasting for the spiritual destruction that unbelieving Zionism has brought with it. The second is that it is a holiday celebrating the "beginning of redemption." The third is that it is neither a holiday nor a day of mourning, but instead a day of sharpening the senses and self-examination to answer war with war, for light to expel darkness, with clear consciousness of the enemy who aspires to uproot the Torah and Judaism via the press, the media, secular education, and laws against the Torah. We have not heard that the great rabbis of Israel have declared "Independence Day" a day of fasting, and the reason may be so as not to give the stamp of authority to despair and resignation in the face of the loud voices wanting to shout down all that is holy, to destroy every good portion. The meaning of the holiday is indirect identification with the Zionist rejection of God and his Torah, and the rule of a regime that does not recognize the laws of Moses's Torah as the sole element of Israel's leadership. . . . We have not heard that the great rabbis have declared a holiday on this day. . . . "Independence Day" is for us a day of self-examination for renewed momentum to answer war with war, not with shouts and sticks but with deeds that will expel darkness by kindling light.[13]

Independence Day is somewhat upsetting for the haredi community. The day is commemorated among Israeli Jews, and even among Diaspora Jews, as the day of the establishment of the State of Israel. There are two groups of religious Jews who are clear about how this day should be to commemorated. The first group (Neturei Karta, the Satmer Hasidim, Toldot Aharon) defines itself as unalterably anti-Zionist, and thus considers Independence Day a day of mourning and fasting. The second group, the national-religious movement (including, perhaps, the Habad Hasidim with their nationalist ideology), considers the establishment of the State of Israel as the beginning of the messianic redemption, and so makes Independence Day into a religious holiday like other Jewish holidays. But most of the haredi community has an unsolved problem with Independence Day, and these are the people that Pollak is addressing. This group maintains ongoing contact with the government authorities. It has representatives in the Knesset and sometimes in the cabinet, and receives funding from government sources. Its children take tests required by the Ministry of Education and the Ministry of Labor and Welfare. Sometimes, when there is no other choice, its sons serve in the Israeli army. For this group, Independence Day symbolizes another paradox.

On the eve of Israel's Memorial Day for the fallen soldiers of the Israeli army (which is the day before Independence Day), Hannah and I had the following conversation:

Hannah: I stood on the balcony today, hanging up the laundry. From there I could hear the principal of the Revivim school speaking to the children in the morning. I wondered to myself why she was having them stand in military formation instead of having them recite the morning prayers. She had them stand in rows and said that the rows weren't straight, as if that was important. Afterwards they began to rehearse for Independence Day. I heard a girl read the *yizkor* prayer [the Jewish memorial prayer]. Better that they shouldn't read yizkor, is that a way to say yizkor, a girl reading and a choir humming? Is that how to show respect for the soldiers who died?

I: And how will you show your respect? What will you do when the siren sounds tomorrow at 11:00 A.M.?

Hannah: I won't listen to music on the tape player, I won't dance in my house. But I don't stand silently either. Jews have their own way to remember, and there are other memorial days.

The boys go to heder as usual. For the girls who go to the Gur Beit Ya'akov school it's different, there they talk about what to do on that day, how to deal with it. But with my girls at their school they don't say anything, good or bad, it's a regular day.

Israeli flags do not decorate the Development's balconies, even though the political representatives of its residents are members of the Knesset and of the ruling coalition. The children of the Development do not make campfires on the night of the holiday and do not go to school dressed in blue and white (the national colors) like other Israeli children do. On this day, when the country's citizens divide into two publics, Jewish and Arab, the Jewish haredim stand apart, especially "other" in their surroundings. On the day on which the establishment of a Jewish state was announced, before the coming of the Messiah, the dividing lines within the Jewish collective in Israel become very clear. The haredi public's spiritual guides tell them not to concede to others the authority to define the character of this collective, not "to give a stamp of authority," says Yisrael Pollak, quoting the admor from Tsanz. Haredim must fight, nonviolently, for the quality of Jewish life, in the belief that the truth will be victorious. By examining the meaning of Independence Day for this community, one can assess the community's connection with its surroundings, the nature of the strings that tie it to the collective, and the essence of the gap that separates it from other Israelis—the areas of contact and separation.

The general division between similar and different provides the broad framework for deciphering social reality. However, the paradoxes within this reality are not caused entirely by this dichotomy. Understanding Jewish life in Israel and even outside it deals also with details. The paradox does not exist only on the "for us/against us" level. It also relies on the unending desire to understand *why*, the desire of a public that assumes that every effect has a cause.

The lines of contact and separation, moments of closeness and extended periods of distance, load social reality with fundamental problems that require solutions. The answer to such problems is again (as in the case of relations with gentiles) leveling its paradoxical complexity and redefining it in simpler terms. The problem posed by the presence of secular Jews is resolved in several interesting ways, which break down this global separation of "for us/against us" into subdivisions that are closer approximations of daily reality. The most important solution of the paradox of secularism is that called "captive children."[14]

Captive Children

The newspaper supplements for Yom Kippur 5749 (1988) contained several articles about the relations between haredim and the secular. In *Hadashot*, journalist Amnon Levy spoke with Rabbinic Counsel Tsvi Weinman, considered the most important rabbinic counsel in Israel. Levi held a kind of mock trial with Weinman, God's trial of Israel's secularists. Weinman was supposed to plead in the defense of secular Jews. Before the two of them began to discuss the charges that could be brought against the secularists, Weinman made two preliminary arguments that were meant to serve as background for his defense. The first was:

This generation is one defined by Jewish law as a "captive child." Jewish law recognizes that a man who was imprisoned among gentiles and desecrated the Sabbath, ate forbidden foods, and committed transgressions will not be punished. Or, alternatively, he will receive a lesser punishment than a [sinning] man who grew up his whole life in a religious home, with a Torah background. We, in this generation, are in the category of a "captive child." The old Zionist leadership cannot, perhaps, be put in this category, but we may be. Ya'akov Hazan and Meir Ya'ari [the two senior leaders of the left-wing socialist-Zionist Mapam Party] for instance, cannot use this defense because they came from the families of famous admorim whose name I will not mention—why should I slander those admorim. We should not accuse the Sabbath violator of today. Instead, we should accuse his teacher at school.[15]

The admor from Klausenburg explains the troubling question of the secularism of the Jews who returned to Zion in a similar way:

. . . of course, disastrously, even in Israel the majority are non-believers and heretics. This fact is one of the enigmas that have no answer—what does a Torah-observing Jew have to do outside Israel and what does one who casts off the yoke of the Torah have to do in Israel. In both cases there is something illogical. The question is, how should we act with regard to the secularists. . . . In fact, there is no need to be like Rebbe Levi Yitshak from Berditchev in order to offer a defense for this miserable generation that has been through the destruction. The great majority of the children of the Holocaust, as well as the natives of Israel, fall into the category of captive children; what can we expect of them in the Jewish area?[16]

The term "captive children" serves the haredim as a key for resolving the paradox of the existence of secular Jews. This category includes all Jews who never received a religious education. Their secularism is explained as a situation they were born into and as a way of life that was not chosen. They are the captives of their circumstances and know nothing else. Even if they behave in such a way as to abuse observers of the commandments, even if their entire lives are lived in contradiction of their Jewishness, the lack of malicious intention absolves them of guilt. This huge human class of "captive children" is also a source of ba'alei teshuva. The secular way of life is not seen as an alternative to Jewish existence, chosen from among a variety of possibilities, but as an unfortunate mistake that is the product of the times. Such an interpretation does not allow for the possibility that there are different ways of being Jewish, and relieves the haredim of the need to treat the secular as heretics. It makes it possible to engage in the range of relations with them that I will describe further on. In looking at the "society of captives," the haredim tend to suppose that their secularism is in fact an intermediate stage, a period of sinful life whose error is imminent, and that will therefore lead to the destruction and disappearance of secularism. Such a view can lead to ignoring the secular, to restricting

one's dealings with them in the name of caution, to paternalistic indul-
gence or attempt to bring them back to religion. But living together in
Israel does not allow this interpretation to remain on the theoretical level;
the two groups meet and put to the test the assumption that the secular are
"captive children." The two following cases describe the continuing fric-
tion between the religious community and the "captive children."

How can you let a woman like that into your home? Not long after Lag
B'omer, a new Torah scroll, was brought to the synagogue, Hannah invited
me and my son Uri to the ceremony held to celebrate the event. The synagogue is not in the Development itself, but in the adjacent neighborhood.
There, in the basement of the Sephoradi synagogue, the Gur Hasidim have
been given a large room. The philanthropist who contributed the scroll (a
new Torah scroll costs upwards of $25,000) was staying with his son in the
Development. The son's apartment had been decorated on the outside
with colored lights, and small loudspeakers on the balcony played Hasidic
music. A large crowd gathered in the parking lot. All the boys between the
ages of six and thirteen held torches in their hands and made ready to
accompany the scroll, which would be carried by avrechim from the Development to the synagogue. Hannah hoped that Uri, who was then eight,
would join her nine-year-old son, Binyomin, and march in the torchlight
procession with him. But Uri stuck close to me from the moment we
arrived at the Development. It was his third visit there, but his first involving such a large crowd. He was dressed in a simple sweat suit, and had on
his head a blue knitted kipah that we keep on hand in the house. I stood
among the women who occupied one side of the parking lot, and Uri was
the only boy of his age around. Together with the women were the babies
and smaller boys and girls. The boys of Uri's age had gathered in a separate
corner and were preparing for the parade. Uri was confused and embarrassed. He hugged me with one arm and from time to time would bury his
head in my side. Hannah and the other women tried to tempt him to join
the parade, and Binyomin himself came over every so often to try to persuade him to come along. Nothing worked. Another group of women from
the Development, with whom I had no close contact except for attending
the various classes with them, stared at me and Uri. My outward appearance, which was exceptional in the neighborhood despite my covered head
and long clothes, was already familiar. It was, however, the first time Uri
had been seen in public. When the men's parade set out (avrechim and
boys only), the women and toddlers remained in the parking lot, and then
Uri stood out even more. When he finally accepted a sandwich from Mrs.
Lichtenbaum, everyone saw that he ate without washing his hands and
without blessing the bread. To top it all off, soon after the parade began
Uri and I got in the car, and I drove carefully through the crowd of women
who stepped off the road. They stared at me as I passed by.

During my next visit to Hannah, she told me that three women had come up to her afterwards to ask how she could allow me to visit her at her home.

"Three is a lot," I said.

"And there are others who were afraid to ask," she responded.

This incident pointed to a sharpening of the unspoken opposition that there had always been to me. This opposition grew out of the puzzle of whether I was really a "captive child." Uri's presence fortified the opposition. The women knew that I was married and had two children. This knowledge played a significant part in making me acceptable to them, themselves married women and mothers. The women also knew that I was not observant and that I was not in the process of becoming a ba'alat teshuva. My adoption of their dress code and the connections I had made with them on the level of womanhood and motherhood had dulled the difference between us and had emphasized what we had in common. This allowed them to accept me to a certain extent. The paradox that my presence caused was not an acute one, and could be dismantled with little cognitive or emotional effort. She'll change eventually, they might think. Who can know what God's way is to bring her to Judaism? At least she is seeing good things here. You can find religion through the university, too as well as other responses that I would later hear. But Uri's presence was more problematic: an eight-year-old Jewish boy, without sidelocks, dressed in colorful clothes that these women considered inappropriate for his age. He stood close to his mother, hugging her like a baby. She, for her part, did not push him away, but rather held him close to her body.[17] He ate the sandwich offered him as if he were a gentile, without washing his hands and without reciting a blessing. Finally, he got in the car with his mother, who drove herself. The women felt that this event showed my true face. I knew how to make gestures that would keep my "alienness" from standing out; my son did not. He constituted definite proof that we were lost causes. They suddenly realized that the prison camp is not so innocent, and that those held within may not really be able, or even want, to escape. In such a situation, the women saw no point in continuing to bring me into their society. The paradox was an intense one. In this case, it was not possible to solve it such that my presence would be accepted without comment, as it had been before. Some of the women now wanted an answer to the questions "What are you really doing here among us?" and "How can you let a woman like that in your home?"

"So, what did you say to them?" I asked.

"What did I say? I told them that there are lots of other things that I do and that they don't."

A place of defilement and a place of purity. On the intermediate days of the Sukkot holiday I visited Miri, Hannah's neighbor. I found her at home with her two daughters and oldest son. She related that her husband had gone to Jerusalem to visit the rebbe, taking the younger son with him.

"Why didn't he take the older one, too?"

"Oh, that's a long story. When I was in the hospital with the older one, a woman who had just given birth to her first daughter was in the bed next to me. You know how it is in the hospital. You lie there for hours, it's hard to fall asleep, so you talk. She was a girl from a home where they kept some traditions, like the Sabbath and kashrut. After she got married she didn't keep doing it, and now she works as a secretary at *Al Hamishmar* [the daily newspaper of the left-wing Mapam Party]. But there's still something in her heart, and when she sees a religious woman it comes out. So we talked a lot, and I understood that it wasn't easy for her. After we went home, she would call every so often. She lives in Holon. I'd send her a card on Rosh Hashanah, and that's the way it's been for nine years. Each time she asks me to come visit. And I don't go, I'm not that interested, you know how it is. This year, on the day before Rosh Hashanah, she called and so much wanted me to come. My husband said it wasn't nice, and that during Sukkot I should go with the boy because, after all, the whole connection is because of him. Okay, I called her, and said that I was coming, and asked that they cover the television. And the day before yesterday we went."

"So, how was it, you must have been happy to see each other."

"Yes, it was very moving, the visit was a success, but it was very difficult for me. We sat in the living room, and she had covered the television and gave us soft drinks we could drink[18] in plastic cups, and cookies with a kashrut certificate. The children went to the room to play, but she has three girls, two of them the age of mine. The girls saw all the toys and they were so happy, they didn't want to leave the room. But with Yenki, I didn't know what to do with him, if he should stay by me and listen to the mothers' conversation, which is not for him, or if he should go to the room and be with the girls, and that's not good because we from a young age have taught him not to be with girls. But what could I do, he went with the girls. The whole way home in the bus I thought to myself, why did my husband go to the rebbe, to a place of purity, while he sent me with the children to a place of defilement. This evening I spoke with the children, I wanted to explain to them a little about what we saw there."

"Do you think you'll visit her again?"

"Again? I haven't gotten over this time yet, so how could I go again?"

In various public places haredim cannot avoid making contact with nonobservant Jews, and this leads to a complex of emotions on both sides.

During such an encounter it is possible to take a peek into the other group and see whether one's basic assumptions about it are valid. The haredi woman in the hospital, municipal building, medical clinic, and other public places generally feels like a member of a minority, sometimes a member of a persecuted minority. Yet she also thinks that others see her as a representative of a type of existence that has authentic or nostalgic significance for them. Haredi women are prepared for certain types of reaction to their presence, from humiliation to admiration, from repugnance to envy. Personal connections created as the result of a given daily reality, such as a stay in a maternity ward, are scrutinized with the tools at her disposal as a human being and as a member of a group. Miri kept in limited contact with the woman from Holon because of what had happened between them as women, and as Jewish women. The experience of staying in touch, and its being put to the test of reality, led to disappointment and introversion. The "child from Holon," taken prisoner by her husband and by her job, seemed after the visit like someone who had no intention of becoming religious. The visit to her house and the connection between the children, who had been born on the same day in the same place, were shown to be dangerous, and therefore impossible.

According to the haredim, the mass of secular Jews, ("captive children") is like an entire public sitting in Plato's cave. It believes that the only truth is the truth of the cave. It does not know that outside it there is a rich world of light and color, reflected in the darkness of the cave only as shadows. Those sitting in the cave are not entirely responsible for their ignorance, so it is possible to treat them leniently, but the paternalistic compassion of Jewish law runs into difficulties in the real world.

Amnon Levy's article includes an interview with a former Knesset member from the Sepharadi-haredi Shas Party, Rabbi Ya'akov Yosef, on the subject of captive children. Rabbi Yosef answered:

> The law applies to a person who does not know, and calls him "a child taken prisoner by the gentiles." He is treated leniently. For a child who has been taken prisoner, there is a different definition. We do not judge a person who sins unknowingly the same way we judge one who sins because he is forced to, and we do not judge one who sins because he is forced to as one who sins of his own volition. We have mercy on this man, a poor man who does not know, who stands beyond the mountains of darkness from a spiritual point of view. . . . Some of them have not tasted anything. They don't know the first things about Judaism. A man who falls into the sewer, okay, he doesn't know. But he is filthy and smelly. Take him to the bathtub and wash him off right away. If he didn't know that there was a sewer there, does that mean that he's already clean?

Rabbi Yosef, a former member of the Knesset, grants the secular public the status of "captive children," but does not absolve them of the stench of the sitters in the cave (or, as he puts it, the sewer). Innocent secularists thus become tainted, a fact that will be taken into account even if they become religious, as we shall soon see. Yet, despite the generalization, the haredim distinguish between different grades of stench and filthiness among the secular, and along these lines divide the public of "captive children" into subcategories.

A reading of *Marveh Latsameh* reveals such a classification system, the purpose of which is to interpret the paradox of the "captive children":

1. *There is only one way to live as Jews,* and the majority of the Jewish people do not live this way.
2. Most of the Jewish people may be categorized as "captive children," living in a dark cave without seeing the light.
3. The doors to the cave are open, and the Jews who live in the light call to those in the darkness, but they do not come out.
4. *Therefore, there are many ways to live as Jews.*

To explain this illogical situation the paradox must be leveled. The leveling process includes categorizing different groups of secular Jews, which creates social boundaries between haredim and the secular.

This categorization begins with the two extremes. On the one side is the innocent, pure public, which has gone astray and which is searching for a way out of the darkness of the cave. On the other side, there is a hedonistic, bourgeois, bored mass of people full of stereotypes about religion. This latter group enjoys the darkness of the cave, which conceals its triviality; this group goes around in circles. Guards at the door prevent the cave residents from leaving, and small groups believe they have found their way out of the cave into the light, but actually live in error.

This picture makes it possible to understand, to a certain extent, the circular question presented above, and makes it easier for the haredim to continue to see their choice as absolute, and to continue to engage in selective cooperation with their surroundings.

I derive this characterization of secular society from serialized stories about the life of people who are about to become ba'alei teshuva.

There are no happy secularists. Marveh Latsameh regularly presents stories about ba'al teshuva. The following excerpt is taken from one such story:

Exam time has come. Avital is deep in her books. . . . The diligent student takes notes. . . . Her eyes long for sleep. . . . She arrives at her home, which is in an exclusive neighborhood of private houses, late at night, and again sits down at her desk. The coffee cups pile up in the sink. . . . Her father is a senior manager at a successful industrial firm. Her mother heads the children's department of a large hospital. The two of them see a promising future for their daughter as a full professor. . . . Exam period is over, but now Avital is very busy. She does not bury herself in books, but she takes part regularly in a drama club and a dance group. . . . Should she ever give up the role of the absent-minded professor, she can always look forward to a respectable position as a theater actress. . . . Avital is involved in counseling problem youth, Avital organizes activities, classes, tournaments . . . but something is always missing.[19]

Avital and her family sound like the stereotypically perfect successful bourgeois family; there are no nuances in the description. Painted in broad strokes, Avital and her family have everything—wealth, good jobs, social involvement. But even as they take full advantage of this, their lives are empty. Secular people who are talented, serious, and who care about others take advantage of the good things life offers them (a house, management, university study, the theater, and dance). But then they discover that secularism at its best still comes up short. In this way the haredim construct their interpretation of the status of "successful bourgeois Jews— even though they are not religious." This situation is always a threat to the haredi consciousness. According to the haredim, these Jews are nevertheless dissatisfied; they are successful, but their hearts are not whole. In the haredi view, it is impossible to be a truly happy secular Jew, and this disposes of the paradox. The young woman, who has not yet established her life in this context, will continue to search, will aspire to wholeness, and will find it in religion. The story of Avital's life (written for a haredi readership) demonstrates the haredi resolution of the dilemma created by secular Jews; it is more relevant for this reason than it is for what it tells about secular Jews finding a way out of their spiritual crisis.

Aliza—a vacuous woman.   Another story describes the spiritual decline of "Aliza":

Want to get out? I've got a great suggestion. I've got tickets for a banquet. You know, the charitable projects of the Academics Union. They rented out a hall with a marvelous dinner and a fashion show and you have to donate a few shekels for the fight against religious coercion. Leave the children some sandwiches and come. . . . You've got to.

(A knock on the door.)

—Dalia, open the door and if they ask where I am say I'm not at home.

—Mommy, it's two people collecting for the Israel Association for the Autistic.

—Tell them that we don't have any money.

Later that evening:

—Here I am busy all day with dieting, exercise, and taking care of my body. I can't look like a grandmother. I bought a ready-cooked chicken, you just have to heat it up, and some salads in containers, and afterwards I fell into bed, I was so tired. . . . In the afternoon they invited me to a banquet at a hall and I wanted to look right, and suddenly he showed up.

—Who's that?

—He—the respected professor of science—my dear husband. . . . To make a long story short, you know what he wants, what nerve, he wants someone to serve him at the table. I couldn't, so my daughter Dalia said that she'd put the food I'd left him in the refrigerator in the microwave.

—The what?

—The microwave. Tell me, where are you living, what primitive tribe do you belong to? How can you live without a microwave? I hear him putting the car in the driveway of our house, I put the frozen food in the oven, and five or ten minutes later the food is hot as if I'd cooked it.

—Really? So then what do you do all day?

—What do you mean, I barely have time to breathe! Every week I go to five health clubs and to eight classes—beauty, sport, painting, ceramics, music, and others. You know that I go to the Heart of Fashion every two weeks, and I have charity lunches and lectures in organic eating and vegetarianism. Tell me, what does he think, that just because he has a few academic degrees I have to be his slave?

No! Rina said, but you're his wife!

—So what? Aliza roared. Just because I'm his wife I have to serve him, to bring him his food, to wash and iron his clothes? You know exactly how he treats me—like a manikin in a store window. For him I'm a serving woman and nothing more. We live in the same house like two neighbors who hate each other, and outside play the game of "hello" and "good morning." What a horrible life.[20]

Rina and Aliza are the lost secularist and the searching secularist. Rina will learn a lesson from Aliza's life and will find the "true path." Aliza and her like belong to the group of secular Jews who are not searching for any real content in their lives. They are occupied with pursuing expensive leisure activities and are busy destroying their families. Aliza is prepared to contribute money for the fight against religious coercion, but tells her daughter to lie when there is a collection for autistic children. Aliza is a failure even in secular terms, and she herself is aware of it. The magazine's characteristic descriptions leave no room for the imagination—they paint a glaring picture of decadence. Elsewhere, the magazine attributes the actions of two upper-middle-class Israeli women then on trial in a sensational murder case to a life of the kind that the fictional Aliza leads. The connection is meant to show that this type of secular life can only end in ruin. Any attempt to be Jewish without obeying the commandments of Judaism ("Aliza's option") is interpreted as destructive. Most secular people do not live such lives, it would seem, but the path they are following leads to corruption.

If Avital and her family have exhausted all the positive things secular life has to offer, Aliza represents their negation. Avital is a positive person, and so she reaches the truth. Aliza serves as a foil to her friend Rina and, in fact, to an entire category of secular Jews who do not look to see where they are going. Either way, whether one belongs to the questioning group or the idle group, the possibility of leading a happy life as a secular Jew (a contradiction in terms for the haredim) ceases to be a threat to the haredi interpretation of reality.

It is not coincidental that secular life is equated with wealth. It is meant to show that any deviation from the standard haredi family structure leads to division. A greater sharing of responsibility for housework, leisure, and luxuries are identified with secularism. Secularism is invalid, so role changes in the home (already slipping through the front door) are rendered illegitimate.

The Guards of the Cave

It is hard to understand what prevents the people sitting in the dark cave from leaving it and seeing the light unless one supposes that the "captive children" are being imprisoned by guards at the entrance to the cave. This assumption leads to the second step in the process of dismantling the paradox of secularism—the leadership. Through the social insights valid in their lives, the haredim reach the conclusion that someone is keeping the "children" from getting to the truth. This enables them to continue to assume the relative purity of the majority of secular Jews, and focuses their battle on those who, in their opinion, concoct plots to prevent the truth from coming to light. The haredi community appears to believe that a small but powerful group of leaders stands guard at the entrance. This was Tsvi Weinman's claim, and it is endorsed by the editor of *Marveh Latsameh* magazine and by the admor from Klausenburg, whom I have already quoted:

> Religion-hating leaders are haters of mankind as a whole and haters of the haredim in particular, and their hate is so vast that they ignored opportunities to rescue haredi Jews during the Holocaust, and their vast hatred today wells up in the media and the press. . . . On the other hand, we must not hate the masses that are dragged along behind them. . . .
> . . . We already hear the voices of incitement against haredi Judaism. The Jewish people in Israel are surrounded by millions of Arabs and all the heroism of these non-believers is in sneering at the keepers of the Torah and the commandments, at the Jew who puts on *tefilin*. They love the Arabs, they want a common culture, and they make fun of the Jew who keeps the Torah and the commandments. Moreover, they celebrate themselves for their love of the Jewish people, for saving European Jewry, for loving the land of Israel. . . .

The haredim see the media as the most efficient device for guarding the entrance to the cave. It is clear to them that the press and television, which they have personally boycotted, stuff the public with lies intended to make the haredim hateful to the "captive children."

Yet they seem to be well aware of the problems (expressed in the boycotted media) that concern the secular public, and they make use of this to
understand the state of the secular Jewish community.

One story from *Marveh Latsameh* about a ba'al teshuva centered on the
journalist "Yossi Har-Kesef."

> The editor said: "No one on the staff questions your great talents as a
> respected reporter. Moreover, it would seem that your coverage of events
> in the haredi sector has given you a store of knowledge that no one else
> on the paper's staff has. You will certainly agree with me."
>
> Yossi nodded and the editor continued:
>
> "So, my friend, you must certainly know about the recent phenome-
> non of more and more talented boys from good families, some of the most
> prominent and sharpest brains in the secular world, being swept into the
> haredi net. Surprisingly, these are thinking, educated, college-educated
> people who analyze their every action rigorously, who are not willing to
> buy anything sight unseen. They are swept away by the current and there
> is no one to save them. . . . The editors of *Only for Secularists* has decided
> to take this serious situation in hand . . . and to solve the riddle in the
> most through way. We have succeeded in interesting foreign investors
> who will contribute large amounts of money to this important subject.
> We must uncover the haredi secret weapon," the editor said with pathos.
>
> Yossi held himself back from rolling on the floor in laughter . . . but
> his face reddened and this gave his reaction away to the editor.
>
> "What's so funny?" The editor suddenly grew angry.
>
> "The haredi 'secret weapon?' What's that supposed to be?" Yossi
> broke out laughing.
>
> The editor stared at him angrily as he shook a finger at the reporter.
> "Do you need me to explain? Don't you see what is happening in the sec-
> ular community? . . . Masses of people are going over to the other side. . . .
> The fresh and vigorous forces, the most beautiful flowers we have raised
> and nurtured in our secular greenhouses, where are they disappearing to?
> To beyond the mountains of darkness. To those places where progress has
> stopped. To the most extreme haredism—they turn their backs in scorn
> on the compromisers [i.e., the religious Zionists]—these hold no interest
> for them. Just like they don't interest you! So I ask you." The editor got
> up and shot the reporter a piercing glance. "How do they attract them?
> With magic, witchcraft, incantations? After all, it is clear to everyone
> that there is sophisticated secret fighting going on here. The only prob-
> lem is to pry these well-kept secrets from them. . . . Then they'll be like
> Samson after his hair was cut," the editor chortled.[21]

Journalist Yossi Har-Kesef was sent on an espionage mission. Over the
course of the story, which was published in installments, he and his wife
discover the way to the "truth"; Yossi confesses to being the scion of a family of respected haredi lineage. He ends up as Yosef-Arieh Zilberberg, of
which his Hebraicized name was a translation.

The portrayal of the editor of *For Secularists Only* is one-dimensional
and shallow. The newspaper in the story has a vested interest in fighting
the haredim. The editor does not leave this to the government authorities

or to public organizations. He raises money for this high purpose, to counter the threat to secular society. The editor's monologue to the "correspondent for haredi affairs" reveals the stereotypes that the haredim believe the secular have about them. Special emphasis is placed on progress versus darkness. As far as the editor is concerned, this is war, and the story stresses that. There are barricades, there are tactics and secret weapons, there is brainwashing, and therefore spies must be used. The press, representing the media as a whole, is portrayed as having great power and a sense of mission. The haredim see it as the leader and shaper of secular public opinion. The people running the media are full of plots to get back at and assault the haredim. They adopt a dual strategy: to keep the secular from knowing the truth about the haredim (a truth that Yossi, the honest reporter, is already close to knowing, which is why he broke out laughing at the editor's opinions), and to try to frustrate the haredi attempts to save the "captive children."

The masses, who are prevented from seeing the true path because of the plots of educators, leaders, politicians, and the media, are not perceived to be a uniform group. The haredim divide them into subgroups. The criteria they use for this are also connected to the key paradox. The secular subgroups are distinguished according to the alternative they offer to religious life. In other words, if the key question is, How is it possible to live a Jewish life without religion? what distinguishes the different groups of secularists is the answer each group gives to this question. Apart from the possibilities represented by Avital and Aliza (the good secularist versus the bad secularist, the searching secularist versus the lost secularist, or the decent bourgeois versus the corrupt bourgeois), the haredi community recognizes other versions of secularism.

The Kibbutznikim

The kibbutznikim are not "captive children." (See Tsvi Weinman's reference to kibbutz leaders Meir Ya'ari and Ya'akov Hazan in the "Captive Children" section.) They are seen by the haredim as people who have consciously chosen their way of life and who must be held accountable. For haredi Jews, the kibbutz is the diametric opposite to them. They see it as the most serious alternative that the secular camp can present to religious life. The kibbutz represents people who believe in certain principles and who live by those values in practice. Socialist theory, and the regulations formulated by the kibbutz to carry out that theory on a practical level, run parallel to the haredi Torah and Jewish law, something the haredim can understand. It would seem that they have greater respect for the kibbutznikim than for other secular Jews. The world of the kibbutz arouses great curiosity and a certain amount of fear. The haredim know well the power of an all-embracing framework, the significance of a comprehensive life, and the secret of social unity. They see kibbutznikim as being the most secular of all secularists, the most extreme, who abhor religion and its institutions. Yet they also assume that the kibbutz as a social phenomenon institutionalized a solid and demanding alternative for its members, and they respect this. It is thus no wonder that in the much-discussed 1990 speech by Rabbi Eliezer Menachem Shach, leader of the "Lithuanian" haredim, the kibbutznikim were a central object of his vituperation. Rabbi Shach saw no point in speaking of the secular Jews who lived with an unclear, indefinite ideology. These, the great majority, were not worthy of his attention. (This is why the kibbutzim were wrong to take offense—they should have taken his denunciation as a compliment.)

The resolve of the kibbutznikim is cited in a story from *Marveh Latsameh* called "The Sabbath Wars":

> "Ah, I'm starting to remember! You're that kibbutznik who attacked me so harshly on that stormy Sabbath in Sabbath Square [a main intersection in the center of the oldest haredi district in Jerusalem, the site of haredi demonstrations against the government]?" I asked in astonishment.
>
> " . . . The change came over me," he answered, "about a year after that encounter. I came to that demonstration to repel the religious attack on freedom of conscience, and I did what I thought was my duty. I screamed at you, called you names, threatened you, and even used force."[22]

The kibbutznik is described as one who believes that the haredim threaten his freedom. The article emphasizes that he did not just think that, but took action consistent with his principles. He was ready to fight for freedom of conscience, and he did his duty—he acted.

The news that my husband used to live on a kibbutz spread swiftly through the Development. The women knew that his family still lived there, and that his parents had younger children still living at the kibbutz and that his married elder sister lived at another kibbutz. I was frequently asked about kibbutz life.

Hedvi: Are you saying that the children still don't live in the same house as their parents?

I: At my in-laws' kibbutz, which belongs to the Hashomer Hatsair movement [the most radical of the three kibbutz movements], that's still the case. At his sister's kibbutz, which belongs to the United Kibbutz Movement, the children already live at home.

Hedvi: May God protect us, how can you do a thing like that? It's really cruel. I think that if I had to put Zelig to sleep in another house, he wouldn't sleep all night.

Miri: Just him? I wouldn't sleep all night either.

I: You get used to it. There are a lot of stories now from the first days of the kibbutzim that tell how the parents would stand on the other

side of the walls of the children's house listening to their children cry
but not go in. That's what made some of the kibbutzim decide
afterwards to bring the children back home.

Shoshana: The same way they brought the children home, in
the end they'll find what it all means and return to Judaism, too.
I heard from Malka [the ba'alat teshuva] that once they didn't
celebrate the Sabbath or holidays, that they had their own
version of the Pesah Haggada that had them, God forbid, eating
bread in public. And now, thank God, they're coming back little
by little.

Miri: They ate bread in public on Pesah?

Hedvi: And other things, too, you shouldn't know. Isn't that right,
Tami?

I: That's true, but they always had *matsah* for those who wanted it.

Hedvi: Tell me, do they even teach the children that they're Jews?

I: Of course, they teach them Bible, Talmud, Jewish heritage, Jewish
history.

Hedvi: They teach it, better that they shouldn't learn anything,
better that they should think that they're gentiles.

Another time, after I'd been on an overseas trip and my oldest son had
been left at the kibbutz for the duration, I had the following conversation
in the yard of one of the buildings, where several mothers gathered one
afternoon.

Minda: And he agreed to stay there?

I: Look, after all, it's his grandfather, and he is used to visiting there.
The lucky thing is that his aunt, my husband's sister, is only twelve
years old, and they get along really well together.

Minda: What do they do all day? Is it like here, with school and
homework, or is it a different routine?

I: It's like here, more or less.

Yohi: You weren't afraid that he wouldn't want to come back, that
they'd talk him into staying?

During several conversations with groups of women I was asked to tell
about the kibbutz. The two conversations quoted here in part show how
much curiosity this unfamiliar Jewish way of life arouses among the
women, who have heard details about kibbutz life from secondary and, one
may assume, biased sources. My presence gave them an opportunity to ask

for confirmation of these reports (as happened with other subjects as well, such as the army, secular schools, secular families, and so on) from a primary source.

The technical details arouse the curiosity of anyone who does not know much about communal life, but beyond these details the women wanted to hear about the substance of kibbutz life, especially in the Jewish context. Somewhat naively, they could hardly imagine the depth of the secularism that was part of the life of the people around them ("What, they eat bread on Pesah?"). The kibbutz, a distant and insular community, is conceived of as having great powers, to the point of kidnapping children ("You weren't afraid that he wouldn't want to come back, that they'd talk him into staying?").

In another article, this one about a young girl who was becoming more religious, the girl's parents disapproved of her interest in religion and suggested that she spend a month at a kibbutz. The kibbutz was depicted as a kind of "antibiotic" that would nullify the pernicious influence of a seminar for newly religious people that the girl had attended. Its all-embracing way of life, the connection between theory and practice, its distance from the center of the country, and its geographical isolation paint for the haredim a picture almost as familiar as that of Mea She'arim.[23] In Amnon Levy's interview with Rabbi Yosef, the kibbutz is cited as a total institution. Responding to a question on young religious men who abandon their heritage, the rabbi said: "Any boy who is not interested in religion gets up and goes. He goes to a kibbutz, or enlists in the army."

Haredi society collects information about kibbutz life in order to estimate the size and caliber of the nemesis, and uses this information to denounce this rival way of life. The transition from the kibbutz to religion would seem to be a complex one. Yet the haredim sense that the difference between the two is more technical than fundamental. The kibbutznikim are seen as people who are prepared to accept the yoke of a certain Torah, a yoke that obligates them to act in certain ways. They are different from the unconstrained secularists who take no responsibility for themselves and who have no moral or social commitments. The kibbutznikim are portrayed as people who are in search of the truth; since there is only one truth, they must eventually find it.

Some of the secular have found the "truth." These are the ba'alei teshuva.

Ba'alei Teshuva

There has been much discussion recently about the phenomenon of secular Israelis becoming religious—"returning" to Judaism in the literal translation of the Hebrew term. Despite all the information that has been gathered and all the articles that have been written, it is still difficult to estimate the extent, dimensions, and depth of the phenomenon. The Hasidic communities, with the exception of Habad and the Bratislavers, tend not to absorb ba'alei teshuva. This does not, however, keep the Hasidim from teaching ba'alei teshuva and referring them to appropriate institutions. Most of the Ashkenazi ba'alei teshuva join Misnaged ("Lithuanian") communities.

During the period of my study there were four families of ba'alei teshuva in the Development, one Ashkenazi and three Sepharadi. The families moved to the Development because the apartment prices in the Development are low relative to the nearby areas of Tel Aviv (about $95,000 for a two-bedroom apartment). Apartments were always available in the Development, for rent or for sale, because there were always families returning to Bene Brak after completing the five-year mandatory "exile" imposed by the rebbe (see Chapter 1).

The families of the ba'alei teshuva had normal neighborly relations with the Gur families. Their women made a point of attending the classes organized by the Gur women, and one series of lessons was even held at the home of one of the ba'alot teshuva, Devorit. Riki, who came from a kibbutz, had taken part in organizing parties for the women, and led a separate class for the four ba'alot teshuva. Nevertheless, the fact that they were not part of the Gur community kept these families from being truly integrated. The Gur women's shared past—their years of study together, their family connections—was a barrier. The fact that the children of the ba'alei teshuva families did not attend the same schools that the Gur children attended after graduating from the neighborhood nursery school further segregated these families from their neighbors.

One might expect that the haredi community would embrace the ba'alei teshuva as a miraculous phenomenon: the wide range of backgrounds from which the ba'alei teshuva come—kibbutzim, the academy, the criminal underworld, bohemia—lends validity and added force to the haredi contention that there is only one way of realizing a Jewish existence.

Over the period of two years, *Marveh Latsameh* printed five stories about ba'alei teshuva that presented major options available in Israel for realizing Judaism. All five ways ended in disappointment and failure, which in turn led to religion. This was what happened to the kibbutznik, to the journalist, to the good girl, to the woman soldier, and to the bourgeois family. The haredi press and their public pronouncements point to the ba'alei teshuva as proof that the truth eventually comes to light. In reality, however, the ba'alei teshuva are treated differently. Instead of providing a resolution to the central paradox, their presence creates a new subparadox.

She's a nothing. We were standing and talking outside the synagogue after the Psalms class. These gatherings, which were leisurely on summer evenings, became briefer and briefer as the nights grew colder. I had just returned from a trip to the United States, as a result of which I had not been to the Development for two weeks. Malka, the Development's only Ashkenazi ba'alat teshuva, interrupted the conversation and asked me loudly:

"Tell me, Tami, did you observe the Sabbath when you were in America?"

The group fell silent. I felt both insulted and angry, and I had no intention of answering her.

"Malka, I've been visiting Hannah for more than six months. I've eaten there, I and my family, and no one has asked me such a question. Why do ba'alei teshuva of all people have the nerve to ask me that?"

"We do what they're too bashful to do. Do you think they don't want to know, don't want to ask you? They're embarrassed, afraid of hearing bad things. They prefer not to ask and not to know."

I walked home with Mrs. Lichtenbaum. Having grown up in Mea She'arim, it was not easy for her to speak in Hebrew, so we spoke in Yiddish.

Don't pay any attention to them, you shouldn't know where she comes from. That's the way she talks. Don't take it personally. Once it was even worse. She had such a big mouth. I thought she'd already become a *mensch*, a human being, but look, it's still there. When a person comes from a good family, like you, he's a human being. She's a nothing.

We went up to the entrance of the Lichtenbaum apartment and the two of us, she and I and the Yiddish between us, were closer to each other than to Malka's 613 commandments.

The women of the Development did not consider the religious observance of the ba'alei teshuva to be an entry ticket into their society. Their social world had a precise and careful caste system. Family origin (including ethnic origin, economic position, education, outward appearance, and other factors) had special significance. The fact that certain people had decided to change their way of life and become religious was admirable, but also suspicious. The haredim want to know what it really was that pushed the secularist out of his world, and what price he paid as a result.

How much did Alona Einstein pay? A special event took place in the community center in the adjacent neighborhood. Hannah called one morning to tell me that Alona Einstein, the former wife of an Israeli rock star and a well-known figure in the Tel Aviv bohemian community in her own right, would be coming to talk. The evening was meant for non-secular women, and had been organized by a neighborhood woman who headed a group of ba'alot teshuva. Hannah guessed that women from the Development would also attend. She herself would not. There would be nothing relevant for her to hear there, she said; there would be questions and answers that she had no interest in hearing.

That evening the community center's dance studio was full. Most of the women who had come from the neighborhood were young. A few had come in modest dress and with their hair covered, but most were wearing pants; a few were even wearing shorts. The women from the Development waited together outside the community center until the speaker arrived, and then entered and sat together, slightly separated from the rest.

The pictures of ballerinas in tights, in dance poses, seemed to me very much out of place. I could not help wondering what the women from the Development thought of them. They, for their part, did not seem particularly bothered. Thirty of the 220 women who then lived in the Development had come. A quick glance showed that they were mostly young and married to working husbands, and that they were mostly women who had grown up in the established Tel Aviv Gur community.

Alona Einstein told her audience all about her secular life. She quickly recounted her relations with various men, her drug use, and her bohemian life in Tel Aviv, continually emphasizing the suffering and dissatisfaction that had accompanied all her experiments. Afterwards she spoke of how she began to take an interest in Judaism, and how this reached its climax in a family seminar she had attended together with her young daughter.

"She's so beautiful, look at her face, it must have been hard for her to give it all up."

"That shows even more commitment than just anyone."

"Too bad her husband didn't become religious also, why didn't he go with her, I heard that they weren't together."

"Where did you hear that?"

"How do I know? She said so, didn't she?"

"She said they were divorced."

"But he's married, isn't he? He's got a child, too."

"So she became religious after the divorce, when she was already alone."

"Yes, that's what I think, she didn't get divorced because of that."

"Too bad. I heard that they tried to match her up, but she didn't want to."

"She's got more now than she had before. From what she says, the family she had was nothing."

The abyss that waits at the end of the secular hedonist road is wonderful proof of the imminent error it contains. The ba'alei teshuva are presented as people who have exhausted that road to the limit, who could not keep from falling. Then they found religion and this elevated and renewed them. The fact that the great majority of the secular public has not yet reached the abyss, and that only some have fallen in, is not attributed solely to opportunity and intensity. Sometimes it acts as a boomerang on the ba'alei teshuva.

The haredim see that most of the secular public manages to live a reasonable life that includes family, work, study, and so on. Those who come to religion should be seen as trail blazers, as an elite among the secular, the first to see the truth, but at times they are treated as a plague of undesirables. (Or, in Ya'akov Yosef's words, they saw a sewer, fell in, and came out filthy and stinking.) The community women understood that had Malka not roamed London with the guru's disciples and smoked hashish in Amsterdam, she would not have found the "truth." The haredim do not forget the filth that preceded the purity. They can portray the ba'alei teshuva as searchers for the absolute truth in the streets of London and on LSD trips, but when they have direct and daily contact with the ba'alei teshuva, they are afraid that traces of that filth are still present and infectious.

The ba'alei teshuva demonstrate, in microcosm, what it would be like if the entire Jewish people became religious. They take the central paradox to its logical extreme. This threatens the haredim and makes them reexamine the nature of their own Judaism. When all Jews keep the commandments, who will be the real Jews?

The community of ba'alei teshuva actually creates a new paradox: may the entire Jewish people become religious, and may we remain the only true Jews.

The interpretation of the paradox created by the phenomenon of the ba'alei teshuva in daily life establishes a possible boundary for the traditional-haredi community in a future when a curiosity becomes an actual reality. The imaginary reality, in which all Jews live according to Jewish law, exists in microcosm in the haredi community. Although it seems like a homogeneous block to the unfamiliar, within it there is a division of resources and status. The internal negotiating process creates boundaries that may be studied through the mechanisms for leveling the paradoxes.

Within the Community

The haredi community includes all Jews who live in accordance with Jewish law, and who do not clearly identify with Zionist ideology.

This group, which subscribes to a uniform code of behavior, must create a common social fabric that grows stronger in the face of non-haredi society. Therefore, the attempt to draw internal boundaries focuses on the general tendency to agree to the unification of these groups in a broad ideological way and the everyday reality that calls this unity into question—not to mention political-economic spheres and the power struggles within the leadership of the haredi community.

The magazine *Marveh Latsameh* reflects a kind of general unity within the haredi community. Its editors take care to give expression to all the recognized groups within the community. Each week the cover is graced with the picture of a rabbi or admor, and taken together these represent the whole range of haredi society. Before each holiday, the magazine includes articles about the customs of the various communities and describes their traditional foods, and stories of righteous men and miracle-workers from Eastern Europe, Yemen, and North Africa. The magazine avoids political coverage of the fights among different haredi factions, and takes no clear position on the issues involved in these struggles. The untutored reader of the magazine gets the impression that the haredi community is pluralist and recognizes the equal status of its diverse component groups. All (except the modern religious Zionists) are joined together, it would seem, by religious observance and fealty to Jewish law.

Understanding the significance of diversity in the haredi community does not get easier when one puts down *Marveh Latsameh* and goes out to the street in a haredi community. The divisions between the Hasidim and the Misnagdim, between different Hasidic courts, and between Ashkenazim and Sepharadim are not that pronounced in day-to-day behavior. Drawing boundaries within the community is delicate work, and only foci of social dissonance, exceptional events, ceremonies, slips of the tongue, and gossip give evidence of this delicate dynamic of internal boundaries.

In order to get a sense of its significance and nature, it is necessary to observe the actors and learn what they think and feel. The community I observed lives in a neighborhood considered to be a "Gur colony." Most of the Development's children are educated in Gur institutions, the avrechim study in Gur kolelim, large purchases are made in the Gur supermarket, and important problems are referred to the rebbe. In general, the girls marry Gur hasidim, and the families live in proximity with other Gur hasidim. But a minority sends its daughters to schools where Yiddish is the language of instruction (Gur schools teach in Hebrew) and its sons to a heder run by another haredi group, like Shomrei Emunim and the Vizhnitz Hasidim. Although not commonly done, a Gur hasid with a family problem may ask the advice of the Sepharadi mystic, Rabbi Abu-Hatzera of Be'ersheva, or a wife might go to the "Tunisian witch" in the adjacent neighborhood to get her migraine cured. Gur girls sometimes ask to marry Misnagdim in order to be freed of Gur's strict code of modesty.[24]

The community called "the Gur Hasidim" is not a closed social framework. Tenuous lines connect the Hasidim among themselves and with other haredi groups. These lines lead from the haredim in general into the Gur community and its various strata, and make their way into the family unit as well.

When to Blush?

There is a knock on Hannah's always open door.

"That must be Weisman—they're making a sheva brachot for one of his wife's students, and he's coming to take table settings." (Hannah has table settings and tablecloths for one hundred people. This is her gamah, a charitable operation she runs in memory of her father.)

Hannah takes out the things she has prepared in advance and puts them on the table in the foyer. She clears the area so that Weisman can take the boxes. He waits in the doorway for her to exit the foyer and asks in Yiddish whether his wife had also requested a large pot and ladle for soup. He does not look directly at Hannah as she enters and exits. She answers him from the kitchen, and I notice that as she talks to him she blushes deeply. Here was a woman married ten years, with five children, and she was blushing.

"He'll ask her if she wanted a pot also, she didn't tell me yesterday," Hannah answers in the third person. She gives the pot and ladle to her daughter Tsiporale, prodding her to give it to Weisman. On the pot is a sheet of paper listing the implements that have been borrowed, and Tsiporale has Weisman sign it. Hannah looks at his signature, stuffs the paper into a kitchen drawer, and says to me: "I remember him at his bar mitzvah, and now, thank God, he's an avrech."

Another time I was standing in the foyer ironing tablecloths. A young man of twenty knocked at the door. He was wearing a black velvet kipah and was dressed Sepharadi style—black pants and a white shirt, without a coat. The boy had come to take something that Hannah's husband had left for him. She had received precise instructions in this regard. They conversed directly. Hannah read out a note her husband had left, directing her gaze at the boy and he at her. Their conversation went into the third person only when Hannah mentioned her husband. She didn't say, "My husband left you . . ." but rather, "He left you . . ." The young man did not say, "You" or "Tell him," but, "I request to inform him that . . ."

This was the first time that Hannah met this young man, and she did not blush.

A different encounter happened between Hannah and a man in a kipah who painted the stairwell. Soon after Pesah, after much procrastination, the residents of the building managed to put together enough money to get the job done. Hannah, a member of the housing committee, hired two young Sepharadi men who wore knitted kipot, the badge of the religious Zionist community.

"Mama," Binyomin called, "they want water."

Hannah went out onto the landing, looked at the painters' work, and said:

"I told you to do the stucco up to the height of the light switches. You're making it too low."

"Look, lady, everyone in this building is giving me different instructions. You say one thing and your neighbor upstairs, the fat one, says something else. You two decide. It makes no difference to me."

"So tell the neighbor from upstairs that I gave you instructions in the name of the housing committee, I'm paying you, and you'll do what I said. Otherwise both you and I will go crazy here. The boy will bring you water in a minute. Afterwards I'll make you coffee."

შ

One might assume that men are all alike and should all make one blush. Modesty before men would seem to have no modifying conditions attached. One might even assume that the greatest embarrassment and most severe isolation would be from unfamiliar men, whereas with men closer to them, women could feel slightly freer.

This assumption was disproved by observation. The laws of modesty, like other laws perhaps, are applied within a meaningful framework. Hannah's behavior, like that of other women in the community, demonstrates that she can distinguish these frameworks, which are so internalized that she can produce spontaneous affects like blushing.

Observation of Hannah's cheeks can teach us something about the way in which she draws her social boundaries. Some men (Torah scholars, for example) are worth blushing in their presence. There are those with whom one must speak politely and in accordance with a formal protocol, and there are other men there is no need to hide from, to turn one's face from, or to be especially polite to, even if they spend an entire day outside your door working in their undershirts (or, as Hannah says, precisely because of that).

By Us in Bene Brak

Hannah telephoned me one afternoon. Every call from her made me nervous—I was always apprehensive that she was calling to tell me not to come any more.

"I've got a wedding today, of my husband's cousin. I'm going on the 7:45 bus to Bene Brak. Can you come?"

I was at her apartment by six, so as to have time to do my Yiddish homework with nine-year-old Sarah-Leah. Her two brothers were sick. Hannah does not have her children vaccinated, even though most of her neighbors do, so Binyomin and Shrulik had come down with the measles. The girls prayed every evening and asked God to grant their brothers a full recovery, and to keep them from coming down with the disease. Sarah-Leah looked over my notebook, corrected mistakes, and added to the top of each page the Hebrew letters that form an acronym for "with the aid of heaven." Hannah emerged from her room in a new dress she had just bought, gray with a low waistline and a wide cloth belt. She also wore light-colored stockings and high heels. Under her white kerchief she suddenly had a certain beauty.

My car was parked down below; we passed it on the way to the bus stop. We ran into Rivka, who lives in Hannah's building, walking in the same direction.

"You're also going to catch the bus to Bene Brak?"

"Yes, I have a wedding at the Vegshel Hall."

"Oh, I see you're taking an important guest."[25]

"Yes, for me it's company and for her it's work," Hannah answered, sensing the critical tone in Rivka's voice.

"Why don't you go in her car?"

"A car is a 'male accessory,' and my husband doesn't want me to drive with women. Even when there's a woman driver on the bus, I don't get on, I wait for the next one."

"Really?" Rivka sniffs. "What's the big deal, a lot of haredi women drive."

"Each one does what she understands is best, but anyone who grew up in Bene Brak knows what I mean."

"Do you think that generations of good boys and girls didn't grow up in Tel Aviv?"

"God forbid, of course they did, but I didn't go live in the city. That's why I came here, so that my children would see good things. It's enough that they have to go on buses and into stores I'd rather not have them go into. Even here it's not exactly Bene Brak."

When we had seated ourselves at the back of the bus, Hannah whispered to me that the Gur "Tel Avivians" had grown up that way, that they could no longer discern many bad things. That's the way it is, she said, when your soul breaks down—it's a lost cause, you can't go back, what the eyes have seen remains part of you. In Bene Brak and Jerusalem they grew up differently, and that's why the Development looks the way it does. Ten years and there's no nursery school worthy of the name; there's no mikveh and no synagogue that women can go to.

The "Tel Avivians" in the Development are not really a clique unto themselves, but after I became aware that they were considered to be different from the other women, I realized that they dominated at certain events. At Alona Einstein's lecture for ba'alot teshuva, most of the women from the Development who attended were Tel Avivians. Their dress was distinct, more fashionable. They wore wigs that were more "daring," decorated with sparkling pins. The "Tel Avivians" went once a month to a lecture at the Scharansky College, where they studied. They were more at home with the bureaucratic ins and outs of government institutions whenever such subjects came up.

Within the haredi community, even among the Gur Hasidim, there are options in religious expression. This difference, the existence of alternatives, needs to be explained. If a long-haired wig with jeweled pins is considered a modest head covering, there must be a reason. If one haredi woman drives a car and another won't even get on a bus driven by a woman, the difference must be significant. Since no one can or wants to deny that these women are observant Jews, divergent behavior must be explained as an environmental effect.

Women who come from overseas are given more leeway in the way they dress and what they do at home. Next in line are the Tel Avivians. The Bene Brakers and Jerusalemites grew up in the purest surroundings. Observance of the commandments would seem to dictate homogeneity, but in reality practices vary. This paradox is resolved by attributing divergent practices to "local custom" or "the environment."

In this way the haredim as a group remain united in principles, its internal differentiation being understood as a *force majeure*, an exigency that has a practical explanation in the history of a minority scattered in exile throughout the world. There is a difference between Hannah, who refuses to board a bus driven by a woman, and a haredi woman who drives her own car. Ascribing significance to this difference would, however, make it hard for haredim of different allegiances to live together, and would cast doubt on whether they all really ascribe to the same common "truth." The difference between the two women must, then, be defined as a situational result rather than as a difference of principle. One has grown up near the Warsaw Park in Bene Brak, and the other on Ahad Ha'am Street in Tel Aviv.

By Us in Gur

The special traits of the Gur Hasidim and their place among other Hasidic sects determine the unique experience of being a member of this community. Every person who belongs to Gur is also part of a broader haredi community, and is obligated by both frameworks. Uniqueness, created by drawing boundaries between Gur and other groups, jeopardizes the link with the haredi community as a whole. Boundary drawing is thus fraught with anxiety. The tension between the ideology of unity and distinctive behavior is expressed in the following incident, which includes both the paradox and the way out of it.

At the edge of Bene Brak, at the new Continental Hall, chaste Rachel-Frieda was married to the esteemed avrech Yosef-Arieh.

> You can tell from the invitations that it's not a Gur wedding. With us there's a standard form for the invitation because of the rebbe's

instructions about weddings. All invitations look the same. First there's a separate party for the unmarried men, so they won't be wandering around the hall, because they don't have anything to look for there. Then there's a little party for the immediate family, and only at the end a modest reception for the rest of the relatives and friends.

Rachel-Frieda is the daughter of a respected Gur Hasid, but her mother is from a "Lithuanian" family. Her parents, like many others, decided that their sons should marry Gur women, but that the daughters should marry "Lithuanian" men. In this way there would be a kind of internal justice in the family: the boys would preserve the Hasidic line, and the girls would escape Gur's strict sexual restrictions.

Like at all haredi weddings, the men and women sat on opposite sides of the hall, separated by a dividing screen. The women were waiting for the bride to emerge from the *yihud* (the room where the bride and groom are left alone together for the first time after the wedding ceremony). The girls were wearing sumptuous dresses and thin, sheer stockings. Most of the stockings had a fashionable seam running up the back of the leg or were embroidered with sequins. Ears and necks were graced with pearls and gold jewelry. Except for Hannah and me, wearing kerchiefs, all the married women were wearing elegant wigs. Hannah does not eat at weddings in order to intensify the force of the precept she is fulfilling (that of celebrating with a bride) while keeping her personal enjoyment to the minimum. Three-year-old Sheine-Brocha, who has come with us, knows the rules, but she nevertheless hesitantly takes a *knish* from my hand. Afterwards she eats cake, mushroom casserole, meat and chicken, washing it down with several cups of soft drink. There is no such food at home.

On the boundary between the men's and women's sections stand only married women, who pretend to be looking for their husbands. The unmarried girls either avoid the boundary or go there with a young child in their hands. The divider between the men and women is fixed, bolted to the floor, and not portable as in other halls I have been in.

To reinforce the kerchief on my head I took Sheine-Brocha and held her on my right hip. In this way both of us could peek into the men's section. The men had taken off their coats and had begun dancing to receive the groom as he returned from the yihud.

"By us in Gur, the weddings aren't joyful any more," said Esther, Hannah's sister-in-law, who is standing next to me. "The young boys don't come to the hall, and the older ones have already forgotten how to celebrate. The weddings are 'black'—no one takes off their coats. Even if they dance, they keep their coats on, even in the yeshivas. With the 'Lithuanians' the boys don't wear coats in the summer. When they study, the room is 'white,' but not with Gur, they stay 'black.' At a Gur wedding you won't see the room white like this, everything will be black from the men's coats, and the women won't be dressed so extravagantly either. On the way home, the families organize themselves outside, who's going in the car, who in a cab or bus.

"With us in Gur," Esther continues, appointing herself my tour guide for the evening, "we don't travel together. The husband and wife sometimes come separately from home, and go home separately. He goes with the boys, she with the girls, no one calls from one side of the hall to the other, there's no discussion of when to go. The 'Lithuanians' are freer."

"What do you mean freer?" I demand to know. "Less modest?"

"You can't say less modest, they have their own modesty and we have ours, I'm telling you how we behave in Gur, so you'll know that what you see here is not what they would do by us."

At the exit from the hall, when we had begun walking to the bus stop, I heard the band playing again after having taken a break to eat. They had struck up "The Pink Panther."

"Hannah, that's so funny, it's a song from an American movie."

"Are you sure? Maybe they took it from somewhere else?"

"No, really, it's obviously not a traditional Jewish melody."

"Okay, maybe, it doesn't matter, that can happen too, but I think that the trumpet player is a ba'al teshuva."

&

It may well be that a Gur wedding would have been more modest, Hannah was insisting, but even Misnagdim would not play something from a foreign film unless there was a ba'al teshuva trumpet player. Close encounters with unconventional behavior (that is, things not done "by us in Gur") affect Gur women in two ways. The exceptional event hones their sense of what is proper or typical in their community; and it forces them to search for an explanation for the difference. Unlike a nonorthodox person, who might leave the experience of otherness undeciphered or only partially deciphered, orthodoxy demands a logical and legitimate response to the fact that different haredim carry out the same action in different ways. At first glance, this moral code must define modesty unambiguously. But the social reality shows that this code has many interpretations. The acceptance of one interpretation casts doubt on the validity of others, but that same reality brings these two interpretations together at a single wedding. Rabbi Shach, the "Lithuanian" leader, can allow himself a serious break with the rebbe from Lubavitch; heads of yeshivot can compete fiercely for resources and for the leadership of one community or another, but the women at the wedding experienced the conjunction of the daughter of a Gur Hasid with a Misnaged bridegroom, on their way to establishing a family together. Through this experience, they must find a way of giving meaning to the group they belong to without rejecting its alternatives. This is a charged situation, and the leveling action of the women created a flexible passage between their framework and the other one.

Publicly abandoning one haredi group for another is not always a simple matter with a happy ending like this Hasid-Misnaged wedding. Transferring loyalties from one Hasidic group to another can be a much more abrupt and painful experience, as in the case of Rachel Lichtenbaum.

Gittel Is a Shiksa to Them

"*Ich hab dem shlissel. Efshar a mal, ken men foren ahin, und bazuchen mein mishpocha.*" (I've got the key, maybe one time we'll go and visit my family.)

Rachel Lichtenbaum had a key to the Gur rebbe's burial cave. An important Hasid gave it to her, when she and her family had been living overseas out of fear of retribution from the Toldot Aharon sect. We did not use the key, but we went to the cave on the anniversary of the admor's death. After prayers on the Mount of Olives, Rachel took me on a visit to her birthplace. We got off the bus on Shivtei Yisrael Street, one of the main streets of Jerusalem's oldest haredi neighborhood, Mea She'arim.

> Kik, this is where I live, where I breathe, it's my place, look at all the stores, the children, here I know everyone. This was the border. We would stand at the window and watch the King's [of Jordan] soldiers. We'd wave to them, but then we stopped, because *iz nisht tsnius* [it's not modest].

We entered a typical Jerusalem house with thick walls of rough stone behind the Toldot Aharon Yeshiva. Rachel's pace swiftened as she ascended the stairs, as if the very aroma of the place was pulling her up. The door was opened by her seventy-year-old father, dressed in striped robe, covered by a black *haltal*.[26] His feet were in black boots. He smiled joyfully, and women and children ran in from every corner of the apartment laughing and calling: "*Rochel iz da, Rochel hat gekuman!*" (Rachel is here, Rachel has come!). Her mother, her sisters who live nearby, and a ba'alat teshuva neighbor squeezed into the kitchen. We entered her father's work room—he is a scribe who makes parchments for mezuzot and tefilin. There were grandchildren, Rachel's nieces and nephews, all over the place. A meal appeared in the room: vegetable soup, meat patties, and noodles made by her mother. My fears that they would be cold and bland like the food I had grown accustomed to in the Development were confuted by the piquancy of real Hungarian cooking. Rachel spoke uninhibitedly with her father and sang my praises. Her father, for his part, asked the three key questions:

"*Vi veint ẓi?*" (Where does she live?)
"*Vas macht deineh man?*" (What does her husband do?)
"*Vi lernt er?*" (Where does he study?)

The commotion about us showed no sign of dying down. Rachel's sisters displayed the Purim costumes they made for the children. Her mother had me admire a prayer book Rachel's father had written by hand, and the grandchildren climbed on and off their grandfather's lap, tasting his soup.

Afterwards we visited the homes of other members of the family, asking about the sick and old, delivering holiday greetings. Rachel visited her husband's family, his elderly uncle, and her disabled brother married to a disabled woman who was not from the Toldot Aharon community, but who was accepted because she was an appropriate match for him.

> I like her in particular. She, good for her, you'll see what a good homemaker she is, how she isn't neglectful even when it's hard for her. She grew up in Bene Brak and they're "Lithuanians," but they were looking for a wife for my brother Ya'akov who was disabled but not in her head, and she has a good head, just that she was sick when she was a baby.

As we walked through the nearby Batei Ungarin compound, Rachel glowed. Women stepped out of their houses to greet her, to tell her who had been born and who had died, who was getting married and who had come to visit from overseas. They conversed in Yiddish. Rachel made sure to introduce me to each and every one of them.

Rachel told them a little about Tel Aviv and they listened politely. But for them the names Antwerp, Golders Green, and Williamsburg fall more easily from their lips than Tel Aviv does.

> You understand, they never leave here, they have everything here— stores, friends, family, celebrations, it's all here, there's no need to go anywhere.

On the way out of Mea She'arim, on the border of the Ge'ula neighborhood, Rachel filled her lungs with a last breath of her native air:

> People don't understand it. My life is here. To take a woman from her home, from her family, without friends, that's a great sacrifice to God.

Would you come back here, Rachel?

> Oh, that's hard to say. *Was ken ich ẓugen?* [What can I say?] Gur has nice things that there aren't here. You can't go back after you leave. I miss the family. My children come to their grandfather like

gentiles, they say words in Hebrew. It cuts Grandfather like a knife. My Gittel wears a wig, not the way they are, with shaven heads and a black kerchief, not like me with the colored kerchief. She's a shiksa [a gentile girl] to them. The way Gittel behaves with her husband, they can't. That's the way it is, that's Gur, for Gittel that's home.

In the cab we took from Ge'ula there were also Gur Hasidim from the northern town of Hazor Haglilit coming back from visiting the admor's grave. Rachel felt comfortable among them. The little boy who sat next to her told her that the proctor at his yeshiva was the brother of her son-in-law. Her daughter's marriage to a promising young Gur man had made it easier for her, reinforcing her ties to the sect. Her son-in-law's sister was married to the rebbe's grandson, something that had improved the family's status. The cab descended to the coastal plain, bringing Rachel into her new world.

For those who remained in Mea She'arim, Tel Aviv sounded like Sodom and Gomorrah. For an eccentric, small Hasidic sect like Toldot Aharon, any departure was desertion. It stings Grandfather for him to hear his grandchildren speaking in Hebrew. For him, there is only one way of being a good Hasid. But in Jerusalem, where he resides, there are many neighborhoods. The Hasidim recognize other orthodox groups, and can relate them thematically and socially. The internal division of the haredi community, presented as clear and obvious, is actually in a continual process of evolution. A ba'alat teshuva of Sepharadi origins sits in the kitchen of this same grandfather; she came to Jerusalem from the southern town of Ofakim and became friendly with one of his daughters. His "exiled" daughter could be reconciled to the family, and brings the Mea She'arim home a bit of the flavor of the Gur Hasidim. His handicapped son had to marry a Misnaged girl because of his physical disability, and he lives in a housing project sponsored by Shomrei Emunim (a Toldot Aharon splinter with a long history of conflict with the mother Hasidut), because the apartment there was cheaper.

The movement of people in and out is felt clearly in a group whose life is like that of a walled-off ghetto. The newcomer and the deserter affect the thematic world and, of course, the nature of the barriers it erects. Bans and ostracism perpetuate the paradox of differentiation, so they cannot be valid in the long run. If ostracism fails to bring its object back to her original community, the ban will prove that the ostracizers believe that there is only one way to be Jewish. Such a claim would make life difficult in the heterogeneous haredi community. Ostracism and bans are supposed to serve as a means of oversight and a way of imposing fear, and after the fact as a way of bringing the lost ones home. If they have not committed acts that depart severely from norms of behavior, the community will have to recognize those who have chosen a different way. In order to accept the deserters in their new guise, the community activates a mechanism that reinterprets the situation, so that the paradox is dissolved. Instead of saying there is only one way to be a good Jew, the definition of the right way is broadened to include the internal preference of every group for its own way of life, while allowing for the pragmatic acceptance of alternatives.

From an intellectual, ideological point of view, it would seem that nothing has changed, but everyday reality creates the kind of flexibility that allows life to go on even as uniqueness is preserved. In other words, the mechanism that shatters the paradox allows certain links between orthodox alternatives, and clarifies each of them. The result is that the existence of this connection and the acceptance of differentiation make the dynamic of the different groups possible. The isolation of the groups on the social (as opposed to the political) level is liable to weaken the entire community's ability to survive.

Gur erects temporary and fragile borders between itself and gentiles, secular Jews, ba'alei teshuva, and extreme-haredi groups. Between the aspiration to portray a harmonious haredi community and the desire to give prominence to the special quality of their own group dividing lines are shifted and erased. The need to resolve the paradoxes that arise from daily reality is the driving force behind the construction of the boundaries. Each day the people of the community put these boundaries to the test, but live within them as if they had always been there.

Men and Women

Gender categorization is seen by the haredi community as manifest, ongoing, and explicitly significant for the course of life. Compared to Western secular society, where unceasing attempts are made to gain a new understanding of the differences between men and women, and to reshape relations between them accordingly, haredi society seems to be "an island of conservatism and stability." This "island" image is applied by outsiders to the haredim, and by the haredim to themselves. Yet, as we have seen, actual social action goes beyond the "island" and shows that the community is actually an integral part of Israeli society. This means that the haredim are constantly reexamining, in thought and action, the set of categories they use to decode their social reality, including the categorization of men and women. The social category called "gender" is here part of a cultural structure. Within the discourse of deconstructionism but without a theoretical discussion, the research (ethnography and its interpretation) aims to unveil some mechanisms of that gender structuring.[27]

The structure of "the natural order of things," within which the division of the sexes was presented, was largely researched by the first wave of feminist study.[28] The first order of business was to negate the "factual" disciplines, among them biology, ecology, and economics, and to promote a sociopolitical interpretation of "the natural order of things."[29] The road was then prepared for the study of the sociology of ideologies.

Feminist studies conducted in Western societies have shown that these societies seem to have a democratic, egalitarian ideology regarding economics, education, law, art, the family, and so on. Yet alongside this apparent ideology there are invisible ideologies that undermine this declared equality.[30]

The opposite situation is true in the haredi community. The declared ideology speaks of inequality between men and women, defined as "differentiation." Under the force of this ideology, all things (including power roles, authority, control of resources, dress, education) are assigned. Haredi women accept this ideology a priori. Yet, in their daily experiences, in the society in which they function, within their relevant time and space, they carry out social activity that oversteps the declared ideology and infuses it with themes and behaviors that stem from their existence. This activity is parallel to the hidden ideological level in Western society, but its contents are, of course, different.

I would argue that women have a significant role in the nonautomatic process of being placed within categories. This role, which Australian sociologist S. Burton adds to gender studies, stresses the active side of the women within the daily reality of their lives. Part of this study focuses on the question of how, in practical terms, subordination and dependency between women and men are created. What are the local reasons for this subordination in each context; and how does each group of women, in every culture, live with it, interpret it, give it meaning and validity, and perhaps try to change it?[31] It is therefore not enough to expose the gap between the sexes and its policy ideology, while presenting society as "male." The social sciences must also study the entire input of women into each society.

With the aid of Burton's argument we may show the transition from enthnography to methodology, and from there to the theoretical contribution. Instead of an all-inclusive theory about categorization and its cultural endurance, Burton breaks the argument down from ideology to praxis, to the "how." The study of the praxis illuminates the institutionalization of ideology, which then closes the circle. Anthropology can enrich this method because of its unmediated observation of those social processes.[32]

Observations of haredi women demonstrate the dynamic that creates the categorization, the meaning of the categorization in daily life, and its effects on the behavioral level (the construction of boundaries). My observations revealed two sources of dissonance, at foci of intensive social activity surrounding the status of women: the issue of luxury and the issue of education. Examination of them will aid in understanding the dynamic of the categorization of men and women and its implications for haredi women's lives. The problem of women's education and its social solution have been treated separately, while the subject of luxury will be presented as a part of the enterprise of erecting social boundaries in the haredi community.

The Flour and Torah Paradox

The public discourse in which the haredi community engages, and which may be seen as a "social arena,"[33] treats economic prosperity as a misfortune. Research by Friedman (1986a, b) and by Shilhav and Friedman (1985) provides a good explanation of this public apprehension about wealth, and gives examples of this public attitude towards luxury.

In the post-industrial age, the haredi community exists in a state of permanent and ongoing repudiation of the secular-modern values of the society surrounding it. Yet its existence is possible only within such a society. Relative prosperity, government appropriations, and the deferral of military service allow haredi men to extend their period of study and to avoid working for a living. Their families become dependent on government stipends or the money brought in by working women. They live in economic hardship, which is particularly problematic because the families realize that they could improve their lot considerably if the father stopped his studies and went to work. Thus, economic prosperity allows men to learn because the government has the funds to support them. Yet these same studies create privation. Therefore, public discourse defending the scholars condemns prosperity as a value and the use of resources for needs other than study.

The condemnation of prosperity is evident in the following selections from *Marveh Latsameh*:

We live in a period of material abundance. People have never had so much money, food, so much entertainment and amusement equipment. . . . We live in a period in which spiritual void has brought mankind to a state in which the purpose of life is enjoyment. Crime has increased in proportion to material abundance. . . .

This leads us to the problem of luxury, a problem that grows by the day, which is reaching the dimensions of a matter of life-or-death, bankruptcies, heart attacks, nervous disorders, divorce, bad relations between husband and wife that undermines education in good values, *Hoshen Mishpat* [the section of the *Shulkhan Arukh* dealing with the laws of commerce and property], and laws of monetary dealings. . . . Once and for all we must lance this boil, this inflated colored balloon that sows devastation and destruction in the Torah, in the whole and the pure, values and morals, and the bitter fruits that grow from this we must eat in both worlds, this and the next.

The concept of "being original" is very popular today, everyone wants to be original and innovative, but let us be honest with ourselves and take a look at the small matters of dress, food, or what is called "the culture of consumption"—has the banner of originality not become one big social fraud.[34]

Or as Nava said during one of her lessons on "worms and insects":

> What they say today is that every generation has its trial. There was the emancipation, the Holocaust, Zionism, and now it's luxury. That's what a lot of people say, that our generation is being tested with luxuries. And even if that seems much less than the previous trials, it is very dangerous. First, every generation is less strong, and also because it doesn't seem like a trial. People think it has no meaning, but it is a very great trial.

"Abundance," "luxury," and "the culture of consumption" are practical and valuable components of capitalist society. In the above quotations, however, they are portrayed as a real threat to the existence of the haredi community. Sometimes they are described as a general threat to the Torah, to purity, to values, and so on. (It is necessary to take into account the pathos that is an inseparable part of both spoken and written haredi public discourse.) Sometimes they are broken down into specific dangers, such as divorce, heart attacks, and nervous breakdowns. Either way, there is a contradiction between the condemnation of abundance and reliance on it, between the possibilities it opens for the haredi community and the fear of what it is liable to do, between the desire to foster the community's uniqueness and the integration that economic prosperity creates between the haredi community and the other groups that participate in the market.

Most haredi homes have electrical appliances, such as large refrigerators, washing machines, sewing machines, food processors, and modern ovens; some even have air conditioners, dishwashers, dryers, and other appliances that make life easier for large families. Many babies are dressed in disposable diapers and fed instant cereals. There are, of course, variations among different economic strata, between the families of working men and those of men who study at a kolel, between the various Hasidic groups, and between various places of residence. But in general the economic well-being of the haredi community is rising along with that of the rest of Israel's population.

The great attention lavished on the subject of luxury and its implications demands explanation. The tension between "flour and Torah," (i.e., between the needs for material and for spiritual sustenance) is not new, of course, but a paradox has now formed around these two elements. The sages said: "If there is no flour, there is no Torah." The contemporary discourse states: "If there is no flour, there is no Torah, and if there *is* flour, there is no Torah either." Haredi society seeks to be freed of this paradox, as of others.

Haredi society lives in anticipation of the time in the not-too-distant future when today's generation of avrechim must start marrying off its children. Unlike the previous generation, which had some resources from which to provide financial assistance to its children, the current generation has nothing. It also has a larger number of children than its parents' generation did, and the standard of living is higher.[35] In preparation for this approaching crisis, the public discourse has been enlisted in the condemnation of prosperity and the glorification of living simply. Haredi society's unique organization as a learning society, made possible by prosperity, may be destroyed by the very thing that created it. The haredi community thus chooses to equip its "religious package" with strict, demanding, particularistic, sexist, and puritanic values. These values contradict what is occurring around (and even within) the haredi community, and create the "counterculture" that is supposed to separate the haredi community from its surroundings and protect it. In order to protect itself from other similar communities, the public discourse is charged with values of humra, strictness.[36] It is in this that the counterculture acquires its specific traits. Everything secular society takes as a "value" is revised, and in every area in which other religious groups advocate leniency, the haredim advocate severity. Every community presents itself to its potential members as a club to which it is hard to be accepted. In this way, Friedman argues, communities try to make themselves unique and elitist in comparison with their competitors.

Resolution of the paradox of luxury seems to be assigned largely to the women. The general discourse that describes luxury as this generation's trial leads into specific accusations directed at women. The generation's trial is thus turned into women's most important trial. The haredi community considers itself to be a collection of individuals aspiring to a modest lifestyle, with minimal needs, but this aspiration encounters a barrier on its way to realization—the covetousness of females. This is the reduction of the "flour and Torah" paradox, and it is stated in such a way that it vanishes, leaving the field clear of men. The women are left alone, and they must cope with this "terrible trial" on their own.

In each of the quotations presented above there is a transition from sounding a general alarm to pointing an accusatory finger at women and girls:

A mother must accustom her children from the earliest age and tell the children that what they have is sweeter than honey. . . . My daughter, do not envy your friend or your neighbor. . . . The dress Mommy bought you is the prettiest. . . . What joy is it for a mother that from dawn until dark she has nothing to do but to cook, knit, and sew for her children, grandchildren, and great-grandchildren. . . .

They present themselves with an ultimatum, what do you mean that everyone around me has and I don't. This ultimatum leads to discord and fights that disturb the home's well-being in a way that the girls grow up in such an atmosphere so that they, too, will present their husbands with ultimatums, like their mothers, and the husbands that are not able or not interested in holding up under the pressure of the demands are liable to send their wives back to their parents' house, sometimes along with the children.

. . . We must feel that we are not missing a thing. If we feel that we do not have to wear the latest fashionable coat then our daughters will also feel comfortable in clothes a little bit different from her peers, and will maybe even take pride in her originality. . . .

Hannah: I also heard from my husband about the generation's trial. People talk about it a lot. What I don't understand is how you connect that subject with what we're discussing.

Nava: It begins when someone says that you can go to Levinsky Street and buy fresh by weight, everyone jumps on her. Who wants to take the trouble to go into town to buy at a bargain when you can buy in the supermarket. This is where it begins, when women do not want to cut back, the most important thing is convenience.

An article in *Marveh Latsameh* takes a romantic and accusatory atti-tude to the present generation of women:

But there is no need to go so far afield. One can simply ask how did my mother manage with three babies without a washing machine? . . . She had to prepare Sabbaths and holidays for a large family. . . . And how did my mother lug blocks of ice for her icebox and carry those heavy blocks up to the third floor. . . . And today . . . families buy sewing machines and freezers and even dryers and dishwashers. . . . But still it is obvious that we have no time to visit a sick aunt or to help a friend who needs it because we are very busy people and we have to invent a machine that will visit the aunt for us.[37]

Rabbis, educators, teachers, and important women charge public dis-course with diatribes against the "phenomenon of luxuries." They have much to say about the "generation's trial," about the "threat of luxuries," and about the "filth in money." Despite this, the haredi community, just like other communities in Israel and the West, partially measures a family's or community's success by its economic attainments. Within the universe of values itself, and in conjunction with the social reality, this creates unresolvable and unsolvable paradoxes.

After having brought the issue of luxury into the public discourse as part of constructing its counterculture, haredi society must free itself from the vicious circle that this choice causes practically. It would seem that breaking free of the paradox of luxury, which is, as noted, a typical and prominent example of the entire process of circularity, is largely imposed on females and is linked to the more fundamental value of modesty.

Diapers and diamonds. In the twenty-fifth anniversary book of the Sharansky Beit Ya'akov college in Tel Aviv, David Zaritzky writes as follows:

> Place the woman once more on the throne prepared at the time of creation for the Jewish mother, and she will be happier with diapers than an ostentatious woman is with a diamond-encrusted necklace, and a night up with her child will be more enjoyable to her than a night of dancing in a café.
>
> Beit Ya'akov took modesty, which had been pushed into a corner, and dressed its students, took the light that had not yet been outshone and which was tossing under the feet of the rock-and-rollers and crowned the heads of our mothers with it.[38]

Transferring the generation's trial onto women's shoulders made an additional reworking necessary. It was no longer sufficient to say that women should be more modest in their demands. The request must have a reason and must be accompanied by a threat. The reason added to the demand to refrain from pursuing luxuries was more particularly directed at women than the other reasons we have seen; it is part of observing the rules of modesty.[39]

No one in the haredi community will come out against modesty. As a vague and comprehensive value, everyone in each haredi group accepts modesty submissively. As a result, it becomes an efficient and important tool. Everyone wants to be modest, and everyone may be accused of having violated its rules. So by declaring that a woman must eschew luxury in order to preserve her modesty, one links the demand to a threat to a woman's reputation. This threat exposes women, as a public, to a multitude of reproofs and rebukes.

The observational evidence shows that *every time* women gathered for any purpose (study, celebration, charity, and so on), they were admonished about modesty. The admonishments may be categorized in accordance with four dimensions that each require a separate discussion, but that we will present at only the most basic level:

1. Extent—the proportion of the event devoted to the admonishments.
2. Location—where the admonishment occurs (i.e., at home, in the neighborhood, or outside the Development).
3. Source—who admonishes (man or woman, an external figure invited for that purpose, or a local figure on his or her own initiative).
4. Message—the content of the admonishment and what it is linked to.

Two of many admonishments I observed are described below.

Self-Chastisement. After about six months in which there was no activity at all, the women met at the Beit Ya'akov school that serves the Sepharadi haredi children in the adjacent neighborhood. At 8:45 P.M. some thirty women, most from Gur, were present in one of the classrooms. Two Sepharadi women with kerchiefs on their heads sat in a corner, apart. Some of the young women were new in the Development—young newly-weds who had taken the place of women whose period of "exile" had ended, enabling them to return to Bene Brak or Jerusalem. The room was animated. The women collected in groups; most knew each other from their studies at the Beit Ya'akov college from which they had recently graduated. They were dressed well, in colorful and fashionable knits, and wore modern wigs, some of which reached the shoulder. About a third of the women present were pregnant. Nava stood at the front of the class-room by the teacher's desk. At twenty-three, she had been married for more than two years, but still had no children. She began to speak, but the noise did not die down. She persisted, and slowly silence fell over the room, the girls shushing one another.

"I apologize for the delay," she said. "The teacher refused to come in a cab for reasons of modesty, so she will arrive on the nine o'clock bus."

At the set hour Mrs. Frieda Hertig, a teacher at the Beit Ya'akov col-lege in Bene Brak, arrived. The girls made a gesture of rising (lifting their behinds slightly). Frieda, thirty-three years old, dressed in a plaid wool dress, had a slender figure and wore a short wig of the reasonable type (not modern but not the simplest, most inexpensive type, either). She did not greet us with a "good evening" or "hello"; instead she immediately began:

> There was a flute in the Temple. A pipe flute. Thin, smooth, and
> simple. The flute had an incomparably pleasant and beautiful sound.
> The king so loved the flute that he ordered that it be plated in gold.
> They took it to the best craftsmen and plated it with the finest gold.
> The flute lost its sound. When they took the gold off, it once again
> played with a wondrous sound. This is the way Jewish women are—
> our beauty lies in our simplicity.

Her voice was dramatic. She reads from notes with all her accents cor-rectly placed, her grammar impeccable.

The teacher then explained the metaphor, nearly word by word. She did not leave a single symbol unexplained.

Afterwards she recalled that women from the Development had asked her to speak about modesty. There were giggles from the audience, and the speaker herself smiled.

> Yes, simply that, whoever expected something else can still leave.
> The fact that you live in this Development is a result of you all being

connected to the same righteous man. This is the rebbe's commandment. Even if it is technical, such a community, such a public, has
much power. Not as it would be if we lived scattered around. You are
together, the society has a voice. So in just such a place there is a
problem of modesty. It is true that our generation is being tested with
a great trial in the matter of consumption and modesty and we all
need great changes, but to what point? A woman will wear a slit in
her skirt? Where does that boldness come from? Lord of the
Universe, to be first? The one that comes after her will need much
less courage, but the first one, where does she get the strength from,
from where? A woman who goes out of her house and everything is
exactly in place, every hair, the clothes, that doesn't come naturally,
right? You have to devote time to that, so she leaves the house with
a sign on herself—this is what interests me. She didn't notice? She
doesn't know that that's what people see on her? So let me judge her
leniently—she's simply a fool.

A while ago there was a conference on modesty at the Modi'in
Hall and rabbis spoke there. What have we come to that we have to
talk about this subject in public, that rabbis come before women to
talk to them about this? So our generation is bringing the rabbis
down as well.

Everyone wants to be different. I cut some advertisements out of
Hamodia, nothing special, just advertisements for furniture, clothing,
such things. Every second word is exclusive, special, unique. People
devote so much time to not being like their neighbor. A woman runs
to every store there is to buy a special dress. With my own ears I
heard a very respectable woman who was mazel tov about to marry
off her daughter, and don't get me wrong I haven't married off a
daughter and haven't had to face the test. She said that she had
combed the United States of America in order to find her a special
wedding gown. Who are we doing that for? Do our avrechim deserve
that kind of treatment? Ahhhh . . . It's not for our husbands? So then
we really shouldn't have to think about it. We're a link in a chain
that goes back to Sarah, and we give to our daughters, what will we
give them? They say of Abraham our father that he reached Egypt
with Sarah and they stood on the edge of the Nile. He saw her
reflection in the water and told her "Now I know that you are a
beautiful woman." What did he see in her? The sages say that all the
women of the generation of Egypt knew that their behavior would
cause Israel's redemption. That's our beauty, not outward beauty.

The teacher went on, her tone changing from that appropriate of a
friendly conversation to that of serious preaching. From time to time she
would throw in a midrash or biblical verse (about the Shulamit from the

Song of Songs, for instance). The women sat quietly, most of them staring at the floor.

At the end of the lesson her former students and current colleagues gathered around her, chatting with her happily. Tsipi told her: "Good for you, we've been waiting for this talk for a long time, let's hope that something gets moving." The other women left in twos or threes. Hannah and I exited, leaving a room in which there was a palpable sense of relief.

We stood and talked in the cold of a February night by the fence around Hannah's building. Slowly the women emerged from the school and passed by us. Devorah was carrying a tape recorder, on which she had recorded the lecture. She came up to us.

"That's it, I've done my part."

Devorah, very active in the Development, had invited Frieda Hertig to speak. She had been a resident for seven years. Recently, her husband had been appointed manager of a well-known hotel in Bene Brak, and they were about to move there. His father had a hotel in Lugano, Switzerland, so he knew the work.

Devorah worked at home, styling wigs. She was always dressed with particular elegance, sporting a variety of wigs—long ones, adorned with colored pins—and loud pink lipstick. She and her sister were always together and formed the nucleus of the group of "Tel Avivians" in the Development. As she was standing with us, a young girl approached her and said:

"So, when will you have time for me, I've got to have my second wig, the long one, styled for the wedding. You know that it's urgent for me, I've got to have it styled, it looks horrible."

Hannah smiled at me, lowering her head. What a fitting conclusion for both the lecture and the woman who arranged it.

Devorah also smiled, turned her back, and began to stride towards the stairwell, blurting:

"Leave me alone now, call me on the phone."

Invitation to a reprimand. At the wedding hall on Hamasger Street in Tel Aviv there was a fundraising night for the dining hall of the yeshiva in the Gur Development in Hatzor Hagelilit. The walls were covered with decorated wallpaper with velvet maroon-colored flowers. At the entrance there were huge mirrors, and on the floor wall-to-wall carpeting. The hall was packed. Some 400 women were socializing, dressed in their best clothes. It was Saturday night, and the glow of the Sabbath still remained in the women's faces. The noise in the hall was deafening. The women tried to get places around those tables with the best views of the stage at the front of the hall. In a few minutes there would be speeches by the head of the yeshiva, its patron, and by a respected woman, a teacher from London. Afterwards the girls from the Gur college in Bene Brak were to present a musical entertainment (or, as the program stated, "A Musical with Many Morals").

After the talks by the head of the yeshiva and the fund-raiser, Mrs. Yaffa Mendel of London mounted the stage. She was wearing a simple dark dress and a short wig.

We are the daughters of Eve. Why? We give life. We have a role with regard to others. To be a helpmeet. Helpmeet? Not at the expense of the husband and children. Not to run off in the evenings to fund-raisers. To be public activists. A helpmeet to minimize demands. Yes, you can take a pencil and paper and add it up. How much clothing do you need, how many wigs? What difference does it make where the buttons are and how the collar lies? It will make your husband happy. Maybe it won't make the neighbors happy, but God yes, that's how you can collect money for charity, not at parties. Your husband will study with his mind at rest, the children will be cared for and the woman will be at home with her small demands.

The women slowly reached out for the coffee pots and the chocolate-filled cakes on the tables. Each of them had paid 20 shekels ($10) for the evening, and here an important woman from London was telling them that they shouldn't have come, that this was not the proper way to raise money. They knew that the speech would be over in a few minutes, however; it would be possible to look up from the floor and enjoy the show, even if it was called "A Musical with Many Morals."

"Modesty" is the basic, broadest, and most inclusive standard of a woman's behavior. It can measure an entire range of her activities—her dress, her speech, her education, the way she educates her children, her work at home and outside it, and more. The standard of modesty is enlisted whenever there is a need to oversee what any woman is doing. "Luxuries" are described as a negative phenomenon embracing all of society, powered mainly by women. The standard of modesty becomes a preventative and threatening factor, in order to persuade women that (1) luxury is indeed the curse of this generation, (2) women are the motivating and determining force in the world of consumption, and (3) women have the central responsibility for the success or failure of this generation's "trial." The logical parallels among these three statements are not left to a woman's own comprehension. Every private or public opportunity is used to explain them to her.

The use of the standard of modesty turns each individual woman into a target of evaluation and judgment, and exposes her to the danger of slander. Modesty can also be a standard by which a community is judged, as we saw in Frieda Hertig's talk. This teacher had charges to make against "the women of the Development." She conveyed her message that life in a homogeneous and constricted community obligated them to a higher standard than that applied to other women. The lecturer had been invited by

several local women who felt that "the situation is deteriorating." As I
recall, nothing in particular had occurred in the Development to arouse
the women. In the daily routine a talk about modesty is always appropriate.
The women, for their part, accept such lectures as being part of the obligations of the community, and take great comfort in them. This was made
clear to me during one of my conversations with Hannah.

Hannah: So, did you enjoy Mrs. Hertig's talk?

I: Not particularly. I felt a little like a first-grader getting chewed out.

Hannah: I know, you like really high talk, about Maimonides and
about faith in the Book of Psalms.

I: That's true, but I couldn't help noticing how all the women sat
like good little girls while she gave them a piece of her mind.

Hannah: For you it doesn't make a difference, what do you understand, but they, when they go to Bene Brak to buy a dress, talk about
Maimonides doesn't help them. Maimonides doesn't help you put
the money back in your wallet. You need something that makes you
strong, that gives you the strength, that gives you the strength.

Teacher Frieda Hertig had been invited to come specially from Bene
Brak in order to give the women strength. Some of the women understood
her the way Hannah did; others listened, but were not inclined to carry out
her instructions on a practical level (like the woman who needed her wig
styled for a wedding). There were even those who told me that, in their
opinion, the women in the Development were very modest and that they
did not understand why they were being reprimanded. Nevertheless, the
women accepted the admonishments about modesty as a valid form of discourse. They knew that it could surprise them at a party or a play, in their
homes at the Sabbath table, or among friends in the Development while
the children played. It was plain to them that this was the price they had
to pay so that the show, in both senses of the word, could go on.

Yaffa Mendel, who spoke before a gathering of charity volunteers at a
benefit evening, went even further. She told them explicitly: It's good you
came, because this is the place to tell you that you shouldn't have come. In
other words, those who came to hear the lecture heard the lecturer tell
them that the proper place for women was not at a charity evening but at
home. (Note the parallel to Rabbi Wolf's exhortation: Go to school in
order not to learn.) Mrs. Mendel proposed that women save for charity out
of their personal budget: one less wig meant more for charity. Like many
others, she linked modesty in a women's material demands with her
husband's and sons' success in their studies and with God's will. These

linkages are so consequential for haredi women that the only possible response was what I observed in the hall—to lower one's head and nibble some chocolate cake.

The concept of "modesty" is, then, the central axis for understanding the social and personal existence of the haredi woman. Anthropologist Rhonda Berger-Sofer, who studied the women of Ha'eda Haharedit in the Mea She'arim neighborhood of Jerusalem, tried to show that women serve as the haredi community's shock absorbers.[40] This is why women are drawn towards "nature" while men are pushed towards "culture." Since they are in contact with the mundane, the profane, and the material, women can maintain contact with the "outside," i.e., with the secular environment. "Modesty" is enlisted in this case to defend women from the outside. The importance of a woman's reputation is an insurance policy that ensures that the woman will not take her contacts with the outside too far.

Vimla Jayanti, an anthropologist who worked in the same community, argues that "modesty" is for the most part an educational tool. She found that the ethic of modesty may be found everywhere a female is educated. In her opinion, the use of modesty does not have a particular direction, and in her study she argues that the standard of *balebeitishkeit*, of homemaking, is more relevant to oversight and critique of women. This standard, which is of great significance in other haredi communities (including Gur) as well, is especially strong among Ha'eda Haharedit. The families of this community live in constricted economic circumstances and lack any thorough education for women, and the difficulty of finding work for women outside the home and the neighborhood makes the virtues of the housewife more significant than any others.[41]

In a society in which people sometimes have trouble obtaining food, clothing, and shelter, "abundance" in the normal sense of the word presents no threat. Austerity and getting by with little form part of this dimension of homemaking, which becomes the major criterion according to which women are evaluated and supervised.

Yet in the haredi community outside the walls of Mea She'arim, it is the women who are the agents of breaking free of the paradox of luxury. This generation's success or failure in its trial depends, as we have seen, on the women. But here, as in all else, any possible outcome will be to their detriment. If the generation fails its test, it will be "because of the demanding women"; if the generation passes the test, it will be because the men knew how to oppose women's demands, how not to give in.

Among the many possibilities available to the religious community, it chooses and nurtures the ideological option of modesty. This choice is consistent with encouraging married men to continue their studies and with fostering the image of an "ascetic community," and is even a consequence of it. Puritanism (which itself may well contradict previous Jewish values and be something of a borrowing from Christianity) aids women in their daily lives. It turns their plight into worship, their relative poverty into a social virtue, and their private troubles into "partial comfort."

The counterculture constructed in opposition to secular society is mainly directed at the middle-class members of the community. Wealth is not an undesirable state. The existence of a moneyed class as a small part of Jewish society does not constitute a threat to the "ascetic community." On the contrary, this class supports religious and charitable institutions, and provides mates for poor scholars. The problem of consumption and luxury termed "this generation's trial" is a problem of the middle classes. Life in a Western society with a competitive market enables everyone to experience consumerism and welfare.[42] The sense of unlimited possibilities is an incentive for economic activity. For a very narrow segment of society these expectations are realized, but among much larger segments they remain a dream difficult to achieve, and this causes great pressure in daily life. In traditional Jewish society there were rich and poor, and the division of labor between them, between flour and Torah, was understood by all. In Israel today, the haredi community has chosen to constrain artificially the certain ability that exists to blur the distinction between these traditional classes. As men are induced to extend their years of study, consumption becomes a delaying and pressuring factor, and the battle to restrict consumption is organized socially as a campaign of and against women.

❦

The boundaries drawn by the haredi community for itself within Jewish society exist as a result of a paradoxical situation. The haredim live in a pluralist society that allows them to undermine its foundations. They charge their cultural choice with values that run contrary to the capitalist society of abundance, and present consumption as "this generation's disaster" and austerity as "this generation's trial." In this same way they wish to protect the learning society, which urges men to abstain from entering the labor market; this is the way they present the economic strain that this society creates. Yet only a society of relative prosperity can bear the burden of this choice. Any attempt to resolve and connect the components of this paradox immediately gives rise to new paradoxes, while any attempt to break it down into its components (state and religion, for instance) is still far away.

The subject of women's education and status, which stands at the center of this book, constitutes a classic example of this circuitous process. At the first stage, the orthodox community was provoked into establishing formal education for women, in order to counter the process of secularization and general education that was experienced by most European Jews. Orthodox schools for women were established in order to prevent the girls from being sent to non-Jewish or Zionist schools. In an attempt to circum-vent the process of education, orthodoxy had no choice but to become part of it. Haredi women began to study.

During the second stage, with the move to Israel, the educational dis-course was charged with anti-Zionist and anti-nationalist values. The com-munity was part of the Zionist-nationalist state, economically dependent on its resources and mindful of events on the sociocultural level. This attentiveness to what was happening in the secular arena guided the con-struction of the community's cultural essence. This society, which some assume wishes to close itself off within its own walls, makes a great effort to know what is going on "out there." It turns these findings upside-down and presents them as a behavioral standard to its members.

The haredi educational system for women offers a feminine ideal-type. It is the opposite of the set of feminine traits common in the sur-rounding society, and it is appropriate to the learning men's society. No wonder, then, that women's education has been defined by the haredim as an attempt to recreate a generation of simple and ignorant women like those mothers and grandmothers who never studied at all. This contra-dictory attempt to educate for ignorance has been presented here in all its facets. We have seen that there is methodical direction of the presenta-tion of the pragmatic aspects of knowledge before women. There is a ten-dency to divide knowledge into "masculine" and "feminine" fields (or what the women call the "substantial" and the "practical"). The women's educational system opens certain doors for them and takes care to keep others locked. Yet from the moment women become literate, they them-selves conduct negotiations over the essence of the boundaries between different fields of knowledge. Women still do not study the Gemara, which is the main part of male knowledge and the source of literate and social power in the haredi world. Yet they can cite laws from the *Shulkhan Arukh*, quote homilies from the ethical literature, and recite a midrash to illustrate their point. They overhear their husbands studying the Gemara with their study partners at home, and they go over Talmudic disputations with their sons. Most important, they know how to navigate between the different fields of knowledge and to test one field with the help of another. When they are presented with practical study, they attack it with abstract questions; when they are offered abstract knowledge, they bring it down to earth.

If one speaks with them on Maimonides' view of the barriers between man and his creator, they find a way of interpreting the issue with the aid of their shopping list. If one preaches "thou shalts" and "thou shalt nots" about slander or modesty, they suggest speaking of Torah instead of gos-siping, they make abstract comparisons with the male world, they describe the preaching as "spiritual strengthening," or they let the preaching fly over their heads.

This is how they make their way through their world, a world whose social order they accept a priori. On the one hand they know how to experience this world as ignorant and simple women and accept the rule of the male world; but on the other hand they are sufficiently literate to be aware of the situation they are in and to find meaning in it.

Haredi men have constructed an educational system for women because "there is no need for women to study." Haredi women have learned to be educated (and to educate) in ignorance, in order to survive as educated women.

Notes

1. The positivist school of sociology likens sociological phenomena to physical phenomena (Durkheim 1956). Thus, it is possible to engage in observations and/or to ask questions about social boundaries, just as one would with regard to physical phenomena.

2. Zobrowski and Herzog 1952; Sobel 1956; Kranzler 1961; Poll 1962; Rubin 1972; Shaffir 1974.

3. On the transition from phenomenological philosophy to sociology, see Schutz 1962, 1970; on phenomenology in sociology, see Berger and Luckman 1966; on phenomenology in the study of religions in the modern age, see Berger 1969, 1977.

4. Heilman 1976; Deshen 1978; Friedman 1982, 1986; and in Hebrew: Deshen 5749 (1989); Friedman 5732 (1972).

5. Smith and Berg (1987) have written a book on paradoxical situations in dynamic work groups. For their purposes, they accept the definition put forth by Hughes and Brecht (1975), which says that a paradox is a sentence or set of sentences that has three characteristics: self-reference, conflict, and circularity. An example of a one-sentence paradox is "Please ignore this sentence." Rabbi Wolf's sentence about women's education is therefore paradoxical: "The purpose of their studies is to aspire to emulate our matriarchs, who did not study." We therefore find in the previous chapter that the very fact of the legitimacy of women's education is paradoxical, and leads to a vicious circle. The community invests huge efforts to resolve this paradox, but it does not succeed because it does not deal with the components of the paradox.

The role of the paradox in community life is also discussed in Hazan's article (1988), and in his book (1990).

6. *Marveh Latsameh*, no. 65, 5746 (1986), p. 18.

7. *Marveh Latsameh*, no. 15, 5747 (1987), p. 4.

8. *Marveh Latsameh*, no. 28, 5746 (1986), p. 10.

9. *Marveh Latsameh*, no. 28, 5746 (1986), p. 3.

10. On June 11, 1985, a group of seventh-grade students from a school in Petah Tikva set out on a bar mitzvah trip. As their bus went through a grade crossing on a dirt road near Moshav Habonim, close to the Mediterranean coast, it was hit by a train. The bus driver, one mother, and twenty children were killed.

11. Each of the participants in the conversation that follows began by citing an authoritative reason for turning on the radio. One said that her husband told her to, another heard it on the bus, and the third had heard about the event from her neighbors and only then decided to turn on the radio. When, in the Development,

people mention that they listen to the radio, they are declaring that they have a radio at home and that they use it at times. None of the homes in the Development have televisions, and the strictest buy tape players without radios so that they can listen to kosher tapes without being tempted to listen to the radio. Most of the residents nevertheless have combination radio–tape players in their homes. In public, these people confirm that they listen to the radio only at special times—for instance, in wartime, during a disaster, or during a special call-in program of Hasidic songs. In the case presented here, each woman had to explain how she heard the news that legitimized turning on the radio.

12. *Marveh Latsameh*, no. 35, 5746 (1986), p. 3.

13. *Marveh Latsameh*, no. 24, 5746 (1986), p. 2.

14. The source for this legal category is the Babylonian Talmud, Shabbat 68b; Shavuot 5a, Kritut 3b. These sources discuss the legal status of a Jew who did not grow up among Jews.

15. *Getting Smaller?*" Amnon Levy, *Hadashot*, 20 Aug. 1988.

16. *Marveh Latsameh*, no. 51, 5746 (1986).

17. Physical contact within the haredi family is an interesting subject. To discuss it in depth almost certainly would require the tools of psychology or anthro-psychiatry. In my notes, I found many descriptions of physical contact between children and between children and their parents. The prohibition against contact between the sexes begins at an early age and leaves the family unit as the only arena in which the two sexes can have primary contact. In the families I was acquainted with, care was taken to put the boys and girls in different bedrooms, but they still had many opportunities for contact. With regard to the event described (the physical contact between me and my eight-year-old son), it should be noted that mothers do not generally embrace their children in public, their sons in particular, after they are three to five years of age. In general, from the time a boy can walk on his own, his mother stops touching him. It is common, on the haredi streets in Jerusalem or Bene Brak, to see older brothers or sisters carrying younger siblings who can walk by themselves, and this is, perhaps, an expression for the need for physical contact that goes beyond the minimum necessary for physical care.

18. Haredim drink only soft drinks manufactured by certain companies that have been approved by the haredi kashrut supervisors.

19. *Marveh Latsameh*, no. 34, 5746 (1986), p. 16.

20. *Marveh Latsameh*, nos. 68–70, 5747 (1987), p. 49.

21. *Marveh Latsameh*, no. 65, 5747 (1987), p. 13.

22. *Marveh Latsameh*, no. 63, 5747 (1987), p. 18.

23. On Mea She'arim, see Heilman 1992.

24. Because women belong to a Hasidic community through their fathers or husbands (being born to a Hasid or being married to a Hasid), they can, therefore, change their community affiliation through marriage. Gur Hasidism is known for the strict code of modesty observed by its members. The women do not dress elegantly as do the wives of the Misnagdim or of Habad Hasidim. They meet their intended husbands only twice before their marriage. There is also controversy within the sect over a custom prescribing abstention from sexual relations except for the night the woman goes to the mikveh (i.e., once a month). All these, and other customs, are a burden of which some women wish to be relieved.

25. "Important guest" is a term taken from the Babylonian Talmud (Kritut 71b, Shabbat 59b, Pesahim 108a, Avoda Zara 25b). These sources grant special dispensations to important women, who are permitted to adorn themselves with jewelry and to recline, like the men, during the Pesah seder. In everyday language, the adjective "important" is applied to righteous women, admired teachers, the wives of

wealthy men, and so on. At a Sabbath meal I had at Hannah's home ("Shabbat Hagadol," the Sabbath before Pesah), her husband went over the laws of Pesah with the children. When he reached the subject of who reclines, he enumerated those worthy of this honor: the father of the family who leads the seder, or the grandfather, or another older man, an honored guest, and an important woman. I, who had remained silent the entire meal, heard myself exclaiming:

"What's an important woman?"

"Ah!" he said, his face to the bookcase. "That is a woman who does charitable works, helps others, teaches, a woman who gives of herself and her time to the public, an educated woman—that is an important woman."

The connotation that came out most strongly then, as at other opportunities when the subject came up, was the emphasis on social status. An important woman is one considered such by others, who is recognized for her deeds, who has an established position. She is prominent, so she is important.

Rivka, however, was being sarcastic. Women in the Development generally appreciated the fact that I was studying for my Ph.D. and that I had my own car (a sign of a stable financial position, something Haredi society has no qualms about praising). But in applying a term reserved for righteous woman to me, a secular woman, Rivka expressed the other attitude displayed by her and also, perhaps, other women in the Development as well.

26. The *haltal* is a thin upper gown that men wear in and around the home. It is lighter than the overcoat worn outside.

27. Nicholson 1990.

28. Kristeva 1981.

29. Strathern 1988.

30. Bem and Bem 1971.

31. Burton 1985.

32. Strathern 1988.

33. On discourse as a social field of events, see Foucault 1970, 1980.

34. From *Marveh Latsameh*, in order of appearance: Yisrael Pollak, no. 35, 5746 (1986), pp. 15–19; Elhanan Hertzman, no. 50, 5746 (1986), p. 22; N. Shapira, no. 50, 5746 (1986), p. 42.

35. While I was writing this book, after my observations were completed, I continued to maintain contact with the Gur women, as well as with other acquaintances in the haredi community. I presented several of my conclusions to them. With regard to the coming economic crisis, a man with a key position in the haredi community noted to me that every (middle-class) couple that has married has cost each side of the family about $60,000. This money was raised from personal holdings and from loans from haredi community funds (gamahim). The gamahim are now on the verge of collapse, and private capital has shrunk. There have been attempts to engineer a general restitution of debts involving the entire deficiency of funds on the part of several rich overseas haredim, but these have not brought results so far. In his estimation, the "learning society" may well suffer a severe blow in the near future. Couples getting married will be forced to live in rented apartments, and the stipends provided by the yeshivot to their students will not be sufficient to pay for rent and living expenses. Some of those studying today will have to find work. This may well be the most weighty reason for the haredi community's increasing involvement in the government and public spheres. Such involvement guarantees a steady flow of government funds to sustain the learning society, or at least a large part of it.

36. The distinction between *humra* (strictness) and *kula* (leniency) is made on two levels. One distinguishes between the "greater" and "lesser" religious observances

("Run to perform a kula observance just as to a humra observance" [Avot 4:2, 2:1]). The second distinguishes between different ways of carrying out an observance— whether on a certain question of observance the rule should be lenient or severe (Eruvin 4:1, Pesahim 4:1, Orla 2:6).

It is in this context that what is called "religious extremism" should be understood. The extremism is not motivated by devotion to God; it is a social solution to cultural competition. The groups freed of public responsibility for all of Israel charge their identity with severe demands in order to set themselves apart from the secular masses and from their religious competitors as part of their cultural marketing strategy.

37. "Muvan Me'elav," no. 34, 5747 (1987), pp. 25–26.

38. Zaritzsky, 5769 (1969), p. 94.

39. The significance of modesty in the lives of Jewish women has received much attention, both in internal (orthodox) literature and in the research literature: Halevy-Steinberg 5743 (1983); Ki-Tov 5723 (1963), 5733 (1973); Fuchs 5744 (1984); Naftali 5745 (1985); Rotenberg 5742 (1982); Schenirer 5715 (1955).

40. Berger-Sofer 1979.

41. Jayanti 1982.

42. Lasch 1978.

Afterword

· · · ❧ · · ·

Cultures in Context

In December 1991 television cameras were brought into the living room of Rabbi Moshe Ze'ev Feldman, chairman of the Knessett's Finance Committee. The producers of the weekly talk show "Haleila" must have felt that this time they had good material. Even if they did not predict exactly what would happen there, what the dynamic between the speakers would be and how it would all "come across" on the screen, they could assume that in bringing the cameras, moderator Gabi Gazit, and secular Labor Party Knesset member Haim Ramon together with a haredi home and its residents, they had a winning combination. The motivation for meetings between haredim and secularists feeds in part on voyeurism. This is the way secular Jews get a peek at haredi life—through popular novels by writer and former haredi Yehoshua Bar-Yosef, through reportage like Amnon Levy's book *The Haredim*, and through the frequent articles in the daily and weekly press. So it was no surprise that the television audience was riveted by the opportunity to look into a home in Bene Brak. Yet, at the same time, Rabbi Feldman's family was peeking into the secular world. His wife did not forgo several appearances in the center of the screen. She could have prepared everything in advance so as to avoid "immodest" exposure on the boycotted medium. The rest of the women in the apartment, who were gathered together in the doorway, should also have stayed backstage, avoiding the camera's eye. But they stood there, peeking into the room, into the camera, and at the viewers in their homes.

The television link-up between the secular public and a piece of haredi reality was very intimate. The viewers sat at home, looking into that other home. For a moment it seemed that Haim Ramon could sit down with the chairman of the Finance Committee, drink coffee, eat homemade cookies, and discuss several matters of government in Hebrew. But it became clear how problematic this link is. *The next day the country erupted.* It was just like on other occasions when haredi and secularist world-views clashed: the night of the elections to the Twelfth Knesset, the violent demands against Ethiopian immigrants, the distribution of gas masks to bearded haredim during the Gulf War, Minister of the Interior Peretz's explanation of the Habonim bus accident, and Rabbi Shach's appearance at the Yad Eliahu basketball stadium in April 1990, when his words determined which party would rule the country.

Israeli society has seen a series of close encounters between the secular majority and the haredi minority. These encounters are characterized by great emotional and political intensity at the time of the event, sinking into oblivion a short time after they occur. It may well be that this dynamic is characteristic of Israeli public life or citizenship. Everyone knows that the outcry and wide-ranging press coverage of the trial of soldiers for their behavior in the occupied territories or the misdeeds of political parties will soon be forgotten.

This book, written by a secular anthropologist, is another type of encounter between the two communities. Every scientific work that sets out to decipher human existence suffers from the limitations of our ability to understand "the other." Yet this same limitation implies that we may understand the "similar" (that is, to apply their experience to ours). This encounter should at least serve to raise several issues that cast light on Israeli secular society in particular and secular Jewry in general.

ಈ

The haredim control whether Israeli society is drowsy or alert; the secular are barely aware of it. As long as the haredim keep themselves far from the social and political arena, the anesthetic continues to flow through the veins of both camps. The minute they wish to act within this arena and to take part in national decision-making processes (beyond the traditional issues of Sabbath and kashrut observance), everyone wakes up. Sometimes it is a sweet awakening, like after the annual telethon for the welfare of Israeli soldiers, when the country learned that the haredi minister of the interior, Arieh Dar'i, likes to listen to Bruce Springsteen. But generally it is an angry awakening in which it turns out, for instance, that Rabbi Feldman would like to revoke women's right to vote.

No initiative to codify the relation between religion and the state can be seriously discussed. Secular politicians have preferred to avoid it.

Yet it would seem that the relation between religion and the state is more problematic for the haredim than it is for the secular. From the moment they chose the "learning society" as their strategy for cultural existence in an open and competitive cultural market, they need more and more room to maneuver in the government arena. This choice of the learning society, with its isolationist values, is dependent, ironically, on the haredim's ability to find their place in the national system. They need government money to maintain their bloated educational institutions and to provide mortgages for their young couples, and they need to delay or cancel military or national service for their young men and women. For this reason, the haredim are making their presence felt in the government and public arenas, and secular society is not prepared for such increasingly frequent encounters.

The secularists display two sets of reactions to the haredim: contempt, revulsion, or hatred; and nostalgia, curiosity, and interest in the exotic. These reactions color relations between the two groups. The contempt and hatred derive from the sense that the authorities are imposing religious coercion. Haredi success on this level is not a function of the haredim's "nature" or "shrewdness." It is a sign of secular society's cultural and political negligence. Israeli society has not succeeded in clarifying for itself the nature of the link between nationality and religion. Every haredi advance (halting El Al flights on the Sabbath, forbidding the sale of pork, insisting on conversion for Ethiopian Jews, to name some recent ones) is made possible because of the political structure that the secular public is reluctant to change. Instead of being interpreted in this way, it is transferred to the emotional level and expressed as hatred of the haredim. At the emotional level the haredim are demonized and given an image that is far from reality. People fear "haredization," speak of the haredim in racist terms, and describe them as monsters, at a time when daily life has grown increasingly secular. (The way people spend their weekends in the 1990s is not at all like the way they spent them ten or twenty years ago.) Contempt and hatred are, therefore, dangerous and useless attitudes.

Yet the secular also display a kind of nostalgia and curiosity about the haredi world. These derive, on the one hand, from the natural tendency to be fascinated by something hidden that lies so close by, but it is also fed by the feeling that these "others" are the current incarnation of a lost past, or a possible variation on ourselves.

When people learned that I was carrying out a study of haredi women, many of them asked me a question: "Are they happier than we are?" Since I could not provide an answer to this query, I decided to look into the frequency of the question.

I learned that we sometimes consider the other possibility (i.e., the religious life) as a way out of distress we have been unable to resolve. A society that is structured according to sexist compartmentalization of men and women is nevertheless thought of as a possible source of happiness. Somehow, it seems better than the indeterminate here and now of a society that has, for the last hundred years, been conducting a probing inquiry into the relations between the sexes. People are weary of this. It still seems, even if only sometimes, and briefly, that "there," among women and men who "know their places," life might be easier. Women don't compete in the labor market, and men do not enter the delivery rooms or wear earrings. Secular society's exhausting fight to liberate the sexes makes the sexuality of the haredi world look unconventional and exotic—sometimes even pornographic.

If we suspend this encounter for a moment, before its time also passes and it is replaced by some other social issue, it would seem that handing Jewish culture over to the haredim has not taken the question of Judaism off the agenda. Orthodox Jewry has quickly appropriated this culture, with the collaboration of the secularists, who are happy to rid themselves of the burden.

Israeli culture has presented nationalism as the answer to the Jewish question. Fragments of Judaism (texts, rituals, customs) were adopted or rejected on the basis of their coherence with the new national identity. In the meantime, religious Zionism became more radically nationalistic, and this led to a transformation of its ideological and actual frontier (for instance, by building settlements in the occupied territories). While this attracted secular Judaism for a short while, in the end it alienated secular Jews from modern orthodoxy and ended up stereotyping the entire "knitted kipah public" as fundamentalist. Haredi Judaism, which nurtures its strict and eccentric interpretations of Jewish tradition, is of low relevance for the majority of the Israeli public. The result is that secular culture turns its back on Jewish culture. It is unconcerned about losing its Jewish identity because it is confident that it has an Israeli identity. Unlike Diaspora Jews, who strive to reform, adjust, claim, and reclaim their religious and cultural identity, secular Israelis leave this to the state and to orthodoxy. In the end this is harmful for non-Jewish citizens (namely the Palestinians) and secular citizens and leaves an inadequate arena for the recreation of a contemporary Jewish culture. This task, like so many others, awaits the liberal, secular part of the Israeli public.

Glossary

· · · 🍃 · · ·

adar: sixth month of the Jewish year, in which Purim occurs

admor: rebbe, leader of a Hasidic sect

Agudat Yisrael: an umbrella organization of haredi Jews throughout the world; in Israel it functions as a political party

Al Hamishmar: daily newspaper published by the left-wing Mapam Party

Ashkenazi: a Jew of German or East European ancestry

avrech: a young man who studies full time (plural, *avrechim*)

ba'al-bayit: someone who leaves his studies and earns his living in a craft or profession

ba'al teshuva: "master of repentance," a newly religious person (feminine, *ba'alot teshuva*; masculine plural, *ba'alei teshuva*)

bal tashit: prohibition against throwing away food

balebeitishkeit: homemaking

bar mitzvah: ceremony for thirteen-year-old boys marking their entry into full responsibility for performing the mitzvot

Barukh ata: "Blessed Are Thou," the opening words of Jewish blessings

Batei Ungarin: a section of the Mea She'arim neighborhood

Batya: Haredi girls' movement

b'de'avad: a posteriori (Rebbis may permit a certain practice or action b'de'avad because it reflects an existing reality.)

bein hazemanim: three-week summer break between two yeshiva academic years

beit-midrash: house of study

Belzer Hasidim: a Hasidic sect

Benot Ha'aguda: Haredi girls' and women's movement

birkat hamazon: grace after meals

brit milah: circumcision ceremony

cholent: stew traditionally eaten for lunch on Shabbat

dosit: Israeli slang for a religious girl or woman, derogatory

Eight Chapters: Maimonides' introduction to his commentary on the Avot tractate of the Mishna, which summarizes his philosophy

211

Elul: twelfth month of the Jewish year, immediately preceding the High Holidays

gamah: charitable operation often run by a family, synagogue, or community (plural, *gamahim*)

Gemara: rabbinical discussions and interpretations of the Mishna; together the Gemara and the Mishna form the Talmud

Geula: a Jewish Haredi neighborhood adjacent to Mea She'arim

gornisht: (Yiddish) nothing

groise zach: (Yiddish) a big deal

Gur Hasidim: the largest Hasidic sect in Israel

Habad: a Hasidic sect that proselytizes among Jews, known for its messianic fervor

Ha'eda Haharedit: the smaller and more extreme group of Hasidic sects in Israel

halaka: first haircut, age three

haltal: (Yiddish) robe worn by Hasidic men at home

Hamodia: newspaper of Agudat Yisrael

haredi: "the God fearing," ultraorthodox Jews (plural, *haredim*)

Hashomer Hatsair: left-wing kibbutz movement

heder: haredi boys' elementary school

hevruta: study partners

Hilkhot Beitah: book collection of laws concerning the home, meant for women

Hovevei Tsion: earliest pre-Herzl movement calling for the return of Jews to the fatherland

humra: strictness

kaparot: ceremony before Yom Kippur in which sins are symbolically transfered to a scapegoat

kashrut: Jewish dietary laws

kipah: a cap worn by religious Jewish men; haredim wear black kipot, religious Zionists wear knitted kipot (plural, *kipot*)

kleine menschelach: (Yiddish) little men

knish: (Yiddish) pastry filled with meat, potatoes, etc.

kolel: institution where young men pursue religious study full time

kula: leniency

laminatse'ah: opening phrase of some Psalms

le'ha'avir: to give (a lesson)

lehathila: a priori (A rabbinic lehathila decision mandates a new reality, in contrast with a b'de'avad decision.)

lernen: (Yiddish) study

limsor: to convey

Ma'alot: an opening word of uncertain meaning in some Psalms sometimes translated as "ascent" or "degrees"

ma'aserot: tithes

Ma'asiahu: a prison

maggid shiur: teacher

matsah: unleavened bread eaten on Pesah

mazel tov: "good luck"

me'ayin: from nothing

Menorat Hama'or: a moral book read by women

mensch: (Yiddish) a good person

Mesilat Yisharim: a book of moral teachings

mezuzot: a small parchment scroll with certain verses from the Torah on it; the scroll is affixed, in a casing, in the doorways of Jewish homes

midot tovot: good values

midrash: a rabbinic story or parable from the Talmudic period

mikveh: ritual bath

minayin: from where

Mishna Torah: Maimonides' code of Jewish law

Misnagdim: "the opponents," the Lithuanians; non-Hasidic haredim

mitzvah: a commandment or precept to be obeyed or performed by Jews

Mizrahi: a religious Zionist movement

moshav letsim: an assembly of scorners

Pele Yo'etz: digest of Jewish law

Pesah: Passover, the Jewish holiday commemorating the exodus from Egypt

pikuah nefesh: Jewish legal term meaning a situation in which someone's life is in danger

Poke'ah Ivrim: a moral book read by women

pritsa: a loose woman

Purim: a Jewish holiday celebrating Esther and Mordecai's defeat over Haman

rabbanit: a rabbi's wife, often a teacher and community leader in her own right

rebbe: admor, leader of a Hasidic sect

Rosh Hashanah: the Jewish new year's festival

Rosh Hodesh: the first day of each month

Sanhedrin: the Jewish religious court in Talmudic times

Satmer Hasidim: an extreme anti-Zionist Hasidic sect

schlemiel: (Yiddish) an incompetent or dull person

schlimazel: (Yiddish) an unlucky person

Sefira: seven weeks between the holidays of Passover and Shavuot

selichot: special prayers of repentance during the two weeks preceding Yom Kippur

Sepharadim: Jews whose ancestors come from the Islamic world, especially northern Africa and Asia

Shabbat: the Sabbath; a day of rest when religious Jews abstain from work and creative activity

Shavuot: Jewish holiday commemorating the giving of the Torah on Mount Sinai

sheine zachen: (Yiddish) nice things

Shekhina: God's presence

sheva brachot: "seven blessings," one of the seven festival meals held for a bride and groom during the week after their wedding

shiksa: (Yiddish) a non-Jewish woman

shofar: a specially prepared ram's horn that is blown during Elul and on Rosh Hashanah

Shulkhan Arukh: classic codification of Jewish law

Sukkot: the feast of Tabernacles, beginning five days after Yom Kippur, commemorating the children of Israel's sojourn in the desert

Tania: the classic text of the Habad sect

tefilin: phylacteries worn during morning prayers

tehilim-zager: (Yiddish) poor Psalm reciter

terumot: tithes

Tu Beshevat: tree-planting holiday

tish: (Yiddish) ritual Hasidic meal of a rabbi and disciples on the eve of the Sabbath

Tishrei: September–October; the first month of the Jewish year, the month of the High Holidays

Toldot Aharon Hasidism: an extreme Hasidic sect centered in Jerusalem

Tsena Ur'ena: Yiddish translation of Torah with commentaries and homilies intended especially for women

Tumim: sacred objects of the Temple used in prophecy

ulpanot: religious high school for girls

Urim: sacred objects of the Temple used in prophecy

Yediot Aharonot: the most popular Israeli daily newspaper

yekke: nickname for a German Jew, here standing for his broad education

yeshiva: a seminar for religious study for boys and men

Yeted Ne'eman: daily newspaper of the Lithuanians

yihud: room where bride and groom are left alone together after the wedding ceremony

yishar ko'ah: "good for you" or "bravo"

yishuv: the Jewish community in Palestine prior to Israel's independence

Yizkor: memorial prayer

Yom Kippur: the day of atonement, a mandatory fast for all adult Jews and the holiest day of the year

Bibliography

· · · ક્ર · · ·

Sources in Hebrew

Alfasi, Y. 5738 (1978). *The Gur Founder, Author of Hidushai.* Tel Aviv: HaRim.
———. 5746 (1986). *Hasidism and the Return to Zion.* Tel Aviv: Sifriat Ma'ariv.
Bauer, Y. 5742 (1982). *The Holocaust: Historical Aspects.* Tel Aviv: Sifriat Poalim.
Deshen, Shlomo. 5740 (1980). "Ethnicity and Citizenship in a Tunisian Synagogue in Israel." In Moshe Shokeid and Shlomo Deshen, eds. *Predicament of Homecoming.* Jerusalem: Yad Ben-Zvi.
———. 5749 (1989). "Understanding the Special Charm of Religiosity for Oriental Jews." *Politika,* no. 24.
Friedman, Menachem. 5732 (1972). "The Chief Rabbinate—A Dilemma Without a Solution." *Medina Umimshal,* A3.
———. 5749 (1989). "The Face of Religious Haredi Society Inside or Outside." *Ha'aretz-Yahadut,* Special Supplement, June 1989.
———. 5751 (1991). *The Haredi (Ultra-Orthodox) Society—Sources, Trends and Processes.* Jerusalem: The Jerusalem Institute for Israel Studies.
Fuchs, Y. 5744 (1984). *Laws of the Daughter of Israel.* Jerusalem: n.p.
Funkenstein, A., and A. Steinsaltz. 5747 (1987). *The Sociology of Ignorance.* Tel Aviv: Universita Mishuderet.
Ginzburg, Y. 5748 (1988). *Haredi Women in the New City.* Sapir Center for Development, Discussion Paper nos. 6–88.
Halevy-Steinberg, M. 5743 (1983). *Women's Laws.* Jerusalem: Reuven.
Hazan, H. 5748 (1988). "A Renewal Neighborhood as a Community." *Megamot,* 31(3–4).
———. 1990. "The Exact Opposite." *Iyyunim Behinuh.*
Ki-Tov, A. 5723 (1963). *The Book of Our Heritage.* Jerusalem: Beit Hotsa'at Sefarim.
———. 5733 (1973). *Man and His Home.* Jerusalem: Makhon Le'hotsa'at Sefarim.
Levy, A. 5748 (1988). *The Haredim.* Jerusalem: Hotsa'at Keter.
Marveh Latsameh. A Weekly Magazine for Counselors, Parents, and Educators. Bene Brak: Merkaz Hamahaneh Haharedi.
Naftali, G. 5745 (1985). *Guide/Epistle for the Bride.* Bene Brak: Tefutsa.
Ravitzky, Aviezer. 1993. *Messianism, Zionism, and Jewish Religious Radicalism.* Tel Aviv: Am Oved.
Rottenberg, Y. 5742 (1982). *The Jewish Home, the Jewish Family.* Bene Brak: Netsah.
Schenirer, S. 5715 (1955). *A Mother in Israel.* Tel Aviv: Netsah.

————. 5720 (1960). *The Writings of Sarah Schenirer*. Tel Aviv: Netsah.

Sharpstein, T. 5701 (1941). *The History of Jewish Education in Recent Generations*. Vol. III. New York: Hotsa'at Ogen.

Shilhav, Y., and Menachem Friedman. 5745 (1985). "Spreading within Isolation— The Haredi Community in Jerusalem." Jerusalem: The Jerusalem Institute for Israel Studies, 15.

Stengel, Y. 5741 (1981). *The Holocaust and the Jewish Question*. Tel Aviv: Hotsa'at Alef.

Wolner, Rachel, and Bracha Kaminer. 5742 (1982). *Private Space*. Tel Aviv: Hotsa'at Beit Ya'akov.

Yanai, T. 5749 (1989). "The Heritage." *Ha'ir* no. 6, 8 Dec. 1989.

Zaritzki, David. 5729 (1969). *Anniversary Book*. Tel Aviv: Hotsa'at Beit Ya'akov.

Sources in English

Adler, Morris. 1959. *The World of the Talmud*. Washington, D.C.: B'nai Brith Hillel Foundation.

Apple, M. W. 1979. *Ideology and Curriculum*. Boston: Routledge and Kegan Paul.

Backs, J. 1972. "Racial Prejudice and Black Self-Concept." In B. Y. Grambs, ed. *Black Self-Concept*. New York: McGraw-Hill.

Belenky, M. F., and B. Clincy. 1986. *Women's Ways of Knowing*. New York: Basic Books.

Bem, S., and D. Bem. 1971. "Training the Women to Know Her Place: The Power of a Nonconscious Ideology." In M. Hoffnung Garskof, ed. *Roles Women Play*. Pacific Grove, CA: Brooks/Cole.

Berger, Peter. 1969. *The Sacred Canopy*. New York: Anchor Books.

————. 1977. *Facing Up to Modernity*. New York: Basic Books.

Berger, Peter, and T. Luckman. 1966. *The Social Construction of Reality*. London: Penguin.

Berger-Sofer, Ronda. 1979. *Pious Women*. Ann Arbor, MI: University Microfilms Int.

————. 1981. "Ideological Separation and Structural Interaction." Unpublished paper.

Bloch, Maurice. 1977. *Language and Oratory in Traditional Societies*. San Diego, CA: Academic Press.

————. 1986. "Literacy and Enlightenment." Unpublished.

Bourdieu, Pierre. 1967. "Systems of Education and Systems of Thought." *International Social Science Journal* 19(3).

Bourdieu, Pierre, and Jean-Claude Passeron. 1977. *Reproduction in Education, Society and Culture*. London: Sage.

Boyarin, J. 1989. "Voices Around the Text: The Ethnography of Reading at Mesivta Tifereth Jerusalem." *Cultural Anthropology* 4(4):398–421.

Bryant, Margaret. 1979. *The Unexpected Revolution*. London: University of London.

Burton, C. 1985. *Subordination*. Sydney: George Allen and Unwin.

Clifford, J., and G. E. Marcus, eds. 1986. *Writing Culture*. Berkeley: University of California Press.

Connell, R. W. 1987. *Gender and Power*. Stanford: Stanford University Press.

Deshen, S. 1978. *Israeli Judaism: Introduction to Major Patterns*. Tel Aviv: Tel Aviv University Press.

Dreeben, R. 1968. *On What Is Learned in School*. Reading, MA: Addison-Wesley.

Dumont, R., and M. Was. 1967. "Cherokee School Society and the Inter-Cultural Classroom." In Roberts and Arkinsanya, eds. *Schooling in the Cultural Context*. New York: David Mckay.

Durkheim, E. 1956. *Education and Sociology*. Glencoe, IL: Free Press.

Ellen, R. F. 1984. *Ethnographic Research: A Guide to General Conduct*. London: Academic Press.

Finkelstein, L. 1955. *The Jewish Religion*. New York: Harper and Row.

Foucault, M. 1970. *The Order of Things*. London: Tavistock.

———. 1980. *Power Knowledge*. Brighton: Harvester Press.

Freilich, M., ed. 1970. *Marginal Natives: Anthropologists at Work*. New York: Harper and Row.

Freire, P. 1985. *The Politics of Education: Culture, Power, and Liberation*. South Hadley, MA: Bergin and Garney.

Freire, P., and D. Macedo. 1987. *Literacy: Reading the Word and the World*. London: Routledge and Kegan Paul.

Friedman, Menachem. 1982. "The Changing Role of Community Rabbinate." *Jerusalem Quarterly* 25:79–100.

———. 1986a. "Haredim Confront the Modern City." In P. Medding, ed. *Studies in Contemporary Jewry*, Vol. 2. Bloomington: Indiana University Press.

———. 1986b. "Life Tradition and Book Tradition in the Development of Ultra-Orthodox Judaism." In H. E. Goldberg, ed. *Judaism Viewed from Within and from Without*. Albany, NY: SUNY Press.

Geertz, C. 1973. *The Interpretation of Culture*. New York: Basic Books.

Giroux, H. 1983. *Theory and Resistance: A Pedagogy for the Opposition*. South Hadley, MA: Bergin and Garney.

Giroux, H., and P. McLaren. 1986. "Reproducing Reproduction: An Essay Review of 'Keeping Track' by Jeanie Oakes." *Metropolitan Education* 1:108–118.

Gluckman, M. 1967. "Introduction." In Arnold Epstein, ed. *The Craft of Social Anthropology*. London: Tavistock.

Goody, J. 1968. *Literacy in Traditional Societies*. Cambridge: Cambridge University Press.

———. 1977. *The Domestication of the Savage Mind*. Cambridge: Cambridge University Press.

———. 1988. *The Logic of Writing and the Organization of Society*. Cambridge: Cambridge University Press.

Graff, H. J. 1979. *The Literacy Myth*. London: Academic Press.

———. 1981. *Literacy and Social Development in the West*. Cambridge: Cambridge University Press.

Hazan, H. 1990. *Paradoxical Community*. Greenwich, CT: JAI Press.

Heilman, S. C. 1976. *Synagogue Life*. Chicago: University of Chicago Press.

———. 1983. *The People of the Book*. Chicago: University of Chicago Press.

———. 1984. *The Gate Behind the Wall*. New York: Summit Books.

———. 1992. *Defenders of the Faith: Inside Orthodox Jewry*. New York: Schocken Books.

Heilman, S. C., and M. Friedman. 1991. "Religious Fundamentalism and Religious Jews." In M. E. Marty and R. S. Appleby, eds. *Fundamentalisms Observed*. Chicago: University of Chicago Press.

Henry, J. 1972. *On Education*. New York: Vintage Books.

———. 1976. "Attitude Organization in Elementary School Classrooms." In Roberts and Akinsanya, eds. *Schooling in the Cultural Context*. New York: David Mckay.

Heschel, Abraham. 1966. *The Earth Is the Lord*. New York: Harper and Row.

Heschel, Susannah, ed. 1983. *On Being a Jewish Feminist*. New York: Schocken Books.

Hughes and Brecht. 1975. *Vicious Circles and Infinity*. New York: Penguin Books.

Jayanti, Bimala. 1982. "Women in M'ea Shearim." Master's thesis, Department of Sociology and Anthropology, Jerusalem University.

Kaestle, C. F. 1985. "The History of Literacy and the History of Readers." In E. Gordon, ed. *Review of Research in Education* 12:11–53.

Kerber, L. 1980. *Women of the Republic.* Chapel Hill: University of North Carolina Press.

Koltun, Elizabeth, ed. 1976. *The Jewish Woman.* New York: Schocken Books.

Kranzler, G. 1961. *Williamsburg: A Jewish Community in Transition.* New York: Feldheim.

Kristeva, Julia. 1981. "Women's Time." Translated by A. Jardine and H. Blake. *Signs: A Journal of Women and Society* 7:13–35.

Lasch, C. 1978. *The Culture of Narcissism.* New York: W. W. Norton and Co.

Levi-Strauss, C. 1964. *The Raw and the Cooked.* New York: Harper and Row.

———. 1975. *Structuralism and Sociological Theory.* London: Hutchinson.

———. 1978. *Myth and Meaning.* London: Routledge and Kegan Paul.

MacCormack, Carol, and Marilyn Strathern. 1980. *Nature, Culture and Gender.* Cambridge: Cambridge University Press.

McLaren, P. 1989. *Life in Schools.* New York: Longman.

Marcus, G. E., and M. J. Fischer. 1986. *Anthropology as Cultural Critique.* Chicago: University of Chicago Press.

Meyer, J. 1977. "The Effects of Education as an Institution." *American Journal of Sociology* 83:55–77.

Meyer, J., Tyack et al. 1979. "Public Education as Nation Building in America." *American Journal of Sociology* 85:986–987.

Mills, C. W. 1959. *The Sociological Imagination.* London: Oxford University Press.

Nicholson, Linda. 1990. *Feminism/Postmodernism.* New York: Routledge.

Pelto, P. J. 1970. "Research in Individualistic Societies." In M. Freilich, ed. *Marginal Natives: Anthropologists at Work.* New York: Harper and Row.

Poll, S. 1962. *The Hassidic Community of Williamsburg.* Glencoe, IL: Free Press.

Ramirez and Boli-Bennet. 1987. "The Political Construction of Mass Schooling." *Sociology and Education* 60:2–17.

Reiter, Rayna. 1975. "The Introduction." In Rayna Reiner, ed. *Toward an Anthropology of Woman.* New York: Monthly Review Press.

Rubin, I. 1972. *Satmer: An Island in the City.* Chicago: Quadrange Books.

Sangren, P. S. 1988. "Rhetoric and Authority of Ethnography." *Current Anthropology* 29(13):405–435.

Schutz, Alfred. 1962. "Phenomenology and the Social Sciences." In D. Emmet and A. Macintyre, eds. *Sociological Theory and Philosophical Analysis.* London: Macmillan.

———. 1970. "Concept and Theory Formation in the Social Sciences." In *Collected Papers,* Vol. 1. The Hague: Nijhoff.

Schwager, S. 1987. "Educating Women in America." *Signs: A Journal of Women and Society,* Winter 1987.

Scott-Firor, A. 1984. *Making the Invisible Woman Visible.* Urbana: University of Illinois Press.

Shaffir, W. 1974. *Life in a Religious Community: The Lubavitcher Chassidim in Montreal.* Toronto: Holt, Rinehart and Winston.

Shokeid, M. 1983. "Commitment and Paradox in Sociological Research: School Integration in Israel." *Ethnic and Racial Studies* 6(2).

———. 1988. "Anthropologists and Their Informants: Marginality Reconsidered." *Archives* 21(1):31–47.

Smith, K. K., and D. Berg. 1987. *Paradoxes of Group Life.* San Francisco: Jossey-Bass.

Sobel. 1956. *The M'lachim: A Jewish Community in Transition.* Master's thesis, New School of Social Research.

Sokoloff, N. 1980. *Between Money and Love.* New York: Praeger.

Strathern, Marilyn. 1988. *The Gender of the Gift.* Berkeley: University of California Press.

Street, B. 1984. *Literacy in Theory and Practice.* Cambridge: Cambridge University Press.

Stromquist, Nelly. 1990. "Women and Illiteracy: The Interplay of Gender Subordination and Poverty." *Comparative Education Review* 34(1):95–111.

Turner, V. 1975. *Schism and Continuity in an African Society: A Study of Ndembu Village Life.* Manchester: Manchester University Press.

Van-Gennep, A. 1960. *The Rites of Passage.* London: Routledge and Kegan Paul.

Van Velsen, J. 1967. "The Extended Case Method and Situational Analysis." In Epstein, ed. *The Craft of Social Anthropology.* London: Tavistock.

Weidman, Schneider. 1984. "Our Minds for Ourselves." In Schneider Weidman, ed. *Jewish and Female.* New York: Simon and Schuster.

Weissman, D. 1976. "Bais Yaakov—A Historical Model for Jewish Feminists." In E. Kolton, ed. *The Jewish Woman.* New York: Schocken Books.

Zimbalist-Rosaldo, M. 1975. "The Introduction." In M. Zimbalist-Rosaldo and L. Lamphere, eds. *Women, Culture and Society.* Stanford: Stanford University Press.

Zobrowski, M., and A. Herzog. 1952. *Life Is with People.* New York: International Universities Press.

Index

About the Book
and Author

· · · ৵ · · ·

> If we succeed in instilling in our girl students that the purpose of their studies is to aspire to emulate our matriarchs, who did not study, then we have succeeded in educating our daughters.
> —*the late Rabbi Avraham Yosef Wolf*
> Founder and Prinicpal
> Beit Ya'akov College for Girls, Bene Brak

· · ·

This ethnography investigates the meaning of learning in the lives of ultraorthodox Jewish women. Presenting a vivid portrayal of the Gur Hasidic community in Israel, El-Or explores the relationship between women's literacy and their subordination. What she finds is a paradox: ultraorthodox women are taught to be ignorant.

And they perform the role of being ignorant as only educated women can. Preserving their social and emotional ties with their community, these women are at the same time able to observe their surroundings and even their own worlds as if from the "outside." This duality creates the social and personal conditions that allow the women to accept their subordination and help to perpetuate it, even at the end of the twentieth century.

Tamar El-Or is lecturer in the Department of Sociology and Anthropology at the Hebrew University of Jerusalem.